TECHNIQUES OF SPIRITUAL EXPERIENCE

First published in 2025 by
Sean Kingston Publishing
www.seankingston.co.uk
Canon Pyon

In association with
The Centro Incontri Umani, Ascona

British Library Cataloguing in Publication Data
A catalogue record for this book is available from the British Library.

Paperback ISBN 978-1-912385-56-0

Techniques of Spiritual Experience

West and East

EDITED BY

JEAN-PIERRE BRACH AND THIERRY ZARCONE

Sean Kingston Publishing
www.seankingston.co.uk
Canon Pyon

This volume is dedicated to the memory of ***Angela Hobart*** (25 February 1939 – 16 August 2025), Director of the Centro Incontri Umani (Ascona, Switzerland), whose endless efforts brought researchers to the shores of Lago Maggiore, to study the spiritualities, philosophies and music of the East and the West together.

Contents

INTRODUCTION JEAN-PIERRE BRACH AND THIERRY ZARCONE 1

I – EREMITISM AND THE SECLUDED BODY

CHAPTER 1 **Tibetan yogic practice** 11
Training the mindbody in a Tibetan hermitage
GEOFFREY SAMUEL

CHAPTER 2 **A technique of spiritual realization** 39
Retreat and seclusion (khalwa) in modern Sufi Islam
RACHIDA CHIH

CHAPTER 3 **Techniques of spiritual experience in Christianity** 57
Hesychast worship in the Eastern church
MARIE-HELENE CONGOURDEAU

II – DIAGRAMS AND VISUALIZATION

CHAPTER 4 **From rituals to techniques in Jewish mysticism** 81
Between 'East' and 'West'
MOSHE IDEL

CHAPTER 5 **Contemplative practices in Asian Sufism** 117
Dhikr exercise, the subtle body and their diagramed representations
THIERRY ZARCONE

III – PSYCHOSOMATIC TECHNIQUES

CHAPTER 6 **Numinous disorder and self-transformation in Central Asian shamanism** 149
PATRICK GARRONE

CHAPTER 7 **Spiritual techniques among late imperial Chinese literati** 163
VINCENT GOOSSAERT

IV – CORPOREITY

CHAPTER 8 **An insuperable citadel?** 189
Corporeity and incorporeity in Indian Buddhism
CRISTINA SCHERRER-SCHAUB

CHAPTER 9 **In between body and soul** 217
The 'subtle body' as a spiritual technique in nineteenth-century occultism
JEAN-PIERRE BRACH

CHAPTER 10 **The lotus mandala and Prince Sutasoma in Bali** 229
A poet-priest's techniques and experiences of the sacred
ANGELA HOBART

Contributors 267

Index 268

Introduction

Jean-Pierre Brach and Thierry Zarcone

The present volume came about as the result of exchanges between Jean-Pierre Brach and Thierry Zarcone over the opportunity to organize an international conference on the techniques of spiritual experiences in the West and East (such as meditation, visualization, repetition of words, seclusion and breathing exercises). Thierry Zarcone was at the time organizing regular international meetings at the Centro Incontri Umani at Ascona in Switzerland, in association with the director of the Centro, Angela Hobart, and consequently asked her about the possibility to devote a meeting to such a topic. Angela warmly welcomed the proposal, and a conference was subsequently held at Ascona, in Monte Verità, in May 2016, close to the villa where the famous Eranos Society used to gather on a yearly basis, only a few decades ago.

It is a well-known fact that mental/cognitive and physical 'techniques' used by ascetics, shamans or mystics belonging to different religions, cultural areas and historical periods are to be considered part and parcel of the universal quest for a full knowledge of God or the Absolute, or – in other words – as essential tools for experiencing altered states of consciousness, or even (re)union with the Self. The chapters of this book are dedicated to critical examinations, from various perspectives (history, anthropology and religious studies), of several different instances of these techniques and practices; for example, kabbalistic meditation and visualization methods, hesychastic prayer and breathing control, Sufi *dhikr* and seclusion, Buddhist and Tantric *dhyana* and visualization practices. As underlined by almost all the contributions, the physical postures and corporal *savoir-faire* (such as breathing skills, movements and gestures, dance, visual and verbal tools and expertise) intrinsic to these 'psycho-techniques' are of primordial importance for our topic. Moreover, some chapters have elected to elaborate on the reports of 'spiritual experiences' allegedly derived from such practices. The emphasis can either be on their ritual and narrative dimensions, as well as on their importance for both the individual and the collective spheres (whether of a religious, magical, or socio-cultural order); or on the specific forms of consciousness experienced by these religious virtuosos, while taking into account their cultural significance within a given context. Among other subjects investigated is the concrete dimension of the performance of such techniques and/or movements; for example, the psycho-physical dimension of the preparation involved in dancing or – on a different plane – in the elaboration of teaching manuals. The traditional threefold division between the body, the psyche and the spiritual is also carefully examined, along with its extensions into the ritual and anthropological realms. Equally worthy of interest is the role of the spiritual master and of the practical aspects of his teachings: conditions and modes of transmitting a technique; design or layout of training places; difficulties to be addressed during the training itself; specific ways and requirements of ritual learning etc. Furthermore, some chapters question the actual process of recording a spiritual experience, particularly given that such a transcription constitutes our only contact with the experience itself, the contents of which we have otherwise no direct access to: these include the mapping out of the itinerary of the soul via symbolic diagrams, supposedly resonating with the layout of the universe, and naturally implies taking into account the rhetoric of self-transformation as well as, from a different perspective, the eventual criticism stemming from religious orthodoxies.

The present collective work is divided into four sections: 1) 'Eremitism and the secluded body', 2) 'Diagrams and visualization', 3) 'Psychosomatic techniques' and 4) 'Corporeity', even though the respective arrangement of the chapters, in some cases, may be regarded as somewhat subjective.

Eremitism and the secluded body

This first section explores the topic of spiritual retreat in Christian monachism, Tibetan Buddhism and Sufism. Rachida Chih – 'A technique of spiritual realization: retreat and seclusion (*khalwa*) in modern Sufi Islam' – points out that such a retreat may in fact be performed in a solitary cell as well as in the midst of a crowd. As shown in the relevant chapters, the retreat is a time of considerable mental activity, accompanied by various forms of asceticism. Such practices have remained for the most part (albeit not exclusively) the prerogative of monks in Buddhism and Christianity. In his own essay ('Tibetan yogic practice: training the mindbody in a Tibetan hermitage'),

Geoffrey Samuel examines three central components of the training of Tibetan Buddhist ascetics, mentioning the well-known prolonged retreat of three years, three months and three days. The aim of the ascetic is to control the inner processes of the mindbody; using 'deity yoga' he also performs visualizations, especially of Tantric deities who finally lead to more and more potent and realistic experiences. Another technique called 'internal yogic practice', writes Samuel, aims at providing control over the *praṇa* that flows through the so-called subtle channels of the body. The strict asceticism of the Sufis when performing the retreat (*khalwa*), as observed by R. Chih, is based mainly on fasting, wakefulness at night, silence and solitude. Such a practice, however, as is normally the case in all spiritual currents, is performed under the close supervision of the Sufi master. The most popular exercise is the forty-day retreat, which is supposedly reminiscent of Moses' retreat on Mount Sinai. The retreat mainly consists of the constant invocation of God (*dhikr*), preferably silently, sitting cross-legged with the eyes closed or half closed and the hands resting on the thighs. The goal is to experience the extinction of the self, to be replaced by the divine presence. Hence, the Sufi becomes dead to himself and spiritually reborn, a metaphor common to many other spiritual movements in the West and East. In addition, Chih underlines the diversity of the manners of performing the *khalwa* within the Sufi brotherhoods, a diversity which spans the entire Muslim world.

The technical aspects of spiritual retreat in Christianity are, in turn, explored in Marie-Hélène Congourdeau's chapter ('Techniques of spiritual experience in Christianity: Hesychast worship in the Eastern church'). Named 'Hesychasm' (calm, stillness), the main technique used by the monks of the (mostly) Eastern churches, combines a number of specific postures with breath control and the reciting of a brief invocation centred on the name of Jesus Christ. More precisely, writes Congourdeau, the technique aims at obtaining, through repetition of a given prayer or divine name, the 'descent of the intellect into the heart' to attain *hesychia*, a state of inner peace pervaded by the presence of God. Here, the heart is therefore not solely a physical organ, but also the seat of animated or psychic life and, lastly, the vehicle of spiritual intelligence, leading to a direct and intuitive perception of the divine, uniting the spirit of man with the Holy Ghost. This resonates with a verse from the Gospel which reads 'the kingdom of God is within you' (Luke 17:21). Initiated by the Desert Fathers, who sought God through solitary prayer, fasting and penance, Hesychast practices equally require, as in the cases of Buddhism or Sufism, the assistance of a master. It is also to be noted that different theologians or even *milieux* belonging to Orthodox Christianity have occasionally shown a certain amount of defiance vis-à-vis these technical and physical aspects of prayer, and have warned of the absolute necessity of spiritual guidance.

Diagrams and visualization

The chapters in the second section ('Diagrams and visualization') illustrate specific aspects of the spiritual techniques performed within the contexts of Jewish Kabbalah and Asian Sufism. Moshe Idel's chapter ('From ritual to techniques in Jewish mysticism: between "East" and "West"') describes the way in which rabbinic rites metamorphosed into techniques. These techniques, reports Idel, may be rooted in a belief in the magical powers of words, i.e. the invocation of names of deities, angels and demons, as well as in the astral forces or energies animating the universe. One technique is a mandala type of visualization that leads to experiences of the structural correspondences and analogies existing between the divine One, the Torah, the religious commandments (*mitzvoth*) of Judaism and the human body. The chart used during this visualization actually aims at being more than a mere 'cosmogram', limited to displaying the essential structure of the hierarchical universe, but rather purports to be a dynamic prayer guide. A similar representation is also at the centre of Thierry Zarcone's chapter ('Contemplative practices in Asian Sufism: *dhikr* exercise, the subtle body and their diagrammatic representations'), which analyses several diagrams depicting the 'centres' in the subtle body that are supposedly activated by Sufis in order to reach higher states of consciousness, interpreted as a 'death before death', i.e. a state of spiritual 'extinction' (*fana*) akin to physical death but on a different plane. In doing so, Asian Sufis rely on an eleven-fold set of principles, named 'sacred precepts' (*kalimāt-i kudsiyya*), which comprise a method designed to develop mindfulness, spiritual awareness and silent recollection (*dhikr*).

Psychosomatic techniques

Dedicated to 'Psychosomatic techniques', the third section deals with the use of spiritual techniques that were purportedly taught by gods, deities and spirits to Buddhist and Taoist monks, and even to Central Asian shamans. As shown by Vincent Goossaert ('Spiritual techniques among late imperial Chinese literati'), Chinese Taoists rely on mediums to establish contacts with gods and deities, thanks to a method named 'spirit-writing' that requires all the revelations of the spirits to be put down on paper and circulated in manuscripts or printed books. The techniques taught include daily meditation, breathing techniques, sleep regimens and the nurturing of *qi* energy. Other types of techniques concern the recitation of sacred formulas and inner alchemy. For example, the recitation of Buddha Amitabha's name aims at preparing the practitioner for a rebirth in the Pure Land, where he will in turn become a Buddha. Spiritual techniques taught by deities, spirits and saints are also dealt with in Patrick Garrone's chapter ('Numinous disorder and self-transformation in Central Asian shamanism'), which shows that in various forms of Islamicized Shamanism belonging to Central Asia there exist kinds of spiritual technique quite different to those familiar from other religious currents elsewhere. The way to become a shaman starts with an 'initiatory sickness', actually a 'numinous disorder' and a sign that the person has been elected by certain spirits. Later, through prolonged contact with the supernatural world of spirits, the future shaman is given the means to fulfil his quest. Hence, Garrone points out that the spiritual technique of 'making' the shaman takes place within the 'supernatural realm', through an alliance between the future shaman and the spirit world itself.

Corporeity

Chapters in the fourth section illustrate several aspects of the specific outlook of ascetics and mystics toward their own body, including taming the physical body and gaining control over the 'subtle' or 'astral' bodies. Cristina Scherrer-Schaub ('An insuperable citadel? Corporeity and incorporeity in Indian Buddhism') examines specific Buddhist practical exercises of visualization that lead to a progressive detachment from 'corporeity' as such. The aim is to liberate the practitioner, usually a monk, from the transiency of this world by discerning and 'seeing' the real nature of physical items. One abrupt yogic technique, among others, consists of a meditation upon a skeleton or decomposing corpse, generally while staying in a burial place.

As Jean-Pierre Brach observes in his chapter ('In between body and soul: the 'subtle body' as a spiritual technique in nineteenth-century occultism'), nineteenth-century occultism developed a new kind of spiritualism (beyond that based on contact with disembodied spirits in the séance room, otherwise called 'table-turning'), one advocating the 'liberation of the double' or 'vital astral body'. Such a subtle corporal organ is supposed, if illuminated from above by the divine spirit, to allow the practitioner to turn him or herself into an immortal entity. The techniques called upon in this process range from fasting, sexual continence or abstinence, vegetarian diet, refraining from tobacco and alcohol, to the eventual use of drugs and concentration on the 'magic mirror'.

Angela Hobart's chapter ('The lotus mandala and Prince Sutasoma in Bali: a poet-priest's techniques and experiences of the sacred') addresses Balinese shadow theatre and the activities of a master puppeteer, who is both a healer and an ascetic, using techniques from yoga and even shamanism to obtain effects directed both at himself and at the spectators. The aim is to evoke invisible entities: the deities, spirits, ancestors and demonic beings belonging to the supernatural world. Central, however, to his pursuit of liberation, writes Hobart, is his concern for the well-being of the whole village community, and to enchant and guide the spectators imperceptibly to enhanced modes of consciousness.

Comparative remarks

Looking at the spiritual techniques presented and analysed in these four sections, one of the first questions that come to mind about the techniques shared by the ascetics and mystics of different religions and cultures, is whether they are actually borrowing from one another or are basically inherent to all gnostic traditions in general. Judging from the present studies, it seems the great majority of the ascetics were inspired by Hindu and Buddhist spiritual techniques, generally of yogic origin, such as the seated so-called lotus posture, breath control, the continuous repetition of words or names (see Idel, Scherrer-Schaub). Another instance of this is present in Zarcone's chapter, which mentions Indian Sufis performing a yoga posture (*asana*) and adopting hand gestures typical of Indian religious culture (*mudra*). Other authors point to the fact that the transmission of certain techniques from India was probably handed down, through Islam and Sufism, to the practitioners of Hesychasm and, possibly, to the kabbalists. That being said, as argued by Samuel, the theme of 'directing and controlling the flow of spiritual energies through the subtle body was developed in elaborate forms within Chinese material several centuries before it can actually be traced in Indian sources'.

Aside from the mutual borrowings between practices belonging to varied cultural contexts, techniques inherent to different traditions can equally exhibit deep similarities. This is the case with the repetition of words, visualizations and concentrative meditations found in Sufism (Chih), Orthodox Christianity (Hesychasm – Congourdeau) and Kabbalah (Idel). In addition, Idel draws our attention to the transition from religious ritual to proper techniques, as well as to the complex nature and esoteric meaning of language and letters in Sufism, notably in Hurufi speculations (letter symbolism), Christian mysticism and Kabbalah. Some ideas and practices may in fact have been borrowed by a given tradition from another, though the practice of meditation on, and manipulation of, letters was nevertheless inherent to these trends.

Another aspect is the mixing of techniques stemming from different origins, one example (Zarcone) is the hybridization of the subtle physiology of yoga with that of Sufism, while being aware that the famous subtle centres of the yogic body (*chakra*) are not identical with the *latifa* in Sufism (or those of Hesychasm), but that they may nevertheless serve the same purpose or share common locations, such as the middle point between the eyebrows or the summit of the head (Scherrer-Schaub, Samuel, Zarcone). Another case in point is the blending of Chinese/Taoist spiritual techniques with those of Buddhist monks (Goossaert). Less well known, however, as pointed out by Samuel, is the considerable resemblance of deity yoga, and of the Tantric mandalas, with some 'theurgic' traditions pertaining to Western magical rituals. This 'theurgic tradition', especially insofar as it makes use of considerations pertaining to the subtle body, is partly derived from ancient Greek material, more or less transformed by Renaissance thinkers and early modern magi, such as Ficino or Agrippa. But it is also largely dependent on the reinterpretation of Hindu and Buddhist sources presented to Western readers by the Theosophical Society (from 1880 onward) and competing within the context of nineteenth-century occultism, with an insistence on *Hatha-Yoga* postures and breathing techniques, stressing the importance of the physical (not astral this time) body, and mingled with meditational exercises stemming either from Oriental practices or from Western, spurious 'Rosicrucian' literature.

Lastly, we would naturally like to express our gratitude to all the contributors to this volume, to Angela Hobart and the Centre Incontri Umani, who welcomed us at Ascona in the Swiss shore of the wonderful Lago Maggiore, and to Sean Kingston, who has agreed to publish the proceedings of the meeting.

I

EREMITISM AND THE SECLUDED BODY

1

Tibetan yogic practice

Training the mindbody in a Tibetan hermitage

GEOFFREY SAMUEL

Historical background: Buddhist practice in India

Ascetic practice has a long history in Buddhism, presumably going back to the time of the historical Buddha, Śākyamuni, who is described as the founder of an order of male and female ascetic renunciates in what is now the north-eastern part of India. Śākyamuni (also known as Siddhārtha Gautama, or Gautama Buddha) probably lived in the mid to late fifth century BCE (Bechert 1991–7; Cousins 1996). However, our knowledge of the ascetic practices of this early period is limited. Śākyamuni's teachings were said to have been compiled immediately after his death, and transmitted orally from then onwards in the form of *sūtra*, narratives which describe what the Buddha is claimed to have said on various specified occasions. These texts, along with other associated documents including the Vinaya, the disciplinary code of the order, were written down in a number of different recensions from the first century BCE onwards.

Some of the material written down at this time is undoubtedly earlier in origin, though it is hard to know how far back any specific content might date. The *sūtra* and the Vinaya code describe ascetic practices, but rarely in much detail, and different schools developed specific traditions of practice over the subsequent centuries. It is nevertheless clear from the early Buddhist *sūtra* and from the Brahmanical and Jain sources that ascetic practice was already an established part of the north-east Indian scene by the time that the Buddhist teachings were first written down, and it seems safe enough to assume that this had been the case for some centuries earlier, at least back to the presumed lifetime of Śākyamuni himself. In the *sūtra* texts, Śākyamuni is presented as studying with other ascetics before his attainment of Buddhahood, and as interacting with other ascetics throughout his later career. These included both Brahmanical ascetics and the ancestors of the Jains. Early Brahmanical and Jain material present much the same picture, as does the Buddhist and Jain sculptural material that begins to appear at this time. Thus, it makes sense to see the origins of Buddhism in a common ascetic milieu that had already existed for some time before the presumed lifetime of Śākyamuni. We can see various refractions of this common milieu in the Buddhist texts, as in the Jaina scriptures and in early Brahmanical texts such as the Upaniṣads.

The Buddhists had a particular take on ascetic practice, focusing on the use of specific meditation techniques and the avoidance of extreme asceticism, but they also had much in common with their fellow ascetics, including the Jains (Bronkhorst 1998). The generic term *śramaṇa* was applied to members of all the non-Brahmanical ascetics, though the precise relationship between the various *śramaṇa* groups, and between the *śramaṇa* and the early Vedic and Brahmanical context, is uncertain (Gombrich 2006; Bronkhorst 2011). Buddhism and the other *śramaṇa* traditions are however historically associated with the north-eastern region of India (Johannes Bronkhorst's 'Greater Magadha'), an area which was probably not yet dominated by Brahmanical religion in this early period. There were Brahmins in the north-eastern region, including Brahmin ascetics, but the Brahmanical heartland was in northern India (parts of present-day Western Uttar Pradesh and Punjab). The society and culture of the two regions probably differed substantially from each other (Bronkhorst 2007; Samuel 2008).

The key ascetic role for the early Buddhists was that of the *bhikṣu* (male) or *bhikṣūṇī* (female), the fully ordained ascetic practitioner. While the life of the *bhikṣu* and *bhikṣūṇī* was certainly ascetic, with several hundred rules governing their behaviour in various respects, including restrictions on food (no solid food after midday), clothing, living conditions and so on, the Buddha's own life story involved his realization of the limits of extreme asceticism, and the need for a more moderate approach. Thus the fifth-century CE *Visuddhimagga*, as well as other relatively early sources, includes a list of further ascetic practices (the so-called *dhutaṅga*, e.g. living outdoors under a tree, wearing robes made of cast-off rags, having one's meal at one sitting). These are allowed by the Vinaya, but are explicitly not required of members of the order. In the traditional Buddhist term, the Buddha's teaching was a 'middle way', and the Vinaya teachings recommended proper care for the body and a general avoidance of extremes.

India had had cities at the time of the Indus Valley civilization, but they disappeared with its collapse in around 1900 BCE. A second period of urbanization began in around 600 BCE, though precise dating is difficult. This took the form of medium-sized cities, each with a substantial rural hinterland, linked by long-distance trade routes. Many scholars have linked the growth of the ascetic traditions with this second revival of Indian urbanism. Certainly, the merchant classes of the new urban centres were important early patrons of the *śramaṇa* orders. They provided much of the lay support that maintained the Buddhist and Jaina ascetics, who in theory at least lived a simple life, supporting themselves from offerings of food, and living in communities outside the urban centres.

By the Buddha's presumed lifetime, these mercantile city-states were being absorbed into larger-scale political entities. The rulers of several of these new expansionist kingdoms also became supporters of the *śramaṇa* groups. The *śramaṇa* orders acquired substantial land-holdings, built permanent monastic centres and a network of sacred places associated with past holy men, which in time became major pilgrimage sites. For the Buddhists, the great Indian ruler Aśoka, whose third-century BCE empire covered most of modern India, Pakistan and Bangladesh, was an exemplar of the just and moral king who ruled according to the principles of the Buddhist dharma or teachings, and who provided financial support for the growth of Buddhist institutions. In turn, the growing Buddhist community, or *saṃgha,* helped to bind together the new Indian states (Bailey and Mabbett 2003; Samuel 2008). The *saṃgha* also provided ritual services, particularly in relation to death, the afterlife and the spirits of the dead (DeCaroli 2004). Later rulers, up to the Muslim conquests at the end of the 1st millennium CE, generally continued to support Buddhism, although the revival of Brahmanical religion that eventually led to the development of modern Hinduism provided increasing competition, as did the growing presence of Islam. Thus Buddhism was progressively marginalized, remaining strongest in the far south (South India and Sri Lanka) and in the north-east (Bihar, Bengal, Orissa, Nepal and Kashmir), eventually disappearing from most of the Indian subcontinent with the exception of the Nepal Valley and Sri Lanka. However, by this time it had spread to Central Asia, East and Southeast Asia, and many of these areas retained a strong Buddhist presence until modern times.

The various early ascetic traditions shared a sense of the unsatisfactoriness of everyday life, particularly perhaps the life of the newly developing Indian cities, and an orientation towards more or less radical withdrawal from that life. This withdrawal involved both physical relocation away from the city, and a set of techniques for training body and mind into detachment from the concerns of everyday life, such as family, prosperity and reputation. The objective was a state of liberation or freedom known by a variety of different terms in the various ascetic traditions. The key term in the Buddhist tradition is *bodhi*, generally translated as awakening or enlightenment. To attain *bodhi* is to become a Buddha.

The techniques (*bhāvanā* in Sanskrit and Pali, *sgom pa* in Tibetan) for the achievement of *bodhi* are what we generically refer to as 'meditation'. The term *yoga* (*rnal 'byor* in Tibetan) is also used in the Buddhist tradition, particularly in reference to Tantric (Vajrayāna) meditation, of which more later. Self-cultivation would also be a good generic translation in English for both *bhāvanā* and *yoga*, except that a critical feature of the Buddhist approach is the denial of the concept of a personal self, and this makes self-cultivation sound less than fully appropriate. But the idea of conscious work on the bodymind as a whole, involving both the integrated disciplining of the body and training of consciousness, seems to have been central from early on. The use of breathing as a key focus of attention, linking both body and consciousness, also seems to go back to the early stages of the tradition.

Numerous new *sūtra* appeared from the first century BCE onwards, including the texts that were to form the basis of the Mahāyāna tradition. These also included what appear to be new forms of practice, including the visualization or imaginative recreation of various forms of the Buddha. Detailed practice manuals began to be compiled, of which the best-known early examples are the Pali *Visuddhimagga* ('Path of Purification') of the fifth-century CE author Buddhaghoṣa, which achieved canonical status for the so-called Theravāda tradition (on which cf. Skilling 2009), and the probably somewhat earlier *Vimukti-mārga* ('Path of Freedom'), which survives in a sixth-century CE Chinese translation. Even these, however, give idealized presentations that include a wide variety of techniques, and their relationship to the actual practices of the time are unclear.

Contact between the Theravāda and the Mahāyāna schools of north India, Central Asia (including Tibet) and East Asia was increasingly limited in later centuries, and regional schools of practice developed in relative independence from each other. Theravāda meditation today has been radically reshaped by a series of innovatory teachers in the early to mid twentieth century, and while there is continuity with the practices in the *Visuddhimagga*, current modes of practice are often significantly different (Braun 2013; Cousins 2022; Dennison, 2022). Ascetic practice in Tibetan and Himalayan regions was reshaped at an earlier period through the growth of Vajrayāna (Tantric) Buddhism, a tradition which also survives in various forms in Mongolia, Japan and elsewhere. Other East Asian schools, including the Ch'an (Zen) and Pure Land traditions, developed their own modes of ascetic practice. Rather than seeking to reconstruct the practices of some past period and region, I have chosen here to concentrate on the Tibetan and Himalayan tradition in modern times, since this gives us a reliable picture of one form of Buddhist asceticism as actually practised.

An early classification of Buddhist meditation into *śamatha* and *vipaśyanā* is nevertheless worth referring to here.[1] These terms are often translated as 'calm' and 'insight'. Initially perhaps referring to aspects of a single process, and still often understood in that sense, they also came to represent different sets of techniques. The *śamatha* techniques were aimed at calming and stilling the mind and achieving a series of trance states (*dhyāna*), and the *vipaśyanā* techniques at duplicating the specific insight into the nature of reality that the historical Buddha was held to have attained, and which was classically summed up in the Four Noble Truths and similar formulations (Bronkhorst 2007). The terms *śamatha* and *vipaśyanā* (Pali *vipassanā*) are still widely used, though their contemporary application varies between traditions and contexts.[2] In the last few years, modernized versions of *vipassanā* and other Buddhist practices have been popularized in the form of 'mindfulness' courses, both in psychiatric contexts and in the wider population (Samuel 2016a).

By the fifth and sixth century of the common era, a substantial literature on meditation techniques had developed, both in the Theravāda tradition, which was establishing itself in South India and Sri Lanka, and among the Mahāyāna traditions, dominant in north India and among the growing Buddhist communities outside the subcontinent. On the Mahāyāna side, as mentioned above, this literature included practices oriented around visualization of Buddha forms of various kinds, seen as ways of recalling and accessing the power of the Buddha. For the Mahāyāna, the Buddha was understood as a cosmic force underlying the universe, of whom the historical Buddha was only one specific manifestation. The various Buddha forms became deities of a kind, through which the underlying Buddha nature of the universe might be realized, accessed and also employed for this-worldly purposes.

By this period, Buddhist monasteries had become large institutions providing substantially for the needs to the lay population. Some of this doubtless went back to the early period: the narratives of the early *sūtra* already speak of the Buddha's lay supporters, and provide roles and teachings

1 These are the Sanskrit versions of the two terms. They are *samatha* and *vipassanā* in Pali, *zhi gnas* and *lhag mthong* in Tibetan (Cousins 1984).

2 Thus the terms of Antoine Lutz *et al.*, focused attention (FA) and open monitoring (OM), while building on the *śamatha*/*vipaśyanā* contrast, refers more to specific modern versions of these practices than to their historical identity (Lutz *et al.* 2008). Even within the Tibetan tradition, there are radical differences between how these terms are understood within different contexts (see Samuel 1993:509, 535).

for these lay followers who were unable or unwilling to take on the full-scale renunciation required of the *bhikṣu* and *bhikṣūṇī* roles. Since the *bhikṣu* and *bhikṣūṇī* were dependent on the lay followers for their livelihood, this was a necessary development, and was based on an exchange of interests between the two parties (DeCaroli 2004). Buddhist monks and ritual specialists provided services for the wider community, including that of the ruling elites. Since all this was taking place in a world in which spirits and deities were understood to be real, and sorcery and destructive magic to be at least potentially efficacious, this meant that Buddhist ritualists needed to be experts in these areas too. They were responsible for rituals for healing, for protection against supernatural harm and the creation of prosperity, and also for rituals of overpowering and destruction. These all became part of what a competent ritualist was expected to do, and ascetic training therefore came also to include training in relevant ritual techniques. This essentially involved accessing the power of the Buddha through a relevant divine form.

Such techniques were evidently part of the material out of which grew the Tantric or Vajrayāna Buddhism that was later transferred to Tibet. In the following section, we move to look at ascetic practice in Tibetan Buddhism.

Development of Vajrayāna practice in Tibet

Vajrayāna or Tantric Buddhism appeared in north and north-east India (including parts of what are now Pakistan and Bangladesh, and perhaps areas further afield as well) from the sixth or seventh century, and was transmitted onwards to Tibet (Davidson 2005; Kapstein 2000; Samuel 2008; Snellgrove 1987). Thus Tibetan Buddhism derives in large part from the late Indian Buddhist milieu of the Pāla empire, in part also from Nepal, Kashmir and China. The great monastic universities of the Pāla empire, of which the best known to the Tibetans were Nālandā and Vikramaśīlā, served as educational centres for lay people as well as monastic training centres. Their curriculum, continued in the new monastic institutions of Tibet and the Himalayas, included much of the scholarly learning of India in the first millennium, including medicine, philosophy, poetics and other disciplines. These institutions, supported by the Pāla rulers and their successors, had an active and complex ritual life, but the Tibetans saw spiritual self-cultivation to be found more in the evolving lineages and schools of Vajrayāna or Tantric Buddhism, associated with teachers who, initially at least, were mostly located outside the monastic institutions and who were not necessarily themselves monks. These charismatic teachers and ritual practitioners also acquired the patronage of local rulers and powerful people, and set up hermitages where their followers could gather and practise.

Figure 1.1 Jangsa ('Bhutanese') Gompa, Kalimpong, West Bengal, India, February 2009 (photograph by G. Samuel).

The dichotomy between the scholastic tradition of the monastic universities and the advanced spiritual practices of the Tantric gurus was not absolute, even in India, particularly perhaps in the last couple of centuries before the destruction of the Pāla state and the monastic universities in around 1200 CE. In Tibet, the overlap was considerable, with the Vajrayāna in time developing a very substantial scholarly literature of its own. Nevertheless, the Tibetans retained a sense of the large monasteries as hierarchical and structured institutions oriented around scholarly study and collective ritual on behalf of the wider community (Figures 1.1 and 1.2), and ascetic practice as more appropriately taking place in small hermitages and places of retreat (Figures 1.3 and 1.4).

In pre-modern Tibet, as had already happened in India, ascetic training was increasingly entwined with the need to provide competent ritual performers, as Tantric ritual progressively became a key part of Tibetan society and to the functioning of Tibetan communities. If virtually all Tibetan agricultural communities in pre-modern times included a small- to medium-size monastery or temple, often on the hillside up above the village, this was not only because of respect for the Buddha's teachings. It was because the protection and welfare of the community was understood to be dependent on the rituals carried on in the monastery or temple.

Figure 1.2 Monks at Tango Gompa, Bhutan, September 2009 (photograph by G. Samuel).

By this stage, therefore, the purpose of training was not just the pursuit of spiritual benefit. It was also a training in techniques held to be of benefit to the lay community. This is a source of tension within Tibetan Buddhism, between the desire to follow one's personal spiritual practice, and the need to provide religious services to one's followers, including the lay population. Both are appropriate, indeed normative, aims for a lama or yogi, but they can pull in different directions.

Despite the large number of celibate monastics in Tibet in the pre-modern period (perhaps around 10 to 12 per cent of the male population in the more centralized agricultural regions, along with smaller numbers of women – Samuel 1993:578–82), the number of seriously committed ascetic practitioners was relatively small, and they were not necessarily celibate monastics. These people were however valued by the general population as source of spiritual power, for pragmatic and everyday purposes, as well as respected as exemplars of central Tibetan spiritual values. Some of them became heads of substantial communities, while at more humble levels village Tantric practitioners (*sngags pa*) were respected and valued members of local communities.

The term 'lama' (*bla ma*) is of more generic application. It is used to translate the Sanskrit term *guru*, and applies at one level to religious teachers, and most particularly to one's personal teacher of Tantric practice. More

Figure 1.3 *Machik Labdron Cave Shrine near Taktsang Gompa, Paro, Bhutan, September 2009 (photograph by G. Samuel).*

Figure 1.4 *Yeshe Tsogyal meditation cave, Taktsang, Paro, Bhutan, September 2009 (photograph by G. Samuel).*

specifically, it applies to someone who has mastered religious knowledge (particularly Tantric expertise) and so is a competent practitioner. Such people may also be heads of Buddhist communities, or hold positions of authority within them. In pre-modern Tibet, they might also hold positions of political authority in wider society. Lamas might come from hereditary lama families. Others were recognized as reincarnations as children, and trained to take over the role they had occupied in their previous life. This happened mostly to children in wealthy families, or families with political or religious importance.

Tibetans can be quite realistic about the politics involved in the reincarnation system, and a lama's status depends on personal reputation as well as formal position. It was also always possible, therefore, for individuals from undistinguished backgrounds to establish a reputation for sanctity and spiritual power that led to recognition by the wider community. Thus, ascetic practice is, among other things, a career pathway to establishing oneself as a lama (ibid.). While lamas might be fully ordained monks or *bhikṣu* (*dge slong* in Tibetan), they were not necessarily so, and this led to a certain relativization of the status of *bhikṣu* in Tibet. *Bhikṣu* are undoubtedly highly respected, but the status of *bhikṣu* is a matter of the observance of rules, rather than of inner attainment. The higher stages of the Tantric path were initially seen as incompatible with monastic celibacy, since they involved sexual practices with partners of the opposite sex. In Tibet, these practices came to be observed, in most cases, symbolically rather than physically, they still suggested that the status of fully ordained *bhikṣu* might not be compatible with high levels of Tantric attainment. Thus many lamas and yogic practitioners were lay people, not monks (Figures 1.5 and 1.6).

One of the features of Tibetan Buddhism is the multiplicity of its forms. The regions over which it spread were vast and rarely had much in the way of effective centralized control. Local communities were free to develop their own spiritual traditions with distinctive local features. Over time, these traditions became associated with a number of major groups of monastic orders. These are the rNying ma pa, bKa brgyud pa, Sa skya pa and dGe lugs pa.[3] The dGe lugs pa were the largest and most centralized of these, though the larger teaching monasteries in particular had considerable autonomy. The Dalai Lama, head of the government at Lhasa until 1959, was the most senior lama of this tradition, though not the formal head of the dGe lugs pa order. The other orders were less unified. Two dominant orientations can be seen in the late nineteenth- and early twentieth-century Tibetan Buddhist practice,

3 A fifth group, the Bon po, were technically non-Buddhist, as they traced their origins to an earlier Buddha figure, gShen rab mi bo, but were institutionally similar to the Buddhist groupings in most ways.

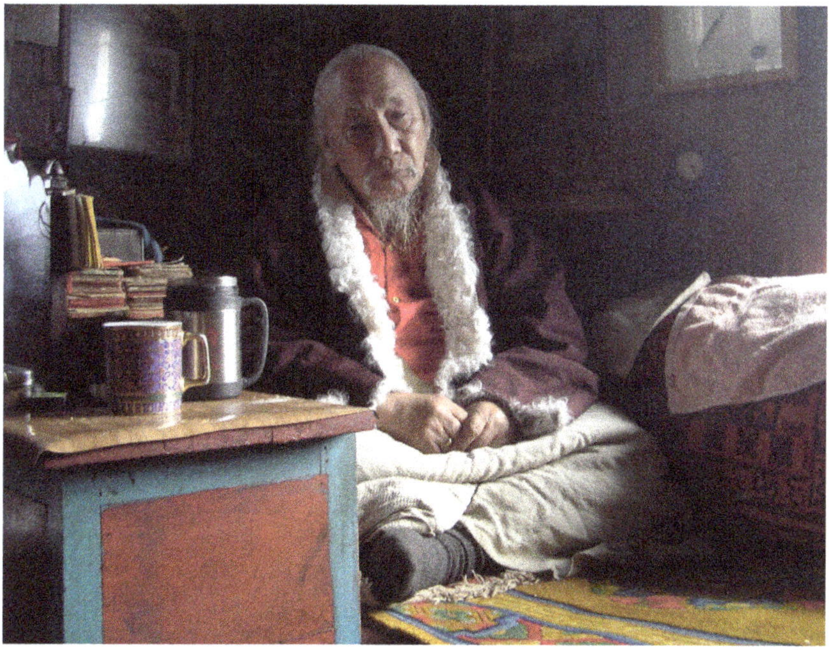

Figure 1.5 *Lama Chime, Zangdok Pelri Gompa, Durpin, Kalimpong, West Bengal, India, February 2009 (photograph by G. Samuel).*

Figure 1.6 *Thubten Repa, yogic practitioner, Chandragiri, Orissa, India, January 1991 (photograph by G. Samuel).*

one giving more attention to scholastic study and monastic discipline, the other to yogic practice and Tantric attainment. By and large, the dGe lugs pa were in the first group, the others in the second, though the contrast is by no means absolute. The bKa brgyud pa, Sa skya pa and dGe lugs pa all go back to the so-called 'New Tantra' lineages that came to Tibet in the tenth to twelfth century. The oldest rNying ma pa lineages claim to derive from the 'Old Tantra' transmission in the seventh to ninth centuries, but were supplemented and extended by a large body of additional practices (*gter ma*, 'treasure' or 'discovered' teachings) revealed by visionary lamas (*gter ston*) from the eleventh century through to modern times. New *gter ma* practices are still being discovered, and while the innovatory side of *gter ma* has perhaps been exaggerated, the *gter ma* tradition provides a mechanism for the progressive introduction of new practices and approaches (Mayer 2013–14; Samuel 1993).

By the twentieth century, forms of ascetic training were therefore complex and various. I focus here however on three central components of the training of Tibetan Buddhist ascetics. The first of these consists of the so-called 'preliminary practices' (Tibetan, *sngon 'gro*). The others are deity yoga (*lha'i rnal 'byor*), which consists of the visualization, or more precisely the imaginative bringing into presence, of Tantric deities; and internal yogic practice (often referred to in Western sources as 'subtle body' practice, and most generically known in Tibetan as *rtsa rlung* or 'channels and *praṇa*' practice).

Preliminary practices, deity yoga and internal yogic practice

Deity yoga and internal yoga may be undertaken as part of daily practice while living an ordinary life, but they are ideally performed in prolonged retreat conditions, along with a range of preliminary and supplementary practices. The standard retreat period in modern times, outside the dGe lugs pa order, which works somewhat differently, is three years, three months and three days (sometimes given as three years and three fortnights).[4] This is often thought of as basic training to qualify as a lama (in the sense of Tantric officiant/performer). Internal yogic practices involve learning to operate with and control the inner processes of the mindbody, including the channels (*rtsa*) and chakras (*'khor lo*) that are shared with Hindu tradition. These techniques have analogues in Chinese and perhaps also Sufi tradition, and have become well-known features of the contemporary Western New Age (Samuel and Johnston 2013). They form a key part of Tibetan ascetic practice. What is learned in a three-year retreat is a basic level of control over both the Tantric deity

4 The three-year retreat is described in detail by Jamgon Kongtrul (1994), who gives both general prescriptions and a number of specific retreat programmes.

Figure 1.7 The Tantric meditational deity Vajradhāra. Painting at Zangdok Pelri Gompa, Durpin, Kalimpong, West Bengal, India, February 2009 (photograph by G. Samuel).

practices (Figures 1.7 and 1.8) and the internal flows in the subtle body (Figures 1.9 and 1.10). This is expected to bring about a level of spiritual maturity in the retreatant, and to provide a basis for the employment of Tantric practice for this-worldly purposes when required.[5] The general expectation, though, is that the training should continue, in or outside retreat conditions, for the remainder of one's life.

Preliminary practices

The preliminary practices serve as a preparation for, and also introduce the basic elements of, Tantric meditation. All traditions have their own version,

5 For a detailed description of one such set of this-worldly practices, aimed at health and long life, see Samuel 2016b:145–64.

Figure 1.8 The Tantric guardian deity Mahākāla. Painting at Hemis Gonpa, Ladakh, India, July 2012 (photograph by G. Samuel).

with varying details.[6] They all begin however with the so-called ordinary or non-Tantric preliminaries, the recitation of verses based on a series of contemplations intended to develop the correct motivation of practice. These are the 'four thoughts for turning the mind to the dharma': the preciousness of the human condition, the fact that death is inevitable, and could come at any time, the inevitability of the law of karma (the connection between action and its result, usually in a future life), and the inevitability of suffering within *samsāric* existence. These 'ordinary' preliminaries ('ordinary' in the sense that they are part of the standard Mahāyāna teachings rather than containing

6 Two accessible versions are the *Karma bKa' brgyud sngon 'gro*, originating with the ninth Karmapa, dBang phyug rdo rje (1556–1603), downloadable from archive.org/details/NGNDROPrayerKarmaKagyuNgondroTheChariotTraversingTheNoblePath (accessed 22 March 2021), and the *kLong chen snying thig sngon 'gro*, which forms part of the kLong chen snying thig thig gter ma – revelations of 'Jigs med gling pa (Ling-pa 1982). Jamgon Kongtrul's (1977) *The Torch of Certainty* is a detailed commentary on the former; Patrul Rinpoche's (2010) *The Words of My Perfect Teacher* is a classic introduction to the Buddhist teachings structured as a commentary on the latter.

Figure 1.9 *Tibetan thangka showing location of six cakras, circa nineteenth century, Los Angeles County Art Museum. Gift of Dr Mark and Dorothy Stern. M91.118 (public domain image, LACMA).*

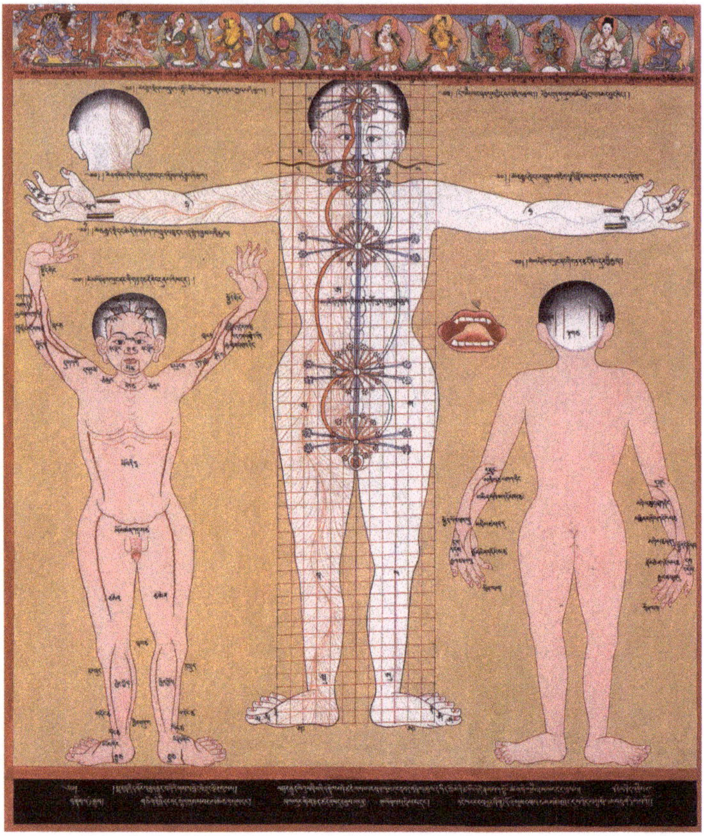

Figure1.10 Tibetan anatomical diagram showing main figure with five chakras, channels and secondary channels. Wikimedia, origin uncertain (public domain image, Creative Commons).

anything specific to the Vajrayāna) precede the 'non-ordinary' Vajrayāna or Tantric preliminaries proper.

The standard components of Vajrayāna preliminary practice involve:

- performing the practice of taking refuge and cultivating *bodhicitta* 100,000 times before the visualization of one's teacher (guru or lama) in the form of a Tantric deity;
- the performance of 100,000 full-length prostrations before the imagined visualization;
- the offering of 100,000 symbolic representations of the universe to the visualized lama; and
- the practice of guru-yoga, which involves 100,000 recitations of the 100-syllable purificatory mantra of Vajrasattva.

Vajrasattva is a Tantric deity who is especially associated with purification. The Vajrasattva practice involves visualizing the deity above one's head, and imagining a stream of white nectar from the deity flowing into and through one's body, purifying all past bad actions and defilements. At the end of each practice session, Vajrasattva dissolves into light and merges into the practitioner.

Performing each of these four or six items (they can be enumerated in various ways) 100,000 times typically takes a minimum of three or four months, and acts as an introduction to more advanced practices, as well as providing a basis to which the yogic practitioner may return in his or her daily practice. The basic elements of visualizing the deity in front or above, making offerings, reciting mantras and merging with the deities are central components of all Vajrayāna practice.

The development of the altruistic motivation towards the achievement of Buddhahood, or 'awakening mind' (*bodhicitta*), is also regarded as critical for Vajrayāna practice, as for the Mahāyāna more generally; it is what, in the Tibetan perspective, distinguishes Buddhist practice from non-Buddhist practice.[7] A key text here is the classic Indian Mahāyāna work by Śāntideva (1995), the *Bodhicāryavātara*. This text forms the basis for a series of contemplations that develop compassion for the sufferings of other beings and the desire to liberate them from their suffering. This is not just a cognitive or intellectual exercise. *Bodhicitta* is a state of the body as well as of the consciousness, and corresponds to a substance that will over time be focused within the body, and directed into the central channel of the subtle body (see below). In subtle-body theory, the flows through the channels and chakras of the subtle body are closely related to consciousness. Learning to direct and shape them is thus equivalent to learning to cultivate and direct what Western languages would refer to as emotional or motivational states. Physical exercises such as the prostrations of the *sngon 'gro* are themselves thought to act on the subtle body, as do the physical yogic exercises (*'phrul 'khor*) generally undertaken in combination with Tantric training. However, direct work with the subtle body is generally reserved to a later stage.

Deity yoga

The specific deities involved in deity yoga, and the specific details of the inner yogic practices, are transmitted from the lama (here in the sense of Tantric

---

7 For the Tibetans, it is also technically what marks out the Tibetan teachings as superior to Hināyāna traditions, such as the Theravādins. However, historically, the category of Hināyāna functioned within Tibetan schemes of graduated teachings as a preliminary class of teachings and philosophical positions, rather than as a way of categorizing Theravādins, with whom the Tibetans had little or no contact until recent times.

teacher) to the student, forming teaching 'lineages' (analogous to lineages of genealogical descent) down which specific sets of teachings are transmitted. Each of these is centred around a particular set of deities, and usually named for the main deity. Some of these come, it is claimed, from eleventh- and twelfth-century India; others are 'discovered' practices originating in processes of visionary revelation in Tibet. The details of deities, internal yogic practices, preliminary and accessory practices vary between lineages, but the general pattern is similar.

Deity yoga can probably be traced back to the deity visualization practices of the early Mahāyāna (Harrison 1990; Samuel 2008:219). It is likely that the liturgical practice of Indian Buddhist monasteries also included modes of deity yoga. In these ritual practices, specific versions of the Buddha, such as the Medicine Buddha, Bhaiṣajyaguru, or the Buddha of Long Life, Amitāyus, would have been worshipped alongside benevolent deities such as Dzambhala, God of Wealth, and Vajrapāṇi, a local deity who was adopted at an early stage as a protector of the Buddha (Linrothe 1999). There is also clearly an admixture from fierce Śaivite deities of the Bhairava kind, and my assumption is that this is because Buddhist ritualists were increasingly called on to carry out defensive and destructive magic for political purposes – in effect, state sorcery. Bhairava himself was adopted into Tantric Buddhism as the deity Mahākāla (Figure 1.8), and was understood as a protector of the Buddhist teachings and an opponent of those hostile to the Buddha dharma (Linrothe 1999; Samuel 2008).

In time, the number of such deities grew large, and they were systematized in the mandalas of major Tantric cycles, such as the Vairocanābhisaṃbodhi and Tattvasamgraha, the two major sources of East Asian Tantrism, and in other works, including systematic treatises by late Indian Buddhist authors such as Abhayākaragupta. A mandala is essentially a kind of cosmic diagram in the form of an imagined palace centred around a single deity (or male-female couple), with ancillary deities arranged symmetrically around. These diagrams also go back quite early; a simple version appears to be described in a fourth-century Mahāyāna sūtra, the *Suvarṇaprabhāsa* (ibid.:225–6). It may be visualized in three dimensions or as a two-dimensional diagram, which is in effect a map of the palace as seen from above. It can also be seen as an array of deities in the space in front of one, with the principal deity or deity-couple at the centre.

The new deity yoga practices of the eighth and ninth centuries took all this a step further, however. They are often referred to in Western publications as *mahāyoga* or as *anuttārayogatantra* ('Highest Yoga Tantra'), though this latter term is a reconstruction from the Tibetan and does not occur in surviving Sanskrit sources (Isaacson 1998:28n11; Samuel 2008:259n40). A key element of these practices, which resemble new practices appearing around the same time in the Śaiva, Vaiṣṇava and Jaina contexts, is the yogi's encounter with circles of wild and dangerous goddesses, most often referred to in Buddhist sources as *ḍākinī*. The mandalas of these new Tantric cycles, such as the Hevajra and Cakrasaṃvara, typically consist of a male-female couple, surrounded by a circle of female deities or male-female couples. While deity yoga may be aimed at achieving this-worldly ends such as prosperity, good health or the destruction of hostile forces, these new yogic practices were primarily concerned with the attainment of *bodhi* or Buddhahood itself. The central deities, generally male-female couples and often with several faces, arms and legs, seem to represent in their visual symbolism a bringing together of the many different aspects of the awakened state.[8]

To start with, practitioners working with these fierce Tantric traditions seem to have been mostly laymen (and perhaps also some laywomen). By the eleventh and twelfth centuries Tantric cycles, however, such as Hevajra were increasingly being practised by monks at the large monastic universities of north-east India. For the Tibetans, these places were critical centres of Indian learning, both religious and secular. Many of the texts studied there (the *śāstra*) were systematically translated into Tibetan along with the *sūtra* literature. This body of material, including much secular learning as well as specifically Buddhist material, codified as the *bsTan 'gyur* ('Translated Śāstras'), was commented on and developed further by Tibetan scholars. Tantra formed a key part of this heritage.

In contemporary Tibetan practice, before performing deity yoga, the practitioner receives an initial empowerment or initiation (Sanksrit *abhiṣeka*, Tibetan *dbang bskur* or simply *dbang*). This is given by a lama who has been authorized to do this by his or her own teacher, and so on, back in a continuous lineage to an original conferral, generally by the deity itself in some form. Thus, receiving an empowerment places the student into one of many lineages of practice, and into a community of people who have received and perform the same practice. Depending on the deity and the mode in which the empowerment is conferred, it may be an elaborate ceremony lasting a couple of days, or a briefer process. The full version involves a symbolic offering to the guru or lama who is conferring the empowerment, the explicit taking on of the three sets of vows, and a formal introduction to the deity and the

8 For examples, see Cakrasaṃvara with his consort Vajravārāhī, or Hevajra with his consort Nairatmyā (e.g. Huntington and Bangdel 2003:236–326, 454–67).

mandala, as well as a variety of other symbolic elements that I do not have space to discuss here.[9]

The three sets of vows or commitments (*samāya*) are important, and I will introduce them briefly. The first of the three sets are the *pratimokṣa* vows, which are in fact the standard vows prescribed in the Vinaya of all Buddhist traditions. Since Tantric practice is not necessarily performed by celibate monks, the vows taken are not necessarily or normally full monastic vows, but those of the so-called lay follower (*upāsaka, upāsīkā*) or novice (*śramaṇera, śramaṇerika*). The second set of vows are the *bodhicitta* vows, and are associated with the stories of past lives of the Buddhas, in each of which there is a point when the person who is to become a Buddha in a future life takes an explicit vow to achieve Buddhahood in order to liberate all sentient beings from their sufferings. The third set of vows are specific to Vajrayāna (Tantric) practice. All three sets of vows are associated with specific commitments and the maintenance of these commitments is thought of as critical to the successful performance of Vajrayāna practice.[10]

The empowerment gives the practitioner permission to perform the practice. The practice itself generally exists in a number of forms. There is almost always a full-scale formal version for collective practice, involving complex offerings of specially constructed ritual cakes (*gtor ma*) and other substances, musical performance etc., and often lasting several hours. There are also shorter forms, however, designed for individual practice. In these, much of what is acted out physically in the long form may be carried out internally, through visualization. In a retreat context, much of the retreatants' time may be taken up with performing these shorter versions of the practice over and over again, until the internal processes become second nature.

But what is deity yoga meant to do, and how is it supposed to operate? There are several ways in which the Tibetans made sense of what they were doing when they undertook deity-yoga practices. All generally derive from basic Mahāyāna Buddhist ideas which they took from India, such as that of two truths (one conventional or provisional, the other ultimate) and of the Buddha-nature or *tathāgatagarbha* within all phenomena. The various schools developed somewhat different theoretical understandings of deity yoga on the basis of this material. Here I will give a simple presentation of one scheme

---

9 For a classic Tibetan account which deals with empowerment or initiation in detail, see Lessing and Wayman 1968:141–55 on initiation into the Kriyā Tantra, 271–331 on initiation into the Anuttarayoga Tantra).

10 The three vows are themselves the subject of a substantial literature within Tibetan Buddhism, see e.g. Ngari Panchen 1996; Sakya Pandita 2002; Sobisch 2002.

that was particularly important for the non-dGe lugs pa traditions, the idea of pure vision (*dag snang*). In pure vision, everything in reality is understood to be a manifestation, a fractal transform if the reader prefers, of the enlightened Buddha nature (*tathāgatagarbha* or *dharmakāya*). This is the true nature of reality, as opposed to the mistaken and deluded form in which we normally experience it, and it is everywhere present as an underlying and basic stratum. When seen with pure vision, the world (here including experience of both 'external' and 'internal' phenomena, both consciousness and apparent materiality) takes on the form of the mandala of enlightened beings. All vision is of divine form, the manifestation of the deities. All sound is experienced as mantra, as the sonic expression of the inner nature of the Tantric deities. All activity is the enlightened activity of the Buddha. Practising deity yoga allows practitioners access to this pure vision, in which the deity is a true expression of the underlying nature of the world, and so also allows them to share the world as experienced by the deity, and to access the powers that are associated with that particular deity form. The more real the visualization and experience of the deity becomes, the more effective this process. The constant repetition of deity yoga is thus a technique through which the realization of the deity becomes more and more convincing, and the alternative vision of the universe that the deity represents becomes increasingly strong and real.

Internal yoga (subtle body practice)

The internal yoga or subtle body practices work in a different way from deity yoga, and quite possibly have a distinct origin. While the language in which these practices are expressed was taken from India, is clearly Indic, and builds on earlier Indian material, the central concept of directing and controlling flows through the subtle body existed in developed form in Chinese material several centuries before it can be found in Indian sources. The practices appeared in India over a relatively brief period, in the eighth and ninth centuries, and it is certainly possible that their development was stimulated by contacts with Chinese practitioners (Samuel 2008:276–85). The idea of Chinese influence nevertheless remains controversial, especially in modern India, where scholarship is increasingly dominated and overshadowed by Hindu nationalism.

In the Buddhist versions of internal yoga, the internal flows are directly related to the processes of attaining Buddhahood. *Bodhi* or Buddhahood is described not in terms of identification with a central deity, but in terms of 'untying' knots within the subtle body and directing a fluid substance into the central channel. This fluid substance, which has analogies to *qi* and its gradual transformation in Chinese thought, is most often referred to in Tibet as *byang chub sems*, and corresponds, as mentioned earlier, to Sanskrit *bodhicitta*, the term for the central motivation to achieve Buddhahood. *Bodhicitta* comes in two varieties, white and red, corresponding to masculine and feminine, semen and menstrual blood, sun and moon, and to a variety of other central dualisms, though both are understood to exist in all human bodies, male or female. Their uniting in the central channel thus becomes another version of the non-dualism that is a pervading theme in Mahāyāna and Vajrayāna Buddhism, and which is also represented by the concept of *mahāmudrā* (Tibet. *phyag chen*) and by a set of corresponding rDzogs chen concepts, of which the most central is *rig pa*.[11]

The key ascetic practice here is work with the *rtsa rlung*, that is gaining control over the *praṇa* (Tibetan *rlung*) that flows through the channels (Sanskrit *nāḍī* = Tibetan *rlung*). This is in part carried out through physical exercises, the so called *'phrul 'khor* practices (Loseries-Leick 1997), nowadays often referred to in Western contexts as *yantra yoga*, though as far as I know that term is not witnessed in Sanskrit. Breathing practices are incorporated into the later stages of many Tantric meditations, and there are also dietary and other practices that assist in gaining control over the *rtsa rlung*.

In the 'New Tantra' lineages associated with Sa skya pa, bKa' brgyud pa and dGe lugs pa orders, Tantra is divided into four classes, and the highest of these, the 'Anuttarayoga' Tantra (Tibetan *bla na med pa'i rgyud*) is divided into two stages, the 'generation' and 'completion' stages (Tibetan *bskyed rim* and *rdzogs rim*). The generation stage primarily emphasizes deity yoga, and the completion stage is mainly based on subtle-body practice. One key set of completion stage practices is the 'Six Teachings of Naropa'. A version of this was translated by W.Y. Evans-Wentz (1967) in 1935, and other versions were subsequently translated by Herbert Guenther (1963:53–85) and others, so there has been some Western knowledge of these practices for many years, though the texts are not all that straightforward to understand outside the actual context of practice. There are various listings of the six practices but the basic set is:

- the generation of inner heat (Tibetan *gtum mo*);
- the generation of bliss (which may involve physical sexual practices, but generally does not in contemporary practice);
- meditation on appearance as illusory;
- yoga of the dream state;
- yoga of the intermediate state between death and rebirth; and
- yoga of the transference of consciousness at death.

---

11 *Rig pa* is also the ordinary Tibetan translation for Sanskrit *vidyā*, science, art or knowledge, but here carries the sense of direct intuitive knowledge of the world beyond duality.

The point here is to attain stability and control over one's internal state within all these various experiences, a process which is equivalent also to gaining control over the internal flows within the subtle body.

Whether the processes of subtle-body yoga can be interpreted in terms of contemporary Western science is a question on which I have written on a number of occasions (e.g. Samuel 1989, 2013). My suggestions, building in part on the work of Alex Comfort (1979), have mostly focused on the possibilities of interpreting subtle-body practices as ways of operating with the human nervous system. Thus, the channels and psychic centres (*cakra*) can be seen not as an inaccurate representation of physical structures within the body, but as a map or guide through which the practitioner can learn to make conscious use of aspects of the nervous system that are generally automatic and unconscious.

Recent neuroscientific work on meditation seems to offer the possibility of taking this argument somewhat further (Samuel 2019; Samuel and Kozhevnikov 2022). Building on Herbert Benson's work on the relaxation response, dating from the 1970s and 1980s (e.g. Benson 1985), much of the earlier neuroscientific work on meditation regarded it, and related practices, as concerned primarily with the stimulation of the parasympathetic nervous system, leading to a general physiological state of relaxation. It now seems clear that this is much too simple. Many meditation practices, including such Tibetan practices such as *gtum mo*, the inner-heat generation process in the Six Yogas, appear to work primarily with the sympathetic nervous system and are associated with physiological arousal (Amihai and Kozhevnikov 2014, 2015; Kozhevnikov *et al.*:2013; Samuel and Kozhevnikov 2022).

This is hardly surprising, in one sense, since the central image of *bodhi* is awakening (Britton *et al.* 2014). However, it suggests that we might see meditation processes, such as those of Buddhist or Saiva Tantra, not simply as accessing a pre-given relaxation or trophotropic response within the organism, but as involving the acquisition of new and more complex modes of operating with both sympathetic and parasympathetic aspects of the nervous system. Jeffrey Lidke (2016:132) has recently made this suggestion in relation to Śaiva Tantra, and Jeff Ruff (2016:113) has argued that the model might be generalized to other contemplative traditions. Maria Kozhevnikov has suggested (2019) that the retraining of the nervous system involved in Vajrayāna practice might enable access to otherwise unavailable modes of human functioning. In Vajrayāna terms, the redirecting of the flows that support consciousness from the outer two channels to the central channel might be seen as linked with a transcendence of the duality of sympathetic and parasympathetic nervous system to a higher and different level of experience and activity. We are at the early stages of exploring these possibilities, but they suggest that the Tantric map of the subtle body may, if understood properly, have much more meaning and validity than has generally been supposed.

Closing reflections

I return to the scheme of impure and pure vision for some final comparative reflections. I begin by suggesting that one could consider the process of deity yoga, and the Tantric mandala, as having considerable resemblance to the theurgic traditions of Western magical ritual, and that the general project of restoring an underlying order that has been disturbed through human ignorance and misbehaviour also has Western analogies, for example in the Kabbalah.

How, though, should we understand the specific state of awakening or *bodhi* at which Vajrayāna Buddhism is directed? *Rig pa* and *phyag rgya chen po* (=Sanskrit *Mahāmudrā*), the terms used to describe this state in the Old and New Tantra traditions respectively, are thought of as very simple and direct matters, though at the same time as extremely difficult to achieve. They stand for reality 'as it really is', the actual state of being, the natural condition of things, something which is by definition beyond any specific verbal formulation. This natural state of being follows on the often complex and elaborate material of monastic discipline, Buddhist philosophy, non-Tantric mind-training and deity yoga. Simplicity in the Tibetan tradition tends to come at the later stages, not at the beginning. In large part this is because it is assumed that most of us are not capable of the direct unmediated perception of things as they are. At the same time, Tibetan tradition retains the idea of the crazy saint, somewhat like the holy fools (*yurodiviy*) of Russian orthodoxy, or the crazy holy men of the *baul* and *faqir* traditions in Eastern India, who can go straight to the core of things, and see through the pretences and delusions of ordinary *saṃsāric* life (Samuel 1993:302–8).

For most people, however, the Tibetan traditions see a need for a gradual deconstruction of the conditioning of everyday life, progressively weakening and dissolving the ways in which our experience of the world is entrained by deeply engrained emotions and habitual tendencies, before it is possible to move to the levels of direct experience.

This need for progressive training, and the occasional exceptions, can be read in political terms too. Pre-modern Tibetan society had a tension between 'wild' and 'tame' dimensions, and while wildness, and the power that was associated with it, was valued and indeed seen as necessary, it also had to be kept under control (Samuel 1993:217–22, 570–2). Within Tibetan Buddhism, most religious personnel, at least in the more centralized regions, were monks living in large, disciplined monasteries. To become a committed yogic practitioner gave access to a different kind of life, potentially more open, free and self-directed, but undertaken at what could be considerable personal cost in terms of comfort and security, quite apart from the austerity involved in the practice itself. It was never the choice of more than a small minority, but those who followed this path successfully could expect at least a modicum of social respect, and possibly acceptance as high-level spiritual leaders in their own right. The dialectic of structure and anti-structure, hierarchy and rejection of hierarchy, dualistic thought and its transcendence, is characteristically Tibetan. It is grounded in the physical realities of Tibetan existence, with the contrast between fluid pastoral and settled agricultural lifestyles, the low population density, long distances and difficult environment all allowing and mandating both co-operation and self-reliance. Vajrayāna Buddhism in Tibet was shaped by this environment, and provided an important part of how the Tibetans learned to cope with it. Ascetic practice in Tibet grew out of this situation, and its practices and orientation reflect that history and that environment.

References

Amihai, I. and Kozhevnikov, M. 2014. 'Arousal vs. relaxation: a comparison of the neurophysiological and cognitive correlates of Vajrayana and Theravada meditative practices', *PLoS One* 9:7, e102990.

——— 2015. 'The influence of Buddhist meditation traditions on the autonomic system and attention', *Biomed Res. Int.*, Article ID 731579.

Bailey, G. and Mabbett, I. 2003. *The Sociology of Early Buddhism.* Cambridge: Cambridge University Press.

Bechert, H. (ed.) 1991–7. *The Dating of the Historical Buddha = Die Datierung des historischen Buddha,* 3 vols. Göttingen: Vandenhoeck & Ruprecht.

Benson, H. 1985. 'Stress, health, and the relaxation response'. In W. Doyle Gentry, H. Benson and C.J. de Wolff (eds), *Behavioral Medicine: Work, Stress and Health,* pp. 15–32. Dordrecht: Martinus Nijhoff.

Braun, E. 2013. *The Birth of Insight: Meditation, Modern Buddhism, and the Burmese Monk Ledi Sayadaw.* Chicago: University of Chicago Press.

Britton, W.B., Lindahl, J.R., Rael Cahn, B., Davis, J.H. and Goldman, R.E. 2014. 'Awakening is not a metaphor: the effects of Buddhist meditation practices on basic wakefulness', *Annals of the New York Academy of Sciences* 1307: 64–81.

Bronkhorst, J. 1998. *The Two Sources of Indian Asceticism,* 2nd edn. Delhi: Motilal Banarsidass.

——— 2007. *Greater Magadha: Studies in the Culture of Early India.* Leiden: Brill.

——— 2011. *Buddhism in the Shadow of Brahmanism.* Leiden: Brill.

Comfort, A. 1979. *I and That: Notes on the Biology of Religion.* New York: Crown.

Cousins, L.S. 1984. '*Samatha-yāna* and *Vipassanā-yāna*.' In G. Dhammapāla, R. Gombrich and K.R. Norman (eds.), *Buddhist Studies in Honour of Hammalava Saddhātissa*. Nugegoda, Sri Lanka: Buddhist Research Library Trust.

——— 1996. 'The dating of the historical Buddha: a review article', *Journal of the Royal Asiatic Society* Series 3(6):57–63: www.ucl.ac.uk/~ucgadkw/position/buddha/buddha.html (accessed 3 August 2006).

——— 2022. *Meditations of the Pali Tradition: Illuminating Buddhist Doctrine, History and Practice.* Boulder, CO: Shambhala.

Davidson, R.M. 2005. *Tibetan Renaissance: Tantric Buddhism in the Rebirth of Tibetan Culture.* New York: Columbia University Press.

Dennison, P. 2022. *Jhāna Consciousness: Buddhist Meditation in the Age of Neuroscience.* Boulder: Shambhala.

DeCaroli, R. 2004. *Haunting the Buddha: Indian Popular Religions and the Formation of Buddhism.* New York: Oxford University Press.

Evans-Wentz, W.Y. 1967. *Tibetan Yoga and Secret Doctrines,* 2nd edn. London: Oxford University Press.

Gombrich, R.F. 2006. *Theravāda Buddhism: A Social History from Ancient Benares to Modern Colombo,* 2nd edn. London: Routledge.

Guenther, H.V. 1963. *The Life and Teaching of Nāropa.* Oxford: Clarendon Press.

Harrison, P. 1990. *The Samādhi of Direct Encounter with the Buddhas of the Present. An Annotated English Translation of the Tibetan Version of the Pratyutpanna-Buddha-Sa*[illegible]*mukhāvasthita-Samādhi-Sūtra.* Tokyo: The International Institute for Buddhist Studies (Studia Philologica Buddhica. Monograph Series, V.).

Huntington, J.C. and Bangdel, D. 2003. *The Circle of Bliss: Buddhist Meditational Art.* Columbus, OH: Columbus Museum of Art.

Isaacson, H. 1998. 'Tantric Buddhism in India (from ca. A.D.800 to ca. A.D.1200).' In *Buddhismus in Geschichte und Gegenwart. Band II*:23–49. Hamburg: Universität Hamburg.

Kongtrul, J. 1977. *The Torch of Certainty* (trans. J. Hanson). Boulder: Shambhala.

——— 1994. *Jamgon Kongtrul's Retreat Manual by Jamgon Kongtrul Lodro Tayé* (trans. N. Zangpo). Ithaca, NY: Snow Lion.

Kapstein, M.T. 2000. *The Tibetan Assimilation of Buddhism: Conversion, Contestation and Memory.* New York: Oxford University Press.

Kozhevnikov, M., Elliott, J., Shephard, J. and Gramann, K. 2013. 'Neurocognitive and somatic components of temperature increases during g-Tummo meditation: legend and reality', *PLoS One* 8:3: e58244.

Kozhevnikov, M. 2019. 'Enhancing human cognition through Vajrayana practices', *Journal of Religion and Health* 58:737–47.

Lessing, F.D. and Wayman A. (trans.). 1968. *Mkhas grub rje's Fundamentals of the Buddhist Tantras.* The Hague: Mouton (Indo-Iranian Monographs, 8).

Lidke, J.S. 2016. 'The potential of the bi-directional gaze: a call for neuroscientific research on the simultaneous activation of the sympathetic and parasympathetic nervous systems through Tantric practice', *Religions* 7:132.

Ling-pa, J. 1982. *The Dzog-chen Preliminary Practice of the Innermost Essence. The Long-chen Nying-thig Ngon-dro with original Tibetan root text composed by the Knowledge-Bearer Jig-me Ling-pa (1729–1798),* trans. with commentary T. Thondup, ed. B.C. Beresford. Dharamsala, India: Library of Tibetan Works and Archives.

Linrothe, R. 1999. *Ruthless Compassion: Wrathful Deities in Early Indo-Tibetan Esoteric Buddhist Art.* London: Serindia.

Loseries-Leick, A. 1997. 'Psychic sports – a living tradition in contemporary Tibet?'. In H. Krasser, M.T. Much, E. Steinkellner and H. Tauscher (eds.), *Tibetan Studies I & II: Proceedings of the 7th Seminar of the International Association for Tibetan Studies, Graz 1995*, vol. 2, pp. 583–93. Wien: Verlag der Österreichischen Akademie der Wissenschaften.

Lutz, A., Slagter, H.A., Dunne, J.D. and Davidson, R.J. 2008. 'Attention regulation and monitoring in meditation', *Trends in Cognitive Sciences* 12(4):163–9.

Mayer, R. 2013–14. '*gTer ston* and tradent: innovation and conservation in Tibetan treasure literature', *Journal of the International Association of Buddhist Studies* 36/37:227–42.

Ngari Panchen (Pema Wangyi Gyalpo). 1996. *Perfect Conduct: Ascertaining the Three Vows. Commentary by His Holiness Dudjom Rinpoche, Jigdral Yeshe Dorje,* trans. K.G. Samdrub and S. Khandro. Boston: Wisdom Publications.

Patrul Rinpoche. 2010. *The Words of My Perfect Teacher: A Complete Translation of a Classic Introduction to Tibetan Buddhism,* rev. edn. New Haven: Yale University Press.

Ruff, J. 2016. 'Strange bedfellows: meditations on the indispensable virtues of confusion, mindfulness and humor in the neuroscientific and cognitive study of esoteric and contemplative traditions', *Religions* 7:113.

Sakya Pandita (Kunga Gyaltshen). 2002. *A Clear Differentiation of the Three Codes: Essential Distinctions Among the Individual Liberation, Great Vehicle, and Tantric Systems,* trans. J.D. Rhoton, ed. V.R.M. Scott. Albany: State University of New York Press.

Samuel, G. 1989. 'The body in Buddhist and Hindu Tantra', *Religion* 19:197–210.

——— 1993. *Civilized Shamans.* Washington, DC: Smithsonian Institution Press.

——— 2008. *The Origins of Yoga and Tantra: Indic Religions to the Thirteenth Century.* Cambridge: Cambridge University Press.

——— 2013. 'Subtle-body processes: towards a non-reductionist understanding'. In G. Samuel and J. Johnston (eds.), *Religion and the Subtle Body in Asia and the West*, pp. 249–66. London: Routledge.

——— 2016a. 'Mindfulness within the full range of Buddhist and Asian meditative practices'. In R.E. Purser, D. Forbes and A. Burke (eds.), *Handbook of Mindfulness: Culture, Context and Social Engagement*, pp. 47–62. Switzerland: Springer Publishing.

——— 2016b. 'Tibetan longevity meditation'. In H. Eifring (ed.), *Asian Traditions of Meditation*, pp. 145–64. Honolulu: University of Hawai'i Press.

——— 2019. 'Unbalanced flows in the subtle body: Tibetan understandings of psychiatric illness and how to deal with it', *Journal of Religion and Health* 58:770–94.

Samuel, G. and Kozhevnikov, M. 2023. 'Scientific understandings of tantric practice'. In R. Payne and G. Hayes (eds), *Oxford Handbook of Tantric Studies*. Oxford: Oxford University Press: doi.org/10.1093/oxfordhb/9780197549889.013.6 (accessed 13 De ember 2024).

Samuel, G. and Johnston, J. 2013. *Religion and the Subtle Body in Asia and the West*. London: Routledge.

Śāntideva. 1995. *The Bodhicāryavātara*, trans. and introd. K. Crosby and A. Skilton. Oxford: Oxford University Press.

Skilling, P. 2009. 'Theravāda in history', *Pacific World: Journal of the Institute of Buddhist Studies* (3rd series) 11:61–93.

Snellgrove, D.L. 1987. *Indo-Tibetan Buddhism: Indian Buddhists and Their Tibetan Successors*. London: Serindia.

Sobisch, J.-U. 2002. *Three-Vow theories in Tibetan Buddhism: A Comparative Study of Major Traditions from the Twelfth Through Nineteenth Centuries*. Wiesbaden: Dr Ludwig Reichert Verlag.

2

A technique of spiritual realization

Retreat and seclusion (khalwa) in modern Sufi Islam

RACHIDA CHIH

Sufis practised three different types of spiritual retreat (*khalwa*): temporary retreat to a secluded or enclosed place; peregrination or the perpetual pilgrimage (*siyāḥa*), especially through deserts, mountains and cemeteries (this method was adopted by the early Muslim ascetics); and, finally, solitude in the midst of the crowd (summarized in the Persian phrase, *khalvat dar anjumān*) or interior retreat, in the sense of being socially active while remaining inwardly concentrated on God, a principle that was particularly important for the Naqshbandīs of central Asia and practised only by accomplished masters. The present chapter deals in most detail with the temporary or periodic retreat to a solitary cell, as practised from the thirteenth century onwards in some Sufi brotherhoods, in which it played an essential part in the disciple's spiritual education (*tarbiya*). Sufi handbooks of the time described spiritual retreat as a method allowing disciples to focus on God with constant prayers and invocations, and to attain illumination (in Arabic, *fatḥ*, a spiritual 'opening'). The word *khalwa* designated the retreat itself (with synonyms such as *'uzla, inqitā', i'tizāl*), as well as the space in which it took place; it is constructed on the Arabic root *khala*, which expresses the idea of the void, for one must extinguish the external senses that stand in the way of the pure adoration of God – the disciple becomes dead to himself in order to be spiritually reborn. Thus, the retreat was described as the entrance to a tomb, because the cell in which it took place was required to be dark and narrow, just big enough for a man to accomplish the prostrations of ritual Islamic prayer. In order to kill the carnal soul (*nafs*) while silencing the intellect, the disciple beginning a retreat was challenged by strict asceticism: fasting, wakefulness, silence and solitude. Knowing this, one understands why such a difficult and demanding practice was not allowed to the beginner on the spiritual path and could only be undertaken with the authorization, and close supervision, of the master.

The practice of spiritual seclusion was covered by very strict rules, which had been preserved in Sufi handbooks written by masters for their disciples. The first of these handbooks were composed by Persian Sufis in Khorasan, in today's Iran; they reflected the way of life inside the *khānaqāh* in which these Sufis lived. These buildings, designed specifically for gatherings of Sufis, often contained individual cells (*bayt al-khalwa*) to be used for temporary retreats. 'The Epistle' (*Risāla*), by Nishapur Sufi Abū al-Qāsim al-Qushayrī (d. 1074), remains to this day the Sufi handbook that has been most read. It is a very effective synthesis of all preceding literature, addressed to both masters and disciples, which is why it is still so successful today. This 'Epistle' reveals the importance that the figure of the master had acquired in the author's time, and the function of the master within the life of the emerging Sufi communities.[1] During the thirteenth century, with the development of Sufi brotherhoods, a new generation of handbooks appeared. Written by the founding masters of Sufi brotherhoods, these drew on past authors such as al-Qushayrī, but also on al-Makkī (d. 996), al-Sulamī (d. 1021), and al-Ghazālī (d. 1111), to produce a new kind of handbook – new because the rules of each Sufi path, and especially those of the *khalwa*, were presented in a practical form, which had not been the case in earlier versions. These handbooks responded to the needs of a Sufism that was increasingly institutionalized within the Sufi brotherhoods, and therefore required more regulation. Two of these works very quickly became successful among the masters of other Sufi paths, and were copied numerous times before the end of the nineteenth century: the 'Book of the Gifts of Knowledge' (*Kitāb 'awārif al-ma'ārif*), by Suhrawardī (d. 1234), and 'The Key to Spiritual Realization' (*Miftāḥ al-falāḥ*), by Ibn 'Aṭā' Allāh al-Iskandarī (d. 1309).[2]

In the present chapter, using an approach adopted in the Sufi handbooks themselves, I will present the conditions, methods and effects of spiritual seclusion, as described in Sufi handbooks of the modern period, as well as looking at how the retreat was practised within one particular Sufi brotherhood, the Khalwatiyya, whose very name was taken from the *khalwa*. Its founding master, 'Umar Khalwatī (d. 1397), was given this nickname because he was fond of retreating inside the trunk of a hollow tree. The practice of retreat has evolved a great deal in the course of history, and differently according to local

1 English translation by Knysh 2007.

2 German translation of *'Awārif al-Ma'ārif* by Gramlich 1998; English translation of the *Miftāḥ al-falāḥ* by Koury Danner 1996.

Figure 2.1 *The retreat cell (khalwatkhāna) in the sanctuary of Aḥmad-i Jām, Turbat i Jam, northern Khorasan, Iran, fourteenth century (photograph by T. Zarcone, 2018).*

Figure 2.2 *The tree where ʿUmar Khalwatī was supposed to perform the retreat, village of Avahil, Azerbaijan (photograph by T. Zarcone, 2012).*

and regional contexts. I will show that while it has declined in modern times as a method of spiritual education for disciples, it is still practised by some accomplished masters in their private *khalwa*. Thus, retreat has returned to its origins as an individual and informal practice of spiritual accomplishment.

The preliminary conditions for voluntary isolation from the world

In medieval Islamdom, from the eleventh century onwards, rulers encouraged Sufism and built *khānaqāh* and *zāwiyas* in the urban hearts of their cities, so that Sufi masters and their disciples could meet, reside, study and assemble for prayer and invocations of God there; at times these buildings also offered shelter to itinerants and opened soup kitchens for the poor (Chabbi 1978:1057–8). If space was lacking in town centres, they were built in the sparsely populated areas on the outskirts of the cities, where new neighbourhoods quickly grew up around them. This was the case for the *zāwiya* Demirdāshiyya in Cairo. Its founder, Muḥammad al-Demirdāsh (d. 1523–4), originally from Shirwan in the Caucasus, had arrived in Egypt as a Mamluk (slave soldier) of Sultan Qāyt Bāy (r. 1468–96); later, he and another Turkish Mamluk, Shāhīn al-Khalwatī (d. 1547–8) went together to Tabriz, in Iran, in order to be initiated into the Khalwatiyya by 'Umar Rūshānī (d. 1486), who lived there. This Sufi brotherhood had increased in importance during the fifteenth century, thanks to a master established in Baku, in today's Azerbaijan, Yaḥyā Shirwānī (d. 1463). From there it spread to Anatolia, and thence, thanks to the protection of the Ottoman sultans, into all the territories of the empire (Clayer 1994; Martin 1972:275–305). After having been initiated, Muḥammad Demirdāsh and Shāhīn al-Khalwatī were sent back to Egypt by their master, in order to propagate the Khalwatiyya there. They were soon joined in Cairo by another disciple of Rūshānī, Ibrāhīm Gulshānī (d. 1534), an Anatolian Turk who had fled the Safavids in 1501 (Curry 2005:47–60). In Egypt, all three men benefited from the support and protection of first the Mamluk and then the Ottoman sultans. This was primarily expressed through the construction of edifices for the practice of the rituals associated with their mystical tradition, the most important of which was the cellular retreat.

Their contemporary, the Egyptian Sufi 'Abd al-Wahhāb al-Sha'rānī (d. 1565), wrote a first-hand testimony on the integration and activities of these three Sufis in Cairo (Sha'rānī 1954). As soon as he got back to Egypt, Shāhīn al-Khalwatī retreated definitively from the world, settling on Mount Muqattam – a limestone plateau that borders the city of Cairo to the east and was considered a sacred mountain in Islamic tradition – to live as a hermit. Sha'rānī affirmed that al-Khalwatī did not visit the city for over thirty years, and that Ottoman leaders often climbed the mountain in order to see him and receive his divine blessing (*baraka*). Gulshānī, with the support of Demirdāsh,

Figure 2.3 *Zāwiya Demirdāshiyya in Cairo, the corridor leading to the retreat cells (from Behrens-Abouseif and Fernandes 1982, courtesy of the Institut français d'archéologie orientale, Cairo).*

Figure 2.4 *Zāwiya Demirdāshiyya in Cairo, an example of retreat cell (from Behrens-Abouseif and Fernandes 1982, courtesy of the Institut français d'archéologie orientale, Cairo).*

lived in Birkat al-Ḥajj on the outskirts of Cairo, until the Mamluk Sultan Qānsūh al-Ghūrī granted him living quarters at the Mu'ayyadiyya mosque near Bab Zuwayla (the southern gate of the old city). After the Ottoman conquest in 1517, Gulshānī built his own *khānqāh*, called by the Turkish name *tekke*, in the same quarter: it combined residential facilities, cells for retreat and a domed mausoleum (Behrens-Abouseif 1988:43–60; Behrens-Abouseif and Fernandes 1982:105–21). The mausoleum stood in the middle of a square courtyard with Sufi residences and cells for retreats lining its three sides.

This mix of residences and cells was designed to provide opportunities for communication between the Sufis in retreat and the novices. As part of their initiation, all new disciples (*dervishes*) bid their respects to the Sufis who had been retreating in the cells (Emre 2016:84). Both the hermitage of Shāhīn and the *tekke* of Gulshānī still exist today, but the former is very dilapidated, and activities in the latter have long since ceased. The destiny of the *zāwiya* of Demirdāsh was completely different, for it has remained active up to the present day (Waugh 2007).

On his return to Cairo, Muḥammad Demirdāsh had his *zāwiya* built at the entrance to the city. There he cultivated the land and planted fruit trees, the income from which supported his family and the disciples who spent time in the *zāwiya*, which was described initially as a simple shack where the master lived with his wife. The *zāwiya* was originally a square building upon which was placed a *qubba* (dome). In one of its corners, the wooden shrine (*maqām*) of the shaykh was built on his death. The cells opened onto the space inside the *zāwiya* building. Thanks to the detailed description of it offered in the nineteenth century by ʿAlī Pasha Mubarāk in his great work on topographical history (1969, reprinted 1981), we know that over the course of the years and centuries this *zāwiya* evolved into a great mosque, the largest in the area (which is now called Demirdāsh in his honour), and that it contained about fifty cells (*khalwa*) over two stories, built around two courtyards. In the Khalwatiyyya Demirdāshiyya, as in all other Sufi brotherhoods, the retreat or spiritual seclusion took place in the master's *zāwiya* because his proximity was necessary. The master, when he judged the disciple to be ready, put him in the cell; he decided how long the disciple should spend in retreat, and let him out when this time had elapsed. The master prescribed the invocations that the disciple would utter and offered him boundless counsel and support; the disciple would confide his inspirations and visions in his master when the latter came to see him.

Submission to the master

It was inside the *zāwiya* and *tekkes* that the relationship between master and disciple developed, following the model of the prophet with his companions (*ṣaḥāba*). The ethics (*ādāb*) of this relationship were covered in most Sufi handbooks. Spiritual progress through companionship (*ṣuḥba*) or in solitude (*khalwa*) could not be accomplished without the establishment of this rapport between the novice and the master, who was considered the vessel of divine authority. Sufi handbooks described a master-disciple relationship in which each had absolute confidence in and love for the other, like the act of love by which God created humanity. This relationship, in which each party gave completely of himself, was sealed by a pact of allegiance (*bayʿa*) during a ceremony in which the novice vowed obedience to his future guide. The disciple submitted to and obeyed his shaykh in outward actions (travel, marriage) as well as internal acts (his spiritual progress). The disciple was obliged to confide his every thought, right or wrong, to his master, obey him in everything, submit to him and be with him 'as the corpse between the hands of the washer of the dead', according to the well-known Sufi expression. This pact represented a duty of transmission for the master as much as a duty of submission on the disciple's part. The master acted as guide and an intermediary (*wasīla, waṣita, dalīl*) between the disciple and God, until the disciple had reached the point of separation; that is to say, until he had transformed the love and correct behaviour (*ādāb*) he showed his master into love for, and correct behaviour towards, God. Then, it would be his turn to become a vector of divine love for his own disciples.

Preliminary preparation

The handbooks of the Aleppo Sufi, Qāsim al-Khānī (d. 1697), entitled 'Spiritual Wayfaring and the Journey towards the King of Kings' (*Al-Sayr wa-l-sulūk ilā malik al-mulūk*), was very popular among Egyptian masters of the Khalwatiyya during the eighteenth and nineteenth centuries. In it, the author explains that retreat is a difficult, even a dangerous exercise, which demands previous experience of asceticism and isolation. Therefore, retreat is reserved for initiates who have already reached a certain spiritual level (*maqām*) (Chih 2017:520–44). Khānī described his own retreat from the world after years spent travelling across the Ottoman Empire for his business. Upon his return to Aleppo, he felt the need to isolate himself from other people, abandon commerce and follow the path of humility and poverty:

> I then changed my companions, my vestments and my interior attitude [*gayyartu al-jullās wa-l-ḥullās wa-l-anfās*], I fought my carnal soul [*nafs*] and its enemies [the pleasures of this lowly world] through hunger and wakefulness for seven years under the direction of my masters. For two years I ate only once every sixteen hours, a handful of flour that I made into a soup and sweetened with a spoonful of honey. And I continued to eat very little thereafter, following in this the counsel of my masters. At the end of these seven long years of combat, God brought forth in me the desire to study exoteric science, which I did for two years with great masters before beginning to teach in my turn.
>
> (Murādī 1997:24)

In his treatise Khānī developed a model of spiritual progress with seven stages, corresponding to the seven degrees through which one moves in perfecting the soul, with the final stage being the direct vision (*mushāhada*) of divine manifestations (*tajalliyāt*), seen not through the eyes but with the heart, during which the creature is reunited with his creator: this is the station of mystical union and acquisition of divine knowledge. Spiritual wayfaring is a struggle (*riyaḍa/mujāhada*) against the carnal soul (which obscures the inner vision – *baṣīra*) through exercises aiming progressively to purify the heart and transform the soul, so that little by little it is prepared to receive divine illumination. To each stage corresponds the recitation (*dhikr*) of one of the names of God, with an initiatory aim: the disciple becomes imbued with this name, which acts as an appropriate weapon to kill the ego (*nafs*) (Giordani 2007:117–34). The first part of this struggle consists in reducing the amounts of food, sleep and speech, and cutting oneself off from the world to the point where one forgets family and friends: 'distance yourself from men until it is said of you that you are mad' (Khānī 2005:123). This position follows that of Ibn 'Arabī, who developed the practice of *khalwa* in the 'The Meccan Openings' (*Futuḥāt Makkiya*) and in at least two epistles (Chodkiewicz 1998:45). The great master warns:

> It is incumbent upon you, before entering into retreat, to have submitted yourself to the initiatic discipline [*riyaḍa*]; that is to say, to have purified your character, renounced heedlessness, and become able to tolerate that which does you wrong. The aspirant for whom the *fatḥ* precedes the *riyaḍa* would only exceptionally be able to attain spiritual virility.
>
> (Addas 1989:54–5)

By the fifth stage, the soul has finally been able to detach itself from the world, and to purify itself of everything except God. The soul is then described as satisfied (*raḍiya*, Quran 89:28) and it now walks in God (*fī-Llāh*). Its source is in the *Lāhūt*, which is the world of names and of the divine attributes, and its corporeal home is the secret of secrets (*sirr al-sirr)*. The soul's spiritual state is one of extinction (*fanā'*); its attributes are sincerity, scrupulous devotion (*wara'*), renunciation of all that is not God, and satisfaction with all that may transpire in the universe, without the least shudder or rejection in the face of anything potentially disagreeable, because the soul is completely absorbed in contemplation of absolute beauty. It is at this stage, Khānī (2005:160) writes, that the retreat into a cell (*khalwa*) is particularly appropriate for the disciple.

Entering the tomb

Another important seventeenth-century Sufi handbook is by the Medinese Aḥmad al-Qushshāshī (d. 1661), 'The Glorious Pearl Necklace on the Pact of Allegiance, on the *Dhikr* and its Transmission and on the Spiritual Chains of the People of the Unicity' (*Al-Simt al-majīd fī sha'n al-bay'a, wa-l-dhikr wa talqīnihi wa salāsil ahl al-tawhīd*) (Qushshāshī 1909). Qushshāshī was an influential teacher of the school of Ibn 'Arabī in Medina, and his chapter on the *khalwa* borrows a great deal from the great master's 'Epistle on Cellular Retreat' (*Risālat al-khalwa*) (Chodkiewicz 1986:183; Qushshāshī 1909:81–6). The dimensions of the cell are minutely described: it must be narrow, dark and far from the disciple's entourage. Its dimensions are determined by the postures of the ritual prayer: its height must be that of a man standing upright with his arms raised to the heavens, and its length that of the body in prosternation. The width of the cell must be just sufficient to allow the final position of the prayer, in which one is seated cross-legged. The cell must have no windows, and no light may penetrate it. Its door must be narrow and solid, and only the master is allowed to enter. Thus, one may readily understand why the cellular retreat has been described as an entrance into the tomb (Chodkiewicz 1998:44).

Methods

Sufi handbooks often mentioned the forty-day retreat (*arba'īniya*), reminiscent of Moses' retreat before his meeting with God on Mount Sinai, which is described in the Quran. In fact, the length of the retreat was variable, as Qushshāshī explains (Qushshāshī 1909:81–6): it might also last seven, ten, twenty or thirty days, depending on the disposition of the person undertaking it. Some disciples might attain spiritual opening quite quickly, in just a few days; whereas for others, several forty-day retreats might be needed. During his retreat, the disciple must fast each day – this will fortify him in his struggle with his concupiscent soul and refine his character (*tahdhīb al-akhlāq*) (Qushshāshī 1909:81). At the breaking of the fast, the quantity of food should be suited to each person's constitution. Qushshāshī is here much more moderate than Suhrawardī, who recommends breaking the fast with a little bread and salt. The diet of the retreating disciple should nevertheless not contain any foods that would provoke flatulence or frequency of stools; this would oblige the retreatant to perform the full bodily ablution ritual (*ghusl*) afresh, since one of the rules of the *khalwa* is that one must remain in a permanent state of ritual purity. Qushshāshī recommends the consumption of almonds, hazelnuts, fried chickpeas and crushed sesame seeds with a bit of sugar, unaccompanied or with bread; the sugar may be replaced by a small handful of dry raisins. The retreating disciple must deliberately and progressively reduce his food intake. He will sleep very little and stay awake and alert as much as possible.

The invocation of God

The *khalwa* is not an occasion for meditation or speculative reflection, but rather for the constant invocation of God (*dhikr*), to which it is intrinsically linked. The *dhikr* is the principal pillar of the Sufi path. Qushshāshī, who on this subject repeats almost word for word what Ibn 'Aṭā' Allāh had written in his *Miftāḥ al-falāḥ*, reminds disciples that the *dhikr* is one of the Prophet's commandments: 'Alī asked the Prophet which was the best and shortest path to God, and the Prophet answered: the permanent invocation of God during spiritual retreat.' Qushshāshī 1909:144). Sitting cross-legged with his eyes closed or half-closed and his hands resting on his thighs, the disciple invokes God, using the formula most often prescribed by the masters, the profession of faith, 'There is no god but God' (*Lā ilāh illa-Llāh*); this is defined by Qushshāshī as 'the fundamental or principal *dhikr* that contains all the other *dhikr* [*dhikr al-umm al-jāmi' li-jamī' al-adhkār*]'(Qushshāshī 1909:7). During the cellular retreat, the interior *dhikr*, or *dhikr* of the heart (*dhikr al-qalb*) is preferable to the vocal *dhikr* (*dhikr al-lisān*), which is used during collective sessions (ibid.:13). The interior *dhikr*, that lives inside the heart of the believer, must be 'as light as the buzzing of a bee, neither too loud nor completely silent' (ibid.:12). It ought, in turn, to lead to a superior form of invocation, the *dhikr* of the secret (*dhikr al-sirr*), or of the intimate consciousness; that is, the invocation of God from a place deeper than the heart. Once a Sufi has reached this level of *dhikr*, he experiences *fanā'* (extinction), he is extinguished in himself and nothing remains but the permanent consciousness of the divine presence. This form of *dhikr*, writes Qushshāshī, is practised by accomplished masters.

Entering retreat with a pure intention

Masters warned the disciple who entered retreat in the hope of visions or charismas that he was bound to fail; the retreat, as its name in Arabic indicates, is a void that is empty of all physical desires and of any drive for spiritual gains. Al-Qushayrī defines the spiritual retreat as a shift from 'isolation' (*khalwa*) to the 'evacuation' (*khuluww*) of the heart that derives from the same root: 'It is right that his heart should be emptied [*khāliya*] of all thoughts but the thought of God, of all will but the will to satisfy his Lord, and of all desire for worldly things.' (Knysh 2007; Qushayrī n.d.). The final point of the retreat is an absolute detachment, an initiatory death as a prelude to spiritual rebirth. It seems that it was during the time of Qushayrī (eleventh century) that Sufis for the first time discussed and described occult phenomena associated with spiritual practices (Meier 1999:97). In a brief epistle entitled *The Stages of the Journey to God* (*Tartīb al-sulūk fī ṭarīq Allāh*), which was copied in its entirety by Qushshāshī in his own handbook, Qushayrī describes the physical and psychic effects of constant *dhikr* and asceticism, which provoke an expansion of consciousness accompanied by supernatural visions and sounds, as well as by a deeper understanding of the realities of the terrestrial world; for example, an understanding of the languages of the mineral, plant and animal kingdoms. The senses of the initiate are so heightened that he may hear the tread of ants on the floor of his cell. The greatest challenges for the disciple in retreat lie in knowing how to control the thoughts that assail him (*wāridāt, khawāṭir*) during his silent invocations in the darkness, and in knowing how to distinguish between angelic or divine inspiration and satanic inspiration that comes from his passionate soul and continues to attach him to the material world. Here the disciple needs his master, for the master knows how to distinguish between authentic spiritual phenomena and hallucinations.

The retreat: cultural differences between Arab and Turco-Persian Sufism

The practice of the *khalwa* was diffused at different rates across different areas and periods. It only appeared in the Maghreb at a late date, during the sixteenth century, and seems to have been little practised there. In *Qawā'id al-taṣawwuf* (The Rules of Sufism), Aḥmad Zarrūq (d. 1489) seems to take a very cautious approach to this eastern habit: although he recognizes the benefits of the *khalwa* as a method for the purification of hearts, he also underlines the dangers it poses if not practised under the strict supervision of a master (Zarrūq 1992:84–5). In Egypt at the same time, the *khalwa*, despite having been known in the country since at least the thirteenth century, seems not to have become general practice: it is not mentioned at all in Éric Geoffroy's vast study of Syrian/Egyptian Sufism between the fifteenth and the sixteenth centuries; this leads one to believe that there were few available traces of the practice for this historian to discover. In 1516–17 the Ottoman conquest of Syria and then of Egypt brought with it a new wave of Turco-Persian Sufis belonging to the great Sufi brotherhoods of the empire – the Khalwatiyya of course, as we have seen, but also the Naqshbandiyya and the Mawlawiyya (*Mevlevi*). These Turco-Persian Sufis were sometimes judged negatively by Syrians and Egyptians, often because of cultural differences. On the subject of spiritual retreat, 'Abd al-Wahhāb Sha'rānī, who was the head of an important *zāwiya*, had harsh criticism for the practice of the *khalwa* as a method of initiating disciples. In one of his works, *Laṭā'if al-Minan* ('The Subtle Blessings'), he argued against the retreat when it was demanded of inexperienced disciples by ill-advised masters, saying it should be reserved strictly for advanced disciples. He attacked those whom he called 'people of the retreat' (*ahl al-khalwa*) directly, in a diatribe that even made the grave accusation of heresy:

> They imposed conditions in the [method of] retreat, which the meritorious ones have never imposed, such as little food, abstinence from talk and sleep, and physical seclusion from society, and other things of this kind, which weakened their bodies, induced in them many fantasies, and corrupted their faith. They imagined that they saw beautiful or frightful shapes, shapes that really originated from their own thoughts, a reflection of their personal condition. Thus, at times, phantoms appear to them in their imagination and tell them of matters, the [true] interpretation of which also lies in such conditions. At other times [they imagine seeing] a light, a shadow, ugly or pleasant shapes of dogs and snakes and the like... And hence error entered into the people of the retreat so that some of them became heretics.
>
> (Winter 1982:84–5)

Although Shaʿrānī exempted Shaykh Demirdāsh and Shāhīn al-Khalwatī from his condemnations, his diatribe was obviously aimed at the Khalwatiyya and at Persian Sufism as introduced by foreigners. Cultural and religious differences lay behind the conflicting attitudes displayed by Turco-Persians and Arabs towards the practice of retreat, as demonstrated by the comment of Muṣṭafā b. Aḥmad of Gallipoli (d. 1600) after his visit to Cairo:

> Another point is that in our times, the [Sufi] brotherhoods followed by the pious, the so-called shaykhs of Egypt, are not in harmony with the approved ways of the shaykhs of the Kalwatiyya and Zayniyya brotherhoods and the heads of the Naqshbandiyya of the land of Rum. For they do not put their dervishes into cells and order them to exercise themselves in gradually increasing ascetic discipline, every day interpreting the dreams they have.
>
> (Winter 1977:297n82)

During the eighteenth century there was a second wave of expansion of the Khalwatiyya in Egypt, coming this time from Syria with Muṣṭafā al-Bakrī (d. 1749), in whose definition of its rituals the retreat itself does not figure.

Retreat in modern times

In the long nineteenth century, the practice of the *khalwa* did not diminish; in fact, it was re-emphasized by the great figures who were at the origin of the renewal of Sufism at that time, following the example of the Kurdish Mawlānā Khālid (d. 1827), renewer (*mujaddid*) of the Naqshbandiyya in Syria and then in Palestine, Turkey, Azerbaijan and Dagestan, and as far as Southeast Asia. He introduced the practice of a forty-day retreat, considering this more propitious to initiation and spiritual progress than the traditional companionship between master and disciple (Abu-Manneh 1990:289–302).

The Moroccan master Aḥmad al-ʿArabī al-Darqāwī (d. 1823) re-emphasized the ambulant retreat or peregrination (*siyāḥa*), bringing about a new wave of expansion for the Shādhiliyya in Morocco and as far as Egypt, Syria and Palestine (Trimingham 1998:106–7, 110–14).

In the contemporary period the *khalwa*, like other Sufi practices, was attacked by Islamic fundamentalists, and by nationalists, whether Arab, Turkish or other. Over the course of the period from the seventeenth to the nineteenth century, Sufi lodges and tombs became centres of devotional and communal life for large circles of ordinary men and women affiliated to Sufi organizations through their attachment to a Sufi saint. For the young Republic of Turkey and for newly independent Muslim states in the postcolonial period, the existence of these multiple local powers represented an obstacle to their project of constructing a nation-state around a single leader. A campaign of denigration of Sufism and its practices was carried out everywhere in the Muslim world, where it began to be seen as a symbol of decadence. Personal piety was to be replaced by a strict application of the Islamic law (*sharīʿa*). In 1925 in Turkey, Ataturk made the radical decision to close all the Sufi *tekke*s. And we know that every religious establishment requires its local and geographical space if it is to integrate into a community. The closure of the *tekke*s meant the death of a centuries-long religious culture and its heritage.

The *khalwa* was also under pressure from a modern society that had little space for solitude. As a result, it gradually became less frequent and shorter in duration. It is perhaps among the Naqshbandiyya Mujadidiyya that the *khalwa* as a technique of spiritual realization has remained the most important. However, the *khalwa* takes different forms in the different branches of this Sufi brotherhood: for example, in the Naqshbandiyya Mujaddiyya Saifi a period of ten days in seclusion (*iʿtikāf*) devoted to prayers and meditation is preferred; at the lodge of Sarkar Professor Sahib in Lahore during the month of Ramadan, the retreat ends on the night preceding the festival of breaking the fast (*ʿid al-fiṭr*) (Rytter 2016:232).

The practice has also survived to the present day in Egypt among the members of the Khalwatiyya Demirdāshiyya. During the 1960s, Father Ernst Bannerth, of the Dominican convent of Cairo, enjoyed wandering through Cairo and the Egyptian countryside in order to observe current Sufi practices. He went regularly and often to spend time with the Sufis, and participated in their *dhikr* sessions; the articles he contributed to the periodical *Mélanges de l'Institut dominicain d'études orientales* during the 1960s and 70s remain a unique source of information, because Fr. Bannerth combined his philological analyses with ethnographic data. While preparing an article on the *dhikr* and the *khalwa* in the *Miftāḥ al-falāḥ*, Fr. Bannerth observed that the members of the Khalwatiyya Demirdāshiyya, whose mosque is near the Dominicans' convent, continued to perform the *khalwa* according to the rules laid down by Muḥammad Demirdāsh, dating back to the sixteenth century: 'The Demirdāshiyya mosque contains 65 cells in which the members of the Order, with the permission of their spiritual guides, may remain for three days… This *khalwa* takes place each year, towards the end of the month of *sha'bān* [the eighth month of the Islamic calendar]. It begins and ends with great festivities.' (Bannerth 1964:3–5, 1974:73). The annual three-day *khalwa* was already mentioned by 'Alī Pasha Mubārak in the nineteenth century, and continues to be practised today on the birthday of the founding shaykh of the Khalwatiyya Demirdāshiyya. During the first decade of the twenty-first century, the American anthropologist Earle Waugh was able to observe a ritual that was normally closed to outsiders:

> Early in the morning after the dawn prayer, general instructions are given in the mosque for procedures: the adept is to maintain a silence as if he is in a tomb (some of them even shroud themselves so that their faces cannot be seen). Once these instructions have been given, the process of placing the participants in the cells begins. This is known as the ceremony of the keys. A *naqīb* [chief intendant] will have chosen a cell for each person, identified a verse for him, and generally given him encouragement to endure the difficulties to come. The shaykh, or his *naqīb*, whispers a verse into the ear of each adept outside his cell and unlocks the cell. The adept then enters the cell where he commences his discipline. The disciple [*murīd*] only leaves the cell for prayer or the bathroom. Should anyone speak to him during his time outside, he is to answer with 'there is no god but God', but no more. If he does utter any further, his vow of silence will have been broken and the benefits of the retreat forfeited… In the evening the participants are provided with yoghurt and a biscuit; this is the only food they are to receive.
> (Waugh 2008:64–5)

Waugh noted that despite the exigencies of material life (in Egypt it can be very difficult to take leave from work for three full days), there is avid participation in the retreat and generally all the cells are full.

Conclusion: retreat as a path to sainthood

During the 1990s, when I was in Upper Egypt doing field work on the Khalwatiyya, I heard of individuals who undertook a prolonged *khalwa*, which conferred on them great charisma, and direct access to a career of sainthood. In fact, the history of each contemporary saint venerated in the Luxor region included spiritual retreats that were sometimes very prolonged, as established by Shaykh Mūsa Abū 'Alī, the saint from the village of Karnak, who died in

1988, and lived for much of his life, and until his death, in a single windowless room. In 1972, Fr. Bannerth visited him in Karnak, where the saint opened his door just a crack in order to shake his hand. Shaykh Mūsa Abū ʿAlī left his cell only at night, in order to preside over *dhikr* sessions, and the entire population venerated him so much that his annual festival (*mawlid*) was celebrated while he was still alive (Bannerth 1974:74; Hoffman 1995:109). Around the same time, Shaykh Raḍwān (d. 1967) was venerated by President Nasser, who, while being an ideologue of socialism Egyptian-style, also respected holy men, as did most of the inhabitants of Upper Egypt, where Nasser was born and raised. On his death, this saint left behind a number of autobiographical notes and mystical utterances, which were published by his son (Raḍwān n.d.). Shaykh Raḍwān undertook his first retreat at the age of twelve, in an isolated room in his home. Later, he retreated for weeks into the desert that spreads beyond the narrow valley of the Nile, where he heard the stones invoking the Names of God (Chih 2000:104–5). Another local saint, Shaykh Muḥammad al-Ṭayyib (d. 1988), spent lengthy retreats in his cell, an alcove abutting on the mosque of his *zāwiya*, from which he came out only to attend prayers. According to witnesses, at the end of his life he would break his fast with only a few sips of milk (ibid.:188). And it is not just the legends of local saints that feature the retreat as a sign of divine election. Ṣāliḥ al-Jaʿfārī (d. 1979), a great scholar at al-Azhar, the most famous mosque-university of the Muslim world, and the founder of the Jaʿfāriyya Aḥmadiyya Muḥammadiyya brotherhood, ended up practising his retreat inside the al-Azhar mosque: he never left it except to undertake pilgrimages to Mecca or to the tombs of the descendants of the Prophet's family (*Ahl al-bayt*) in Cairo. He ordered that a cell be built for him inside the former college (*riwāq*) of the Maghrebi students at al-Azhar Mosque, and in this cell he gave himself over to the *dhikr*, to reading the Quran, and to prayers of blessing upon the Prophet, in addition to teaching in the mosque. Finally, beyond Egypt, we can cite the example of the Cypriot Turk, Shaykh Niẓām al-Ḥaqqānī, who died in 2014 at the age of 92, and played a central role in spreading the Naqshbandiyya order in the west. He was regarded by his followers as a saint who performed many miracles. He said that during his thirty years of intense training under Shaykh ʿAbd Allāh Daghestāni, he was placed in numerous seclusions. He was 33 years old when he was first ordered into seclusion by his master, who told him: 'I have received an order from the Prophet for you to make seclusion in the mosque of Shaykh ʿAbd al-Qādir Jilānī (d. 1166) in Baghdad. Go there and enter into seclusion for six months.'[3] About this same seclusion Shaykh Naẓim stated:

3 This and following quote are from: seekerofthesacredknowledge.wordpress.com/biographies-of-awliya-allah/shaykh-nazim-al-haqqani (accessed 21 April 2021).

> I only emerged from my room for the five daily prayers. I was able to reach such a state that I was reciting the whole Quran in nine hours. In addition to that I was reciting the *dhikr*, '*Lā ilah illa Llāh*' 124,000 times, and 124,000 prayers of blessing on the Prophet, and I was reading the entire *Dalā'il al-Khayrat* [collection of prayers for the Prophet]. Added to that I was regularly reciting '*Allāh Allāh*' 313,000 times every day, in addition to all the prayers that were assigned to me. Vision after vision was appearing to me every day. They used to take me from one state to another and give me a state of complete annihilation in the Divine Presence.

Shaykh Naẓim went into retreat with his own master Shaykh 'Abd Allāh in Medina, where they rented a tiny room near the tomb of the Prophet. He then prescribed retreat to his close disciple, Muḥammad Hishām Qabbānī, who would become his successor as master of the Naqshbandiyya Ḥaqqāniyya, and who described his experience in a book written in English and aimed at a transnational readership, *Fifty Days: The Divine Disclosures during a Holy Sufi Seclusion*, available on Amazon. For today's Sufi masters, the prolonged retreat from the world remains an effective support for spiritual realization and a visible sign revealing to their followers their intimacy with God (which defines sainthood in Islam).

References

Abu-Manneh, B. 1990. 'Khalwa and râbita in the Khâlidi suborder'. In M. Gaborieau, A. Popovic and T. Zarcone (eds.). *Naqshbandis, Cheminements et situation actuelle d'un ordre mystique musulman*, pp.289–302. Istanbul: Isis.

Addas, C. 1989. *Ibn 'Arabî ou la quête du Soufre rouge*. Paris: Gallimard.

Bannerth, E. 1974. '*Dhikr* et *khalwa* d'après Ibn 'Ata' Allah', *Mélanges de l'Institut dominicain d'études orientales* 12:65–90.

——— 1964. 'La Khalwatiyya en Égypte'. *Mélanges de l'Institut dominicain d'études orientales* 8:1–74.

Behrens-Abouseif, D. and Fernandes, L. 1982. 'An unlisted monument of the fifteenth century: the dome of Zawiyat al-Damirdash', *Annales Islamologiques* 18:105–21.

——— 1988. 'The Takiyyat Ibrahim al-Kulshani in Cairo', *Muqarnas* 5:43–60.

Chabbi, J. 1978. 'Khānkāh', *Encyclopédie de l'Islam* 2(IV):1057–8.

Chih, R. 2000. *Le Soufisme au quotidien. Confréries d'Égypte au XXe siècle*. Paris: Sindbad-Actes Sud.

——— 2017. 'Le livre pour guide: *éthique* (*adab*) et cheminement spirituel (*sulūk*), dans trois manuels soufis d'époque ottomane'. In F. Chiabotti, E. Feuillebois-Pierunek, C. Mayeur-Jaouen and L. Patrizi (eds.), *Ethics and Spirituality in Islam: Sufi Adab*, pp. 520–44. Leiden: Brill.

Chodkiewicz, M. 1986. *Le Sceau des saints. Prophétie et sainteté dans la doctrine d'Ibn 'Arabî*. Paris: Gallimard.

——— 1998. 'Les quatre morts du soufi', *Revue de l'histoire des religions* 215(1):35–57.

Clayer, N. 1994. *Mystiques, Etat et société: Les Halvetis dans l'aire balkanique de la fin du XVe siècle à nos jours*. Leiden: Brill.

Curry, J. 2005. 'Home is where the Shaykh is: the concept of exile in the hagiography of Ibrahim-i Gülsheni', *Al-Masaq: Islam and the Medieval Mediterranean* 17(1):47–60.

Emre, S. 2016. *Ibrahim-i Gulshani and the Khalwati-Gulshani Order*. Leiden; Brill.

Geoffroy, É. 1995. *Le Soufisme en Syrie et en Égypte Sous les Derniers Mamelouks et les Premiers Ottomans*. Damascus, Presses de l'Ifpo.

Giordani, D. 2007. 'Le metamorfosi dell'anima e gli stadi della via spirituale: considerazioni intorno a 'Al-Sayr wa-l-sulûk ilâ maliki-l-mulûk' dello 'shaykh' Qâsim ibn Salâh al-Dîn al-Khânî di Aleppo (1619-1697)', *Divus Thomas* 48(3):117–34.

Gramlich, R. 1998. *Die Gaben der Erkenntnisse des 'Umar as-Suhrawardī ('Awārif al-Ma'ārif)*. Wiesbaden: Steiner Franz Verlag.

Hoffman, V. 1995. *Sufism, Mystics, and Saints in Modern Egypt*. Columbia: University of South Carolina Press.

Kabbani, M. H. 2010. *Fifty Days: The Divine Disclosures during a Holy Sufi Seclusion*. Fenton: Islamic Supreme Council of America.

Khānī, Q. 2005. *Al-Sayr wa l-sulūk ilā malik al-mulūk* (ed. and annot. I. Shams al-dīn). Beirut: Dār al-kutub al-'ilmiyya.

Knysh, A. 2007. *Al-Qushayri's Epistle on Sufism: Al-Risala Al-Qushayriyya*. Reading: Garnet Publishing.

Koury Danner, M.A. 1996. *The Key to Salvation: A Sufi Manual of Invocation by Ibn 'Aṭā' Allāh al-Iskandarī*. Cambridge: The Islamic Text Society.

Martin, B.G. 1972. 'A short history of the Khalwatiyya order of dervishes'. In N. Keddie (ed.), *Scholars, Saints, and Sufis: Muslim Religious Institutions in the Middle East since 1500*, pp. 275–305. Berkeley: University of California Press.

Meier, F. 1999. 'A Book on etiquette for Sufis'. In F. Meier, *Essays on Islamic Piety and Mysticism* (trans. J. O'Kane), pp. 49–92. Leiden: Brill.

Mubārak, 'A. 1969. *Al-Khitat al-tawfīqiyya al-jadīda*. Cairo.

Murādī, M. 1997. *Silk al-durar fî a'yān al-qarn al-thānī 'ashar*. Beirut: Dār al-kutub al-'ilmiyya, IV.

Qushayrī, A. n.d. *Risāla*. Beirut: Dār al-Kitāb al-'Arabī.

Qushshāshī, A. 1909. *Al-Simt al-majīd fī sha'n al-bay'a, wa-l-dhikr wa talqīnihi wa salāsil ahl al-tawḥīd*. Hyderabad: Dā'irat al-ma'ārif al-nizāmiyya.

Raḍwān, A.M. n.d. *Al-Nafaḥāt al-rabbāniyya*. Kom Ombo.

Rytter, M. 2016. 'By the beard of the Prophet: imitation, reflection and world transformation among Sufis in Denmark', *Ethnography* 17(2):229-49.

Sha'rānī, 'A. 1954. *al- Ṭabaqāt al-kubrā*. Cairo.

Trimingham, J.S. 1998. *The Sufi Orders in Islam*. Oxford: Oxford University Press.

Waugh, E.H. 2007. *Visionaries of Silence: The Reformist Sufi Order of the Demirdashiya al-Khalwatiya in Cairo*. Cairo, AUC Press.

Winter, M. 1977. 'Sheykh 'Alî b. Maymûn and Syrian Sufism in the sixteenth century', *Israël Oriental Studies* 7:281–308.

— — — 1982. *Society and Religion in Early Ottoman Egypt*. New Brunswick: Transaction Publishers.

Zarrūq, A. 1992. *Qawā'id al- tasawwuf.* Beirut: Dār al-Jīl.

3

Techniques of spiritual experience in Christianity

Hesychast worship in the Eastern Church

Marie-Helene Congourdeau

❋

'And the Word was made flesh' (John 1, 14). This phrase from the Gospel according to John expresses the singularity of Christianity. God in a human body, the resurrection of the flesh, the consumption during the Eucharist of Christ's body: these elements demonstrate the extent to which corporeality is central to the Christian mystery, yet the religion in question is often said to be one in which only the soul's salvation counts, one that promotes contempt for the body. Under such conditions, spiritual life would consist of detaching oneself as far as possible from any physical, bodily element, in this respect following the neoplatonic model of the experience of awakening, as described by Plotinus: 'Often, I awaken to myself and escape from the body' (Enneads IV, 8, 1). This awakening would be the result of a dis-incarnation.

Responses to the importance of the (sometimes extreme) ascetic recommendations made in the Christian monasticism that took root in the deserts of Egypt and the Near East during the fourth century may have amplified this tendency towards dis-incarnation, which is illustrated by the definition of monasticism as an angelic state. But the radical asceticism of the Desert Fathers, which sprang from many sources in antiquity, also influenced an even more mystical outlook, in which the primary battle is not against the body, but against thoughts themselves (*logismoi*), and the demons who cause them. The aim of this battle against thoughts is a union with Christ that can be attained by remembering God and repeating certain phrases that gradually become centred on the name of Jesus.

This form of spirituality was forgotten for many centuries, but it was reborn in a mutated form in the mid-thirteenth century, with the emergence

Figure 3.1 *Saint Macarius of Egypt. He lived as a monk in the Egyptian Scetic desert during the fourth century. Most texts attributed to him belong in fact to another, later, author or Pseudo-Macarius. Macarius the Great is considered to be the fountainhead of the hesychastic tradition. Fresco from the Mileseva monastery (Serbia; thirteenth century). © Svetlana Tomeković.*

of a new way of praying – one that would set in motion theological disagreements whose repercussions would be felt even in the political sphere. In fact, this was not the first such event in Byzantium – one has only to recall the eighth and ninth century 'image struggle' that tore the Empire in half over a theological dispute.

A spiritual tradition

The experiences of the Desert Fathers, who sought God through solitary prayer, were synthesized at the end of the fourth century by Evagrius Ponticus and Macarius of Egypt, the former initiating followers into a form of prayer that was pure of thought, and the latter recommending a sense-experience of God in one's own heart (Rigo 2008). These diverse spiritual currents had some things in common: guarding one's heart (against the demons who are 'spiritual enemies' and against the adverse thoughts that they may engender); watchfulness towards God and sobriety; a shared ultimate goal, which was *Hesychia*, the heart's peace as a prerequisite for encountering God; and the potential appearance of rewards that could be sensed, such as peace, joy,

Figure 3.2 *Saint Arsenius the Great. He lived as a monk in the desert of Scetes (fifth century). Fresco from the Mileseva monastery (Serbia; thirteenth century). © Svetlana Tomeković.*

a sensation of heat or of light. It is no longer a question, as in Plotinus, of escaping from one's body, but instead of entering into oneself, for, as the Gospel says, in an oft-cited verse, 'the kingdom of God is within you' (Luke 17, 21). From these beginnings was born a form of prayer whose aim was to facilitate access to *hesychia*. These prayers, intended to bring unity where an abundance of words brings dispersal, were composed of a single word or short phrase, repeated indefinitely; little by little the word or formula acquires a structure around the name of Jesus. The name of Jesus, sometimes repeated on its own, then becomes a sort of mantra, providing protection from demons for the person praying, and keeping his/her awareness of God alive.

Specific information on these practices appears in the Mount Sinai monastery during the sixth century. Mount Sinai Hegumen (Abbot) John Climacus underlined the importance of perseverance in prayer with the metaphor of the breath, which never stops while a person still lives: 'May the memory of Jesus be united with your breathing; then you will know the usefulness of *Hesychia*.' (Climacus 1860: rung xxvii, para. 62). Nearly a century later, Hesychius of Sinai writes: 'Join sobriety to the breath of your nostrils, along with the name of Jesus, humility, and meditation upon death.' (Hesychius of Sinai 1974–5: para. 189) Some fourteenth-century spiritual authors would invoke these phrases in order to demonstrate the ancient pedigree of a method of prayer founded on the rhythm of breathing, but among the monks of Sinai this was only a metaphor: the name of Jesus must be as constantly present in one's thoughts as one's own breathing in one's lungs. In fact, no text from before the thirteenth century links the keeping of the heart and the invocation of Jesus's name with any specific physical technique.

To these authors from the Sinai, we can also add a seventh-century Syriac monk, Isaac of Nineveh, whose works, translated into Greek during the ninth century, profoundly influenced Byzantine monks who followed the Hesychast movement. As an example, we can cite the following oft-quoted passage from his works:

> Try with all your might to enter the treasure-chamber that lies within you; then you will see the treasure that is in heaven, for these two are but one, and they are reached through the same door. The ladder to the Kingdom is within you, hidden in your soul.
>
> (Isaac of Nineveh (or of Syria), *Discourse* 30, 11; French trans., Deseille 2006:222)

Over the course of centuries, this type of Hesychast spirituality was part of various currents: these were heterodox to varying extents, but their practices were pushed underground and forced to remain hidden, or to retreat into

Figure 3.3 *Saint Hilarion of Gaza. A monk in Gaza in the fourth century. Fresco from the Studenica monastery (Serbia ; thirteenth – fourteenth century).* © *Svetlana Tomeković.*

Figure 3.4 *Euthymius the Great. He lived as a monk in the desert of Juda (fifth century). Fresco from the church of Tokali Kilise (Cappadocia; tenth century). © Catherine Jolivet-Lévy.*

monasteries outside of the Byzantine empire. This form of spirituality was mistrusted because certain of its adepts were close to deviant movements such as Messalianism,[1] and because they defied political and ecclesiastic authority. During the thirteenth century it mutated in a way that allowed it to gain new adherents, through the appearance of a new method of prayer.

Earliest descriptions of the hesychastic method of prayer

The oldest text that describes this method is by an anonymous author, and is known as *Method of Holy Prayer and Attention* (*Méthodos tès hiéras proseuchès kai prosochès*). This short text is cited in part by several fourteenth-century authors, either favourably (Gregory Palamas, Gregory of Sinai) or with unrelenting hostility (Barlaam of Calabria). Most of these authors attribute it to the eleventh-century mystic Symeon the New Theologian, an attribution that has been refuted by modern historians, so that our anonymous author is sometimes called the pseudo-Symeon. The text itself was published in 1927 (Hausherr 1927).

In this opuscule, the author first describes two forms of prayer, which he rejects. One consists of 'looking up, stretching out one's hands and imploring the heavens to have mercy' (ibid.:151); the other consists of resisting thoughts that come from outside oneself. For our author, these two forms of prayer both lead to illusion. He strongly recommends a third form of prayer, warning his readers that it is very difficult and its practice requires a guide; this is the form of prayer in which we are interested, and here is his description:

> Seated in a peaceful cell, away in a corner, apply yourself to doing as I tell you: close the door, raise your spirit above all vain and ephemeral objects. Then, pressing your beard against your chest, direct [the focus of] your bodily eye and your entire spirit simultaneously[2] on the middle of your belly, that is, your navel. Compress the inhalation that enters through your nose so that your breathing is not easy, and mentally scrutinize the inside of your entrails to discover the location of your heart, in which are found the powers of the soul. At first you will discover darkness and a tenacious weight, but if you persevere, if you practise this exercise night and day, O marvel! you will discover an infinite happiness. For as soon as the spirit has found the heart's location, all at once it sees what it had never seen before. It sees the air that is found inside the heart, and it sees itself entirely

1 A heresy that rejects all forms of ecclesiastic practice in favour of prayer alone. This was condemned at the Council of Ephesus in 431.

2 What I translate as 'spirit' is the νοῦς (*noûs*), sometimes rendered as intellect, the most subtle part of a human being.

> luminous and full of intelligent discernment. From this moment, if a thought presents itself it will not have time to take shape or become an image: [your spirit] will chase it away and destroy it by invoking Jesus Christ. The spirit, in its hostility towards the demon, will awaken the aggressiveness nature has given it against spiritual enemies, and it will expel them with powerful blows. You will learn all the rest with God's help, by practising the keeping of the spirit and retaining Jesus in your heart.
>
> (ibid.:164–5)

The first specific characteristic of this method is the recommended posture: the person praying is seated, whereas in the Christian East prayer was generally practised in a standing position; he bows his head down so deeply that his beard touches his chest; he looks (with his bodily eye, which therefore remains open, as well as with the metaphorical eye of the spirit) at his navel, in the middle of his belly. The second specificity here is the respiratory discipline demanded: the compression of the inhalation (and perhaps also the holding of the breath before exhaling, but this is not demanded in the text). The third is the mental activity, of 'discover[ing] the location of your heart', which is precisely situated 'inside… your entrails'. If the similarity with the above-cited text from Isaac is striking, one should nevertheless note that for Isaac the ladder leading to heaven is 'in your soul', while here the location of the heart, assimilable with the inner kingdom, is 'inside… your entrails'.

At more or less the same period another text began to be diffused, and the author of this one is known: Nicephorus the Hesychast was of Italian origin, a monk on Mount Athos who had been imprisoned and then exiled as a result of his opposition to the union with the Roman Church concluded by the Emperor at Lyon in 1274. His opuscule, written before he had suffered these tribulations, is called 'Very useful treatise on guarding of the heart' (Nicephorus 1865). It is made up of three parts: the prologue is a call to those who wish to know 'through experience and through their senses' (*peira kai aisthèsei*) the presence of the kingdom of heaven within their hearts, made manifest as a light and a fire; it also takes up the metaphor of the 'treasure that is hidden in the field of the heart' and promises that those who so desire may be taught a method (*méthodon*) that will, without pain, lead them to impassiveness (*apatheia*). This prologue is followed by an anthology that provides several short texts, essentially taken from the Desert Fathers, but also from Isaac of Nineveh (the passage cited above), and from Symeon the New Theologian. The aim of this anthology is to demonstrate the traditional character of the author's teaching. The presentation of the method itself is preceded by a warning that it is essential to practise it only with the help of a spiritual guide. This is followed by an excursus providing the physiological principles on which this method is based:

> Know, then, that the breath we exhale is the air itself. And we breathe this air for nothing other than the heart. Indeed, the heart is the source of life, and of the warmth of the body. Thus the heart attracts the breath in order to temper its own heat through exhalation, and give itself a good disposition. The author, or rather the servant, of such an order, is the lung. The Creator has made it to be porous. Like bellows, it makes the air go in and out. Thus the heart, attracting cold through the breath and rejecting heat, keeps the order for which it has been regulated, without ever transgressing it, with a view to dominating the nature of what is living.
>
> (Nicephorus the Hesychast 1865:963)

This excursus borrows from traditional physiology, derived from Plato's *Timaeus* and Aristotle's *De Respiratione*: the soul has its seat in the heart, which is also the hearth, generating inner heat; the heat, which is necessary for life, can destroy the heart if it is too great; the role of breathing is to introduce, through the lungs, a draught of cool air to refresh it. This analysis of physiology was transmitted through Byzantine Christianity, in particular via the treatises of Gregory of Nyssa (*De Hominis Opificio*) and Theodoret (*De Providentia*). For the physiological justification of the method, the fact that air that is inhaled goes directly to the heart via the lungs is fundamental, because this air that is breathed in is the vector of the entry of the spirit into the heart.

What follows is a description of the method itself:

> So, you, sit down and collect your spirit. Make it enter – I mean your spirit – along the path of the nostrils, through which the breath penetrates into the heart. Push it, and constrain it to remain within the heart along with the breath you have taken in. When it has entered, what happens next will no longer be denuded of joy and of grace, but [be] like a man who had been exiled from his own home, for when he returns no joy lacks for him any longer, because he is with his wife and children anew; thus the spirit, when it is united with the soul, is full of an indescribable pleasure and joy. Therefore, brother, make sure your spirit becomes accustomed never to come out quickly from that place. Indeed, at first it is completely opposed to letting itself be shut in and compressed inside. But once it is used to this, it no longer desires to move around the outside world. For, *the kingdom of heaven is in our interiors* [...] Thus, if from the beginning [...] you are entered by the spirit in the place that is your heart, that I have shown you, may grace be rendered unto God! [...]

> You must also learn this: when your spirit is in that place, it must not be silent and remain inactive, but rather it must have as its work and continual meditation the invocation: 'Lord Jesus Christ, son of God, have pity on me', without ever stopping. For these words keep the spirit calm and make it invulnerable and inaccessible to the enemy's suggestions, and they make it grow each day in love and desire for God. If, oh brother, despite your efforts you have been unable to enter into the places of the heart in the way we have described, do as I tell you and, with God's help, you will find what you seek. Know that the reason [*to logistikon*] of every man is in the heart. [...] Thus, after having rid the reason of all thought, offer it the [invocation] 'Lord Jesus Christ, son of God, have pity on me.' Constrain it to keep these words within itself, excluding all other reasoning. When, with time, you have mastered this practice, then the entrance of the heart will open for you, without any doubt, as we have written. We have experienced this ourselves. With much-desired joy and fervent attention, the entire chorus of virtues will follow, charity, joy, peace, etc., and through them all requests will reach our Lord Jesus Christ.
>
> (ibid.:963–5)

Here we observe that the description of the posture to be adopted is more allusive: yes, one must be seated, but there is no mention of bending the head, or of turning the gaze towards the navel. The breathing technique is also slightly different: it is no longer a question of compressing (*ancheïn*, to squeeze, from which is derived the English 'anguish') the inhalation, which induces a long-drawn-out in-breath, but rather of 'push[ing] it, constrain[ing] it to remain', which implies holding one's breath. The instruction to repeat the formula evoking the name of Jesus is only mentioned after the instruction regarding the breath. We must also remember how powerful the notion of constraint is here.

Among the spiritual men and mystics who adopted and described this method, we must accord particular attention to Gregory of Sinai. In the course of a life full of tribulations (captured by Turkish pirates as a young man, he was a slave for a time, escaped, became a monk in Cyprus, visited the monasteries of Sinai, Palestine and Crete, and eventually ended up at Athos), Gregory was initiated to the keeping of the heart and to pure prayer, doubtless on the basis of the *Method of Holy Prayer and Attention*. Gregory spent some time at Athos, where he was reproached for teaching an unknown path, but acquired numerous disciples. He ended his days in a monastery in Bulgaria. His influence on the spiritual authors of the period is considerable and was certainly a major vector for the diffusion of the new method of prayer (Rigo

2002). He wrote about this method in a treatise called 'On stillness and the two ways of prayer' (1865a).

> First thing in the morning, seated on a small stool, draw the spirit out from the reasoning mind and compress it in the heart, and keep it there within. Bend forward painfully, feeling a sharp pain in the chest, the shoulders and the nape, cry out persistently in your spirit or in your soul: 'Lord Jesus Christ, have pity on me.' Then, perhaps because of the contraction, the pain, and the tiredness, all due to prolonged effort, [...] transfer your spirit to the other half,[3] and say: 'Son of God, have pity on me.' Repeat this other half a large number of times. You must not be negligent and change back and forth many times, for plants that are constantly being set out anew do not take root. In addition, restrain the breath from coming back up through the lungs, in order to avoid breathing easily. For the exhalation of breath coming up from the heart obscures the spirit and excites the reason, expelling the spirit from the heart. [...] If you see the impurities of evil spirits, or thoughts, mounting or taking form in your spirit, do not be afraid, and if good reflections on things manifest themselves in you, do not pay attention to them, but restrain the exhalation as much as possible, enclose your spirit in your heart and repeat the invocation to Jesus continually and with perseverance: you will burn them easily, you will oppress them, flagellating them invisibly with the divine name. [...] That you must restrain the exhalation is attested by Isaiah the hermit and many others who have spoken on this subject.
>
> (Gregory of Sinai 1865a:1316)

Several quotations on the union of prayer and breathing follow, but apart from a phrase drawn from the *Method of Holy Prayer and Attention*, all of these quotations refer to the breath in a purely metaphorical way.

In another treatise, called 'How to sit in the cell' (1865b), Gregory gives more details of the method:

> Sometimes on a stool – most of the time, because of the painful nature of this – sometimes even on a bed, but rarely, and just for a brief moment, to rest yourself; you must remain seated patiently, because of he who said: *Continue in prayer* (1 Col. 4, 2), and not rise rapidly through indolence, because of the painful suffering, from the internal cry of the spirit and continual immobility. [...] Instead, bending downwards, introduce your

3 Gregory probably evokes here the second part of the invocation to Christ: the first being 'Lord Jesus Christ' and the second 'Son of God.'

> spirit into your heart, if it is open, and call the Lord Jesus to your aid. If your shoulders hurt and your head is painful, persevere laboriously and with love in this activity, seeking the Lord in your heart. For *the kingdom of heaven suffereth violence, and the violent take it by force.* (Matt. 11, 12)
>
> Certain of the Fathers say, 'Lord Jesus Christ, Son of God, have pity on me,' in its entirety; others say one half: 'Jesus, Son of God, have pity on me,' which is easier because of the weakness of the spirit. [...] Some teach that the formula must be pronounced aloud with the mouth, others that it should be uttered by the spirit. I think one must do both. [...] The retention of the inhalation, keeping the mouth closed, retains the spirit, but only partially, and then it is dispersed.
>
> (Gregory of Sinai 1865b:1329)

What is striking here, by comparison with the preceding texts, is the precision and detailed nature of the instructions, with their insistence on the constraints that the person praying must place on himself, the pain that arises from maintaining the posture, the holding of the breath, and the details on the two types of formula for the prayer. The liberty of the Fathers of the Desert and of Sinai, simply to utter the name of Jesus, is far away now. In addition, the introduction of the spirit into the heart, and its retention there, building on the physiological description of Nicephorus, seem to be the principal aims of this method.

Gregory also describes the effects anticipated from the use of this method, which may be physical or spiritual:

> Some people see a sort of light that rises. Among others there is a kind of trembling exultation. And others feel joy [...] Among others it is trembling and joy [...] and among others still, a good cheer that the fathers have often called a thrill [σκίρτημα], and that is a power of the Spirit and a movement of the living heart. It is also called a pulsation [πάλμος] and a sigh of the Spirit that intercedes for us with God in inexplicable ways. [...] One must be aware that there are two kinds of thrill or good cheer: the serene kind, called pulsation, sigh and intercession of the Spirit, and the other kind, the great [movement] of the heart, that is also called thrill, or leap or vibration, and that is an open-winged jump of the living heart towards the divine air. For, receiving from the divine Spirit the wings of loving desire, and free of the bonds of passion, the soul strives to fly upwards even before its exodus; it seeks to separate itself from what weighs it down.
>
> (ibid.:1308–9)

Other examples of Hesychast prayer and its effects exist in the spiritual literature of the fourteenth century, but these few extracts are, we believe, sufficient, because the same elements recur in all of these texts.

Historians of spirituality have sought the reasons for these modifications of Hesychast prayer. The insistence by fourteenth-century spiritual authors (Nicephorus the Hesychast, Gregory of Sinai, Gregory Palamas) that they conform perfectly to a tradition going back to the first centuries of Christianity cannot hide the fact that novel elements are at the heart of this way of praying: none of the earlier authors had recommended any specific posture, any breath control or any predetermined form of words. At most they may have, in a few places, offered advice that bore some resemblance to the instructions given by our authors.

Several hypotheses on the subject have been put forward: similarities have been detected between some of the characteristic aspects of the method (the seated posture, inclining forward; the gaze fixed on the navel; breath control) and practices found in Buddhism, yoga, Anatolian Sufism, among fakirs, and even in Taoism. But how would these practices have been transmitted to Byzantine Hesychasm? The most convincing theory to date has been advanced by Antonio Rigo (1998): he finds that, at the beginning of the thirteenth century, in a region of Central Asia corresponding more or less with today's Turkestan, that was Islamized but also influenced by Shamanist and Buddhist cults, a method of prayer arose that brought together physical posture, breath control, and the repetition of the Names of God. One of the initiators of this method was the Sufi, Najm al-dīn Kubrā (d. 1221), who founded a Sufi brotherhood in the region. The essential elements of this method for prayer are the posture (seated with the legs crossed), and control of the breath, allied with the pronunciation of the syllables of the Islamic profession of faith (*Lā ilaha illā Allāh*), which can be assimilated to the *dhikr* (rumination on the Name of God). After the death of this Sufi master, his disciples were pushed to the west by the migration of the Turkish tribes of Central Asia as they fled from Mongol expansion; they travelled through Iran and the Caucasus as far as Anatolia. In this way, some of the Sufis of this brotherhood went as far as the Seljuk Sultanate of Konya, where they encountered and mixed with disciples of Jalāl al-Dīn Rūmī (d. 1273), the founder of the Mevlevi Sufi brotherhood of 'whirling dervishes'. Another name for this kingdom was the Sultanate of Rûm (in other words, of 'the Romans', that is, the Byzantines, who were still numerous in this recently conquered region). Here, contact between Christians and the disciples of Rūmī was fairly frequent: Rūmī himself visited the so-called 'Plato's monastery'[4] near Konya, where he liked to speak with the resident monks. It was thus that the psycho-physical techniques of the *dhikr*, brought by Sufis from Central Asia, were diffused throughout the Muslim world, and, through contact with Byzantine monks in the Sultanate of Rûm, into the Christian world. It is indeed striking to observe that the *Method of Holy Prayer and Attention* and Nicephorus's treatise are contemporary with these contacts between Anatolian Sufis and Byzantine monks.

The Hesychast quarrel

This method of prayer, originally confined to monastic milieux, would become more widely known because of a polemic. Let us briefly retrace its origins.

In 1334, Barlaam, a philosopher-monk from Calabria, was invited to discuss with two of the Pope's legates the theological disagreements that divided the Church of Rome from that of Constantinople. The Pope's legates, who were Dominicans, used Scolasticism in their arguments, an approach that Barlaam challenged. Onto this question of the legitimacy of syllogisms in theology, was then grafted an epistolary quarrel between Barlaam (for whom, given that human reason is incapable of attaining God, God was essentially unknowable) and a monk from Mount Athos, Gregory Palamas, who defended the possibility of knowing God. Among his arguments, Gregory happened to cite the experiential knowledge of God that monks could attain through the use of a specific method of prayer. Intrigued, Barlaam undertook an enquiry among the monks of Thessalonica, and declared himself scandalized by what he discovered. He expressed this sentiment in a letter to another monk, Ignatius (who was called 'The Hesychast'). This letter interests us because it provides a precise description (in an ironic mode) of Hesychast prayer:

> Having formed ties with certain men who are called by the same name as you (that is to say, Hesychasts), they initiated me into monstrosities and absurd doctrines [...] They offered up their teachings on marvellous separations and reunions of the spirit and the soul, on the commerce that demons may have with the soul, on the differences that exist between lights that are tawny or white, on the arrivals or departures of the spirit that passes through the nostrils with the breath, on the pulsations that occur in the vicinity of the navel, and, finally, on the union of our Lord with the soul that is produced in the navel in complete certainty of heart, and in a way that is fully accessible to the senses.
>
> (Barlaam of Calabria 1954:323)

4 This is the monastery of Saint Chariton the Confessor, founded during the ninth to tenth centuries and standing about eight kilometres from Konya.

Figure 3.5 *Saint Gregory Palamas. The author of the theological doctrine backing the hesychastic method of prayer in the fourteenth century. Fresco from the saints Cosmas and Damian church in the Vatopedi monastery (Mount Athos),1371. © Georges Fousteris Archives.*

This description includes almost all of the principal characteristics of the Hesychast method of prayer: a posture centred on the navel, breath control as a vector for the spirit, bodily effects. The only thing lacking is the formula for invocation.

Not content only to attack the method, Barlaam also attacked those who practised it, principally on the grounds of their pretension to the attainment of an experiential knowledge of God. He published a treatise, 'Against the Messalians' – known through the Triads of Palamas (1973) and whose title comes from the heresy that was condemned at the Council of Ephesus – denouncing those who practised Hesychasm as heretics before the Synod of Constantinople. Gregory Palamas defended the monks in a treatise composed of three books, known as the Triads, or The Holy Hesychasts (1973). In these, one finds several descriptions and justifications of the method of prayer:

> It is not out of place to teach, especially to beginners, how to look within oneself, and how to send one's spirit inside of oneself by means of the inhalation. Indeed, no man of sense would forbid anyone to use certain procedures to bring his spirit back within himself when it does not yet contemplate itself. Anyone who has only just begun this struggle sees his spirit fleeing continually, barely assembled; he must therefore bring it back to himself just as continually; in his inexperience, he does not realise that nothing on earth is harder to contemplate, and more mobile, than the spirit. This is why some recommend that such people place a strong watch on their breath as it goes out and comes back in; they should hold it in a little bit, in order also to hold in the spirit and watch over it, too, until, with God's help, they have progressed, and fortified their spirit against all that surrounds it, and have purified it, and are able to bring it back to a unified contemplation. And we can observe that this constitutes a spontaneous effect of the spirit's attention, for the entrance and departure of the breath become peaceful during all intense reflection, especially among those whose bodies and spirits are in *Hesychia*. [...]
>
> Among beginners, none of these phenomena occur without tiredness. [...] For when they seek to bring the spirit back within the self in order to push it into the movement that is not a straight line, but rather a circular and infallible movement,[5] instead of letting their eyes wander here and there, how could it not be more profitable for them to fix the eyes on their chests or their navels, as on a firm starting point? For not only will the seeker thus outwardly fall back into himself as much as is possible, in conformity with

5 According to Dionysius the Aeropagite (*Divine Names*, IV, 9), the soul adopts a circular motion when it contemplates itself, and it is in this way that it attains God.

Figure 3.6 The Tranfiguration of Christ on Mount Thabor. Among the expected results of the hesychastic method of prayer is the actual vision of the light of the Transfiguration. Miniature painting from Ms. Paris. gr. 1242, f. 92v. –1 375, © BNF.

> the inner movement sought for the spirit, but also, in adopting such a bodily posture, he will send the power of the spirit, that flows away when one looks to the outside, back towards the interior of the heart.
>
> (Palamas 1973:7–8)

Having thus justified the rational and traditional character of the prayer method, Gregory Palamas goes on to defend the orthodoxy of the effects of this way of praying. Hesychast monks did indeed report physical repercussions from this form of prayer. Gregory gives several examples of these:

> If one asks them: 'Why do you say that the prayer vibrates secretly in your entrails, and what sets your heart in motion?,' they illustrate this by mentioning the earthquake that Elijah felt before the manifest and intelligible apparition of God (cf. 1 Kings 19, 11), and also the bowels and inward parts of Isaiah, that shall 'sound like an harp' (cf. Isaiah 16, 11). And

Figure 3.7 *Ecumenical Council of Constantinople, 1351. Headed by Emperor Jean Cantacuzene, this council definitively endorsed Gregory Palamas' theology and made it an official tenet of the Greek Church. Miniature painting from Ms. Paris. gr. 1242, f. 92v. – 1375.*

if one asks them again, why the prayer produces heat in us, they will speak of the fire that the same Elijah designated as a sign from God before His apparition, a sign that must be transformed into a light breeze if it is on the verge of assuming the divine ray and designating the Invisible to he who contemplates it.
(ibid.:25)

Thus, while the soul is transported and seems to be shaken by irresistible love for the sole Desirable One, the heart, too, is also shaken, and it indicates by its spiritual movement that it is in communication with grace itself, as if it were flying up from this world below to encounter the Lord, when He will come with His body through the clouds, as has been promised. Thus, in continuous prayer, when the intelligible flame is lit and when, through spiritual contemplation, the spirit awakens love in an aerial flame, the body also, in a strange way, becomes light and hot.

(ibid.:32)

Palamas gives still further description of the effects of hesychastic prayer; for example, in a letter to his disciple, Menas:

> Someone who has not received the lively joy of the saviour Jesus, often called a shudder by the Fathers, a power that is constrictive and a movement of the living heart, is someone who has not experienced this joy fully.
>
> What spirit does Isaiah say we must receive and bring forth (Isaiah 26, 18)? Is it not that of the Lord Jesus Christ acting in the fire within his believers and accomplishing their salvation? But which fire whips demons and causes them to flee, as John the divine Father tells us? Is it not that of the Lord Jesus, which burns inwardly in his memory? What other odour is there for the Most High, but the heat of the breath that sometimes comes ineffably out of his nostrils?
>
> (Rigo 1988:57–80)

Quite soon this quarrel extended beyond the practice of prayer. Gaining impetus from the physical effects that monks claimed brought them an experiential knowledge of God, it entered the territory of theology itself, with the help of Barlaam's accusations: these monks claim to attain God's very essence; they are repeating the Messalian heresy. It was in order to respond to this allegation that Gregory Palamas elaborated a theological doctrine that would unleash even greater passions. According to this doctrine, the essence of God remains completely inaccessible, but those who practise Hesychast prayer, and use it to bring their spirits back into their hearts, gain access to the uncreated, and thus Divine, 'energies' (or operations, or activities – the Greek term *energeiai* is difficult to translate accurately) of God that are His light, His grace, His heat, etc. We will not examine the theological implications of this doctrine, but only say that by appearing to introduce plurality into God, Palamas was accused of a return to polytheism through having distinguished between a superior divinity (the inaccessible essence) and several inferior divinities (the accessible energies). In 1341 the Synod of Constantinople decided in favour of Palamas and against Barlaam, and in 1351 it instituted Palamas's theology as the official doctrine of the Byzantine Church. The Hesychast method of prayer acquired the right to exist in the Church, although it remained largely (but not exclusively) the preserve of monks.

If we leave to one side the political issues that perturb one's reading of this episode of Byzantine history, the Hesychast quarrel has two dimensions, theological and anthropological. The theological controversy around the distinction between the essence and the *energeiai* of God, an issue that eventually became all important, was born from the attempt by Gregory Palamas to find a theological justification for the physical effects of the

Hesychast method of prayer (visions of lights, heat, shudders of the heart), which were presented as an experience of God's presence and a foretaste of mankind's divinization. This doctrine relates to God, and is therefore properly 'theological', but its point of departure is an anthropological question: can human beings experience God, not only in their spirits (the acceptance of which notion already means adopting a theological position), but also in their bodies? Thus the question of the place of the body within the religious experience is at the heart of this quarrel, which is not surprising, given that it springs from the advent of a method that demands a specific physical posture, and control of the breath. It is therefore equally unsurprising that two of Palamas's principal adversaries should be Barlaam of Calabria and Nicephorus Gregoras, two Platonic philosophers who believed that in order to accede to knowledge, the human spirit had to purify itself of what was sensed physically. They were certainly more in harmony with the Plotinian ascent than with the Hesychast method of prayer.[6] The existence of two antagonistic movements, one a quasi-dualism that valued the soul to the detriment of the body, and the other an anthropological monism that insisted on the union between these two components of the human being, goes back as far as the origins of Christianity (Congourdeau 2007). As for Palamas's other great adversary, Gregory Acindynus, he never denied the validity of Hesychast prayer, instead refusing to accept any distinction between essence and *energeiai* in God: his quarrel with Palamas was thus strictly theological, and not relevant to the present investigation.

This is thus a question of the relationship between the body and the soul or spirit. The aim of the prayer method is to facilitate the 'descent of the spirit into the heart' in order to attain *Hesychia*, a state of inner peace in the presence of God. From this point of view, the movement is situated in the afterlife of a spiritual tradition that goes back to the Desert Fathers: the aim is to discover the 'inner kingdom', the 'hidden treasure' that is at once internal and celestial. This attempt at interiority is common to Christianity and other cultures, which, in the region of Konya, may have facilitated the contacts and syncretisms between Christian monks and Sufis that were the probable sources of the mutation that brought forth the Hesychast method of prayer.

If we use the word 'mutation', it is because the depths of the interior into which the believer descended, which was until then considered to refer to the interior of the soul, was now situated in the body: the 'location of the heart' is no longer the centre of the soul, but rather it is explicitly placed in the region of the navel and/or in the physical heart, into which, according to

---

6 In this case it is irrelevant that Barlaam and Gregory were adversaries within the same Platonic movement.

traditional physiology, flows the air we breathe (and this is the link between the heart and both the respiration and the posture to be adopted, bent over with the head towards the chest). Although Barlaam's caricature of the method, and his qualification of monks who practised it as *omphalopsychites* (people who identify their souls with their navels), along with certain rather forbidding aspects of the method itself (Gregory of Sinai mentions constraint, pain, difficulty breathing) may give a negative image of this practice, it is nevertheless founded on anthropological essentials, and this is why traces and versions of this approach can be found in numerous cultures, regions, and periods.

If we undertake to 'modernize' the terminology of Hesychasm in order to make it easier to understand in today's world, we could attempt to see conscience in 'the spirit' (*noûs*), and the self in 'the heart' (the intimate centre of a human being). 'Making the spirit descend into the heart' then means bringing about the union of conscience and self. Might we go further, and identify this procedure with what contemporary psychiatrists call 'mindfulness'?[7] This experience of 'mindfulness' – validated by brain-imaging technology – is often identified with a re-appropriation of the body, and can be sought and discovered through physical practices (sometimes borrowed from Buddhism), such as the seated posture, and breath control. One of the potential results claimed for these practices is inner peace, which is not so far from what Byzantine spiritual monks called *Hesychia*. We leave the question open.

Our presentation of these hypotheses does not indicate any denial of the religious dimension of the Hesychast method of prayer that appeared during the fourteenth century, for this 'method' is precisely and only that: a *méth-ode* (μέθ-οδος), etymologically a guide for a journey, and not an end in itself. In his Triads, Gregory Palamas (1973:7) tells his readers that this method is mostly aimed at beginners. The goal is the inner kingdom, the 'hidden treasure' that is God himself. For Palamas, the re-attribution of value to the human body, to which this method bears witness, goes along with an insistence on the importance of the incarnation and the sacraments, especially the Eucharist, during which the believer absorbs into his own body the body of God made flesh. In any case, this Hesychast tradition reveals the existence, particularly within Eastern Christianity, of techniques of spiritual experience that were rooted in an anthropological monism.

---

7 The expression was popularized in France by the psychiatrist Christophe André; it is significant that he mentions his stays in monasteries as being among the inspirations for his thinking on this subject.

References

Barlaam of Calabria. 1954. 'Letter 5 to Ignatius the Hesychast'. In G. Schiro (ed.), *Barlaam Calabro, Epistole Greche*. Palerme: Istituto Siciliano di Studi Bizantini e Neogreci.

Deseille, P. 2006. *Saint Isaac le Syrien: Discours ascétiques selon la version grecque*. Solan: Monastère Saint-Antoine le grand and Monastère de Solan.

Congourdeau, M.-H. 2007. *L'embryon et son âme dans les sources grecques*. Paris: Amis du Centre d'Histoire et Civilisation de Byzance.

Dionysius Areopagites. 2016. 'Divine names I–IV', *Sources Chrétiennes* 378. Paris.

Gregory of Sinai. 1865a. 'On stillness and the two ways of prayer', *PG* 150:1313–29.

——— 'How to sit in the cell', *PG* 150:1329–45.

Palamas, G. 1973. 'Triads for the defense of those who practise sacred quietude'. In J. Meyendorff (ed.), *Grégoire Palamas, Défense des saints hésychastes*. Louvain: Spicilegium sacrum Lovaniense.

Hausherr, I. 1927. 'La Méthode d'oraison hésychaste', *Orientalia Christiana* IX(36):150–72.

Hesychius of Sinai. 1974–5. 'On watchfulness and holyness'. In M. Waegeman, 'Les 24 chapitres De temperantia et virtute d'Hésychius le Sinaïte (édition critique)', *Sacris Erudiri* XXII(2) :218–70.

Isaac of Nineveh (or of Syria). 1770. 'Ascetica'. In N. Theotokis (ed.), *Τοῦ ὁσίου πατρός ημῶν Ἰσαάκ Ἐπισκόπου Νινευή τοῦ σύρου τά εὑρεθέντα ἀσκητικά*. Leipzig: Breitkopf.

John Climacus. 1860. 'The ladder of paradise', *PG* 88 :632–1164.

Nicephorus the Hesychast. 1865. 'Very useful treatise on guarding of the heart', *PG* 147:945–66.

Rigo, A. 1988. 'L'Epistola a Menas di Gregorio Palamas e gli effetti dell'orazione', *Cristianesimo nella Storia* 9:57–80.

— — — 1998. 'Le origini delle tecniche psicofisiche d'orazione del Cristianesimo bizantino'. In A. Vega *et al.* (eds), *Estetica y Religión. El discurso del cuerpo y los sentidos*, pp. 257–66. Seville-Barcelona: Institut Universitari de Cultura. Universitat Pompeu Fabra, DL.

— — — 2002. 'Gregorio il Sinaita'. In C.G. Conticello (ed.), *La Théologie byzantine et sa tradition*, vol. II, pp. 35–130. Leuven: Turnhout.

— — — 2008. *Mistici bizantini*. Turin: Einaudi Editore.

II

DIAGRAMS AND VISUALIZATION

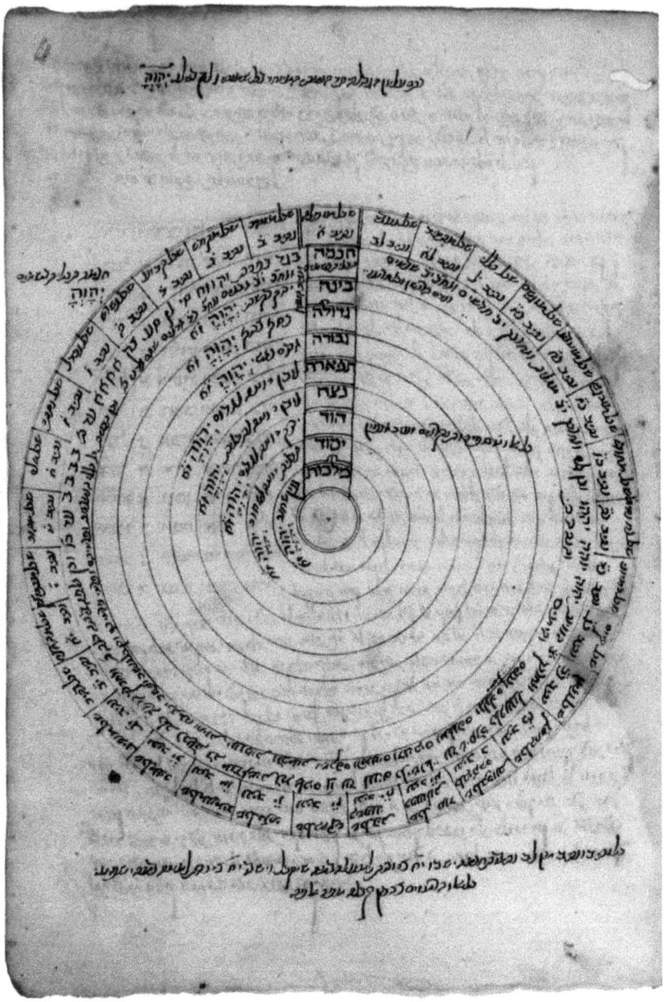

Figure 4.1 A diagram that forms a mandala and belonged to R. David ben Yehudah he-Hasid, a late thirteenth-century kabbalist (ms Milano-Ambrosiana 62, fo. 4a).

4

From rituals to techniques in Jewish mysticism

Between 'East' and 'West'

Moshe Idel

> *'This is the world of performing Commandments and of the Deed.'*
> (R. Moshe Cordovero, *Pardes Rimmonim* 1962, XXXI:6)

The main purpose of this study is to present some aspects of Judaism as a performative religion by the dint of its rituals and techniques. The centrality of those performances has been neglected in the study of Jewish mysticism, given that the type of scholarship in the field privileged the more intellectual aspects of this religion, due to the influence of prevailing scholarship of history of religion as articulated in Germany. The performative nature of traditional Judaism, which continued through the Middle Ages, constitutes the matrix for many of the later developments in kabbalistic literature and praxis, where rabbinic rites metamorphosed in techniques, and eventually appropriated also some new techniques, as we shall see below.

Judaism: from Asia to Europe

The earlier forms of what is conceived to be Judaism, including Jewish mystical literatures, emerged in the Middle East, in a geographical area that includes Mesopotamia and Egypt. For more than two millennia, that was the main region of its different developments. These include manifold contacts with a variety of religions, including Assyrian, Babylonian, Egyptian, Iranian (Zoroastrian and Zurvanite), Ugarit, Akkadian, Hurrian, Hittite, Greek and, later on, Roman, Christian and Islamic, and some of their different combinations, like Gnosticism or Manichaeism. Even contacts with Hindu views and practices of Altaic tribes can be discerned. While borrowing from those religious systems at different stages of its development, the ancient biblical and the late-antiquity and medieval rabbinic forms of Judaism focused their main religious life not on theological speculations, nor even on theologies of monotheism, nor on mythologies, whether autochthonous or eventually adopted from other sources, but on a certain ritualistic *modus vivendi*. When a philosophical understanding of Judaism emerged, such as that of Philo of Alexandria, its content has been completely ignored within rabbinic Judaism. The primary focus of these two forms of Judaism was the performance of the biblical commandments, which had been elaborated in many details in numerous rabbinic treatises, written over many generations. Those various rites are based on the primacy of precise details, which renders those acts as religiously significant. In the huge majority of the discussions of the rituals, no myths are given in relation to their performance (see, for example, Gruenwald 2003; Swartz 2011), and only extraordinarily rarely is some aetiological explanation provided for their emergence. I would define those earlier forms of Judaism as gravitating around the concept of 'performing body', which means that what counted more from the religious point of view were ritual acts and techniques, rather than theological speculations or the centrality of belief.[1]

Ritual performances have been articulated within rabbinic Judaism as being related to the 613 commandments that correspond to the 613 limbs and sinews of the human body. This specific nexus between the imaginary structure of the limbs of the human body and commandments, which is very meagre in early rabbinic literature, turned out to be pivotal for the further developments in theosophical-theurgical Kabbalah.[2] The structuring of the rituals, which sometimes turned into techniques, as symmetrical or isomorphic to the human and the divine bodies, is one of the topics to be treated below, part of an effort to organize a rich body of religious knowledge

1 Idel 1983a:201–26, 1988a:57, 160, 168, 172–99, 232, 245, 1998:3–6, 2009a, 2009b:93–134. See also Idel 1993, 1995, 2002:3, 13, 31, 60, 67, 73–4 etc., 2005a:7, 11, 16–18, 68, 114–15, 120–1 etc., 2005b:33–4, 47, 215–20. Meanwhile, a variety of scholars discovered the importance of performance in Jewish mysticism. See, for example, Elkayam 1990:5–40; Garb 1997:47–67, 2011; Mottolese 2017, 2018:7–61. For some aspects of Kabbalah I refer to as 'ergetic', namely as related to learning by doing, see Idel 1990. For the importance of body as related to technique in human behaviour in more general, basically sociological terms, see Mauss 1943.

2 Though the source of this figure for the commandments is Talmudic (Mak. 23b), it did not play an important role in its connection to the human body in rabbinic literature until the emergence of theosophical Kabbalah in the Middle Ages. See also, Scholem 1974a:279.

in more comprehensive patterns.[3] The leading scheme is the structure of the commandments, and the numbers of the limbs and sinews of the body have been accommodated to that structure. The emphasis on performance includes also a significant role attributed to magical practices, in the stricter sense of the word. In my opinion, this attitude reflects an archaic, probably 'pre-axial' approach (as understood by Karl Jaspers).

Since the last century of the first millennium of the Common Era, great parts of the vast literary production of Jews have made their way to Europe, and the western part of North Africa, triggering a new phase of development, especially since the beginning of the second millennium CE, I designate as the 'great transition' (see, for the time being, Idel 2007:111–127, 2016b). This is comprised by Biblical literature, the Talmud, Midrashim, prayers and liturgical poems, customs, the so-called Hekhalot literature, magical treatises and recipes. The details of such a transition, or the dates of the arrival of these materials, are basically unknown.

What is characteristic of the emerging centres of Jewish culture in those new areas is a more intimate type of relationship with the two monotheistic religions, Christianity and Islam, than previously in the Middle East. More than Judaism, those religions absorbed Greek philosophical influences during the first millennium CE, and developed complex theologies, inspired basically by neo-Aristotelianism and Neoplatonism, which could be described as the axial forms of these religiosities. The focus in these was much more on speculation, contemplation, or belief, while the rituals played a much more modest role in their general religious economy. Under the conceptual impacts of those encounters, theological speculations emerged also in some elite forms of rabbinic Judaism. In some cases, this introduction, and that of Greek philosophy in general, generated tensions with the more concrete, ritually – and bodily – oriented forms of earlier Judaism, the anti-Maimonidean series of polemics since early thirteenth century, being the best known ones.

It is since the twelfth century that we may notice the accelerated emergence of a variety of theologies and theosophies among Jews in Al-Andalus, Catalonia and Castile, and, though much less, so in Germany and France, and, at the same time, the formulation of several types of techniques for, and numerous new interpretations of, the rabbinic rituals (*ta'amei mitzwot* – literally rationales

3 For the importance of the anthropomorphic structures of the Torah, the world of the angels, and of the *sefirot* within the realm of the infinite, see my early studies printed in the early eighties: Idel 1980b (and its enlarged and updated English version, 2009c), 1981 and 1986. See also, Idel 2001 and Wolfson 1989. For the emphasis on organization of knowledge in Kabbalah, see, for example, Idel 1988a:32, 213, 1995b:20, 41–2; 234–5, 257n.58, 272n.14.

for performing the commandments), which were intended to strengthen the importance of the elaborated ritual practices performed in any case of most of Jews.[4] In other words, a more axial understanding of religion has been grafted onto a pre-axial religion based on the centrality of performance. While philosophical theologies, which gravitated around an abstract, intellectual divinity as the main vision of Judaism, have problematized the centrality of the ritual performance, in other cases, such as that of the main school in theosophical-theurgical Kabbalah, the emerging modes of theological thought interacted with the performance of the rabbinic rituals, imagined now as predominantly intended to induce changes within the structure of ten powers found in the divine realm – something I would designate to be theurgy.[5] One of the theses expounded below will be that rituals when performed with awareness of a detailed structure, either divine or human/psychological, and intend to impact them, turn into techniques. The coordination of performance with the details of complex theosophies invites additional mental operations, which amount to an intensification of human activities, in comparison to the earlier, more corporeal acts, and thus an acceleration of actions involved in the new conceptualizations of the ritual, transforming it in a technique.

In a recent interesting observation about the relationship between theology and Judaism, a Christian scholar of the Hebrew Bible wrote as follows:

> Theology has never been a major feature of Jewish religion. The highly theoretical, philosophical constructions that constitute theology are very much at home in Christian thinking, whereas Jewish movements have tended to eschew such speculative constructions in favor of halakhic and textualist procedures. There are, of course, exceptions to these generalizations (e.g., the Kabbala tends to be mystical, speculative, and comprehensive) but generally the nature of the theological in Judaism is different from that in Christianity.[6]
>
> (Carroll 1994:267)

4 For the new genre of commentaries on the rationales of the commandments among the kabbalists, see Idel 1988a:xvi–xv or Wolfson 1988a.

5 See the sources of this view and its different variants in Garb 2004; Idel 1988a:112–99; Lorberbaum 2015:94–99; Mopsik 1993; Wolfson 1988b and 1988c.

6 These are remarks on George Steiner's 1990 Gifford lectures, entitled *Grammars of Creation*.

Though this depiction of Judaism is generally accurate, the emphasis on the Kabbalah as somehow different by virtue of its speculative dimensions seems to me a little bit exaggerated.

However, the role of techniques, which will concern us below, was to induce changes within the human psyche, so that it may attain a variety of extraordinary experiences: revelations, visions, ecstatic states, mystical union or communion. The thousands of recipes found in Hebrew in manuscripts and printed books, where instructions are formulated as to how to obtain a certain specific material effect, are quite technical. These techniques may be rooted in a belief of the magical powers of words and invocations, of names of angels, gods or demons, and of magical bowls; and, alternatively, in the belief in an astral order of the universe, what can be called talismanic, or astro-magic, directed to the astral bodies, sometimes connected to Hermetic literatures. In this category we may include also medical prescriptions.

To be sure, both rituals and techniques, presumably also customs, pre-existed the flowering of Judaism in European regions, and were found, in their vast majority, already in the Middle East, but their elaborations are evident in Europe in the high Middle Ages. In other words, while Judaism developed dramatically in the West in this period, it contained major components of performance as part of an attempt at attaining more intense forms of experience that were characteristic of the 'East'. Therefore, though emerging and flowering in the Latin West, phenomenologically speaking, medieval Jewish forms of mysticism are more similar to the Christian Orthodox forms of mysticism, like the praxis of hesychasm and the ideal of theosis, despite the fact that most of its main medieval developments took place in European regions. Certainly, 'West' and 'East' are quite vague terms when discussing complex topics that develop over centuries, like religions. They are, nevertheless, useful here heuristically, not just in terms of theological differences, such monotheism verses polytheism, respectively, but also in the field that will concern us below: the existence of, the role and the attitude to, techniques and rituals (see Canetti and Piras 2018).

The relative absence of techniques to attain mystical experiences – ascetic practices aside – is more evident in the Christian-Western forms of mysticism than in the Christian Orthodox ones. And they are more central in Hindu, Japanese or Muslim forms of mysticism, than in the Christian ones. It seems that most of Italy[7] and the countries westwards belong, geographically and phenomenologically, to what I shall call 'West', while the Byzantine Empire and the Slavonic regions, as well as the other, more eastern forms of religion,

7 In the south of the peninsula there were some Byzantine cultural and religious centres still active in the second part of the thirteenth century.

belong to what I shall designate as 'East'. Despite the significant divergences between religiosities of 'West' and 'East', the western parts of the 'East' were in contact with the eastern part of the 'West', and some encounters took place at this conjuncture (Idel 2017:7–51). Moreover, some major aspects of Judaism, though belonging to what we called 'East', developed nevertheless in the West, and the impact of the Western visions of this religion is evident in the scholarly treatments, which ignored the performative dimensions: mainly the central role played by rituals and techniques.

European scholarship of religion

Like many other forms of scholarship in the humanities, the critical study of religion first began in west and central Europe, and the intellectual propensities there, from the Middle Ages onwards, have coloured the manner in which religion has been depicted by scholars. This means that the more theological aspect of religion, namely the acquaintance with the nature of divinity, was conceived of by scholars as quintessential for understanding the nature of the religious experience (Idel 2004a:123–74). A corollary is that in the West experiences of contact with divinity were imagined as granted, freely, by the divine grace to the aspirant. The role of the specific path to reach divinity was neglected in the early scholarship of religion. Though certain rules that were part of the general ways of life in specific social-religious frameworks, such as monasteries and orders – to say nothing of cells – have certainly been respected, they were conceived more as a form of preparation, rather than as techniques sufficiently effective in themselves to ensure the attainment of mystical experiences, without mentioning the intervention of the divine grace. The concept of the fallen man, so central in Christianity, left its indelible imprint on the prevailing anthropology. Montaigne, in a passage that has been cited by A.O. Lovejoy (1976:102), regarded the place of man as in 'the filth and mire of the world, the worst, the lowest, most lifeless part of the universe, the bottom story of the house'. This passage illustrates the more general approach inspired by the Aristotelian world-view in the Middle Ages. The place of man in this world was, according to Lovejoy,

> not a position of honor; it was rather the place farthest removed from the Empyrean, the bottom of creation, to which its dregs and baser elements sank. The actual centre, indeed, was Hell; in the spatial sense the medieval world was literally diabolocentric.
>
> (ibid.:101–2)

Even more relevant for our argument, is the diagnosis of C.S. Lewis, another eminent scholar, describing the Christian contemporaries of the medieval Jews in Europe:

> Our highest privilege is to imitate it [the celestial dance as described by Chalcidius, the interpreter of Plato] in such measure as we can. The Medieval Model is, if we may use the word, anthropoperipheral. We are creatures of the Margin.
>
> (Lewis 1967:58)

I assume that the two characterizations are, to a certain extent, exaggerations, but they are nevertheless corroborated by more recent studies (Boia 2000:109–10; Delumeau 1990). In a more moderate manner, Evelyn Underhill, acknowledged 'the total dependence on this free action of God immanent and transcendent, is therefore a true part of worship' (Underhill 1937:11).

This is basically the reverberations of the famous theory, formulated by the leading nineteenth-century theologian F. Schleiermacher, of the nature of religion being that of 'absolute dependence' and 'creature feeling' (Behrens 1998:471–81). This marginalization of humans, especially when compared to the transcendental, perfect, God, is implicit in the centrality of the fallen human condition. The theories of Schleiermacher's most famous follower, the influential twentieth-century scholar Rudolph Otto, gravitate around the concepts of the 'wholly other', the numinous and the holy, and still operate on the basis of some form of human reaction to what he calls the *mysterium tremendum*, which is conceived to be transcendental, his critique of his predecessor notwithstanding.[8] We may describe them as a combination between Kantianism, Hegelianism and some sort of Western Christianity.[9]

---

8 On this topic and its influence in scholarship, see S. Sarbacker, 'Rudolph Otto and the concept of the numinous', *Oxford Research Encyclopedia of Religion:* oxfordre.com/religion/view/10.1093/acrefore/9780199340378.001.0001/acrefore-9780199340378-e-88 (accessed 3 May 2025). For critiques of Otto's view of religion from the perspective of Jewish sources, see Berkovits 2002, who already pointed out explicitly (ibid.:314) the significance of closeness, related to the root QDSh, which is invariably understood by Otto as if pointing solely to the wholly different. See also Idel 2006a; Leiser 1971.

9 See, for example, the emphasis on the Christian dimension of Schleiermacher's view of religion, (and in my opinion, this is pertinent also for Otto's vision) in a statement of another leading Christian theologian, Karl Barth, 'Christian pious self-awareness contemplates and describes itself', as quoted in Macquarrie 2001:210–11.

Ultimately, this privileging of the cognitive functions of humans, following Greek philosophical axiology, is less than consonant with archaic rituals, and provided the Paulinian shift. In Hegelianism, the religious developments do not depend on human activities, but on the inevitable evolution of the spirit.

The impact of this approach, which emphasizes the 'mysterious' and transcendental holiness, is evident also in some scholarly conceptualizations of Judaism.[10] Though in the case of Maimonidean thought, they are helpful;[11] in the case of rabbinic thought, or for most of kabbalistic writings, this approach is very problematic (Idel 2006a).

Martin Buber, for example, describes the tendency of 'the Kabbalah' to schematize the mystery (Buber 1966:69, 141 and 1988:124).[12] After being involved in the first stage of his academic career with Christian mystics like, Meister Eckhart, Nicholas of Cusa and Jacob Boehme, the technical, performative aspects of Kabbalah, as well as of Judaism, became quite alien to him. His main religious concern was the 'mystery of being'.[13] Though different from Buber in many ways, the great scholar of Kabbalah, Gershom Scholem, was also concerned with the mystery in Jewish mysticism. He argued, however, that:

> For kabbalah, Judaism in all its aspects was a system of mystical symbols reflecting the mystery of God and the universe, and the kabbalists' aim was to discover and invent keys to the understanding of this symbolism.
>
> (Scholem 1974b:5-6)

Indeed, the centrality of symbolism played a special role in his general picture of the kabbalistic material he studied.

> In Kabbalah one is speaking of a reality which cannot be revealed or expressed at all save through the symbolic allusion. A hidden authentic

10 See, especially, Scholem 1969:1–2, 1974a:57, 1974b, 1987. On Otto, see Scholem 1960:21. See also, Séd 1987; Werblowsky 1962:243–8, 270. Joseph Ben Shlomo, the main student of Scholem, has dedicated more analyses to Otto's thought than to any other scholar in Jewish studies. See, especially, his afterword to the Hebrew translation of Otto (1999); also Ben Shlomo 1973 and 1974, and the various references to Otto in the last part of Ben Shlomo 1965.

11 See the updated bibliography on this topic in Kellner 2018.

12 See also his description of Kabbalah as Gnosis (Buber 1988:175).

13 Though there is a phrase 'mystery of God' in some few Midrashic texts, this is an issue that can be revealed, and this is also the case in many cases in Kabbalah. Though using the Greek term mystorin, the rabbis intended something much closer to 'secret' than 'mystery'.

> reality, which cannot be expressed in itself and according to its own laws, finds expression in its symbol.
>
> (Scholem 1997:140)[14]

The centrality accorded to symbolism, we may speak of a pan-symbolism, invites an emphasis on alleged acts of contemplation of the 'sublime', as peaks of religious activity.[15] The distance between the human and divine was conceived as so great that it could be hardly surpassed, meaning that symbolism was the only way to approach divinity; thus the experience of mystical union was flatly denied by scholars insofar as Judaism was concerned (Rotenstreich 1977–8; cf. Afterman 2017). Quite a similar approach is found in the understanding of Kabbalah propounded by Isaiah Tishby, a major disciple of Scholem. Here is one example of his uncritical dependence on Scholem's approach:

> At the very core and foundation of this teaching is one particular subject of investigation: the *mystery* of the knowledge of the Godhead. The great themes of the Creation and the Chariot, the existence and activity of the angels, the nature of the spiritual worlds, the forces of evil in the realm of Satan, the situation and destiny of Man, this world and the next, the process of history from the days of creation until the end of time – all these topics are no more than the boughs and branches of the mighty tree of the *mystery* of the Godhead. The knowledge of this *mystery*, which depends on man's spiritual level and on the root of his soul, is the basis of religious faith as seen by the Kabbalah.
>
> (Tishby 1991:229–30, emph. added)

Here, in a way quite reminiscent of Scholem, knowledge of 'the divine 'mystery' is conceived of as the supreme aim of Kabbalah. This Scholemian orientation is evident also the case with Tishby's appropriation of Scholem's theory of symbolism, and the two topics are often interrelated (Tishby 1964:11–22). More recently, the resort to the term 'mystery' as a translation of the Hebrew *Sod* or the Aramaic *Raz*, which actually mean, in most of the cases

14 See also Scholem 1969:22, 36, and my detailed analysis of his view of symbolism in Idel 2010:83–108.

15 For Scholem's strong tendency to depict early kabbalistic prayer as contemplative see, for example, Scholem 1987:243–45; cf. also Elliot R. Wolfson's essentialist stance of Kabbalah as dealing with contemplation (Wolfson 2005a:3–4, also 2005b:55–110). See also, Fine 2003:215–19. For some scholars' emphasis on contemplative prayer in eighteenth-century Hasidism, see the survey in Idel 2019b, and Idel 2020a.

'secret', points in this direction.[16] This is an example of the application of some Western approaches, or categories concerning religion, to what I consider to be an 'Eastern' type of religiosity, from the phenomenological point of view (Idel 2015a). Rituals or techniques are never mentioned in the scholarly contexts in which the core of Kabbalah is defined, as it has been conceived of as a combination of mystery religion and symbolism of the ineffable, an attempt at spiritualizing Kabbalah in order to present it as comparable to Christian mysticism. My problem is not with Buber's philosophy or with Scholem's spiritual quest. These are part of personal religious jounreys, and this is the case for many of their followers, such as Gabriel Marcel, for example. My problem is their attempt to discover their spiritual interests in texts that, in my opinion, do not support them; which means – to put it in more explicit terms – that they project their personal attitudes to texts whose authors would protest against such an interpretation. These are readings 'against the grain' of the texts and their authors that betray the backgrounds of the scholars.

However, from the beginning of the twentieth century we witness a much greater concern with rituals and techniques from a variety of scholars. Most evidently from what was known as the school of the myth and ritual. This first emerged in England, with the work of William Robertson Smith and James Frazer,[17] and was then developed by S.H. Hooke and Jane Harrison, and then subsequently by scholars in Scandinavia, and put the accent on the importance of rituals, especially on the basis of major archaeological discoveries in the twenties and the thirties in the former Mesopotamian areas (Hooke 1953:56–62, 85–92). Those scholars turned their gaze to archaic religions (Semitic, Mesopotamian or ancient Greek) that were much more performative than the later forms of religion that inspired the views of Schleiermacher and Otto.[18] Given the concern of this school with rituals, a concern much traditional Judaism also has, I believe that it is fruitful to adopt it for the study of many traditional forms of Judaism (Hooke 1932; Idel 1988a:197, 1998b).

In comparison to earlier forms of scholarship on the history of religion mentioned above, what happened in this field from the early 1950s onwards, with the emergence of Mircea Eliade's scholarship on European languages, was a paradigm shift. While the earlier scholars were concerned in one way

16 See, for example, the translations of those terms as 'mystery' in the writings of Ginsburg 2006; Wolfson 1995:64, 94, 101, 243n.118 and 2005a. See also Scholem's translation (1974b:5–6, after n.13).

17 See, for example, Smith 1989:17. For more on this school, see the comprehensive anthology by Robert A. Segal (1998).

18 Otto, who was deeply interested in Hinduism, chose to analyse the philosopher Sankara, and compare him to Meister Eckhart. See Otto 1960.

or another to understand the religious environment for the emergence of the Hebrew Bible, Eliade was concerned with unearthing what he considered to be the original religion, which differs dramatically from the Judeo-Christian historically oriented religion. This change can be described as follows: a scholarly field dominated by a monotheistic propensity, coupled with a Hegelian vision of development, was now addressed differently, emphasizing much more Hindu thought and primitive or archaic religion, filtered as they were by Hindu concepts such as *Brahman, atman* and *maya*, and sometimes by Orthodox Christianity, which somehow distinguished Eliade's approach from that of myth-and-ritual theory (Segal 1998:180–9).

Confronting the developmental understandings of humanity and religion, both the general one of Hegel and the Hegelians, and that of the scholarship of religion, as found in James Frazer's opus, Eliade was more concerned with the past and origins than with the future or ends. This focus was in the cause of retrieving some allegedly repressed forms of religion, which were presented as resisting the addition of later layers. This is the case with his presentations of the impact of the yoga techniques of the pre-Aryan culture in India, of the pre-monotheistic religion among the Israelites, and of the Romanian pre-Latin and pre-Christian Dacian religion, which were integrated into what he called cosmic Christianity (Eliade 1958 and 1974). These examples seem to me quite important, as they constitute a pattern. In trying to illustrate the vitality of neglected cultures, Eliade finds common denominators between them, and these serve as the raw materials for his construction of an archaic Pre-Socratic metaphysics, and for his claim of its continuation in a variety of forms much later. His project may be defined as an attempt to provoke a cultural anamnesis of the European culture of its archaic sources, and an encounter between it and Oriental types of thought.[19] In fact, Eliade described the existence of 'a second Renaissance' or a New Humanism, much more comprehensive than the Italian one, and this argument is fundamental for him.[20] This call for a new, expanded humanism, inclusive of many cultures unknown to the Italian Renaissance thinkers, is definitely reminiscent of the Italian new concept of humanism (Eliade 1971:1–11; Faivre 1994:108 and Turcanu 2003:443–6).

19 See, for example, his own formulation in Eliade 1963:142–70. But see, also, his much less integrative approach articulated later on: cf. Idel 2014:227–8.

20 See Eliade 1971:55–7. There were, nevertheless, earlier European calls for the integration of India into European history, such as Schopenhauer's, for example. See Droit 1997:135–52.

Though not always related to Eliade, the concern with techniques became more evident in scholarship in the 1970s.[21]

In lieu of a theological type of constructivism, which is problematic given the diversity of theologies active in the cases of some of the mystics (many of them elite figures and erudite scholars, who also changed their mind), there is also the danger of a constructivism of technique. Nevertheless, there is a substantial difference between the two forms of constructivism: while the theological one is prone to being exclusive, preventing (at least according to the methodology of Gershom G. Scholem and, under his influence, Robert C. Zaehner – see Idel 2005b:4–16) extreme forms of mystical experience in Judaism; technical constructivism can be envisioned as inclusive (a variety of experiences can be induced by the same mystical technique, given the diversity of the spiritual physiognomies of the mystics), with in some cases a variety of techniques being available within the same mystical system. On the other hand, I am not aware of any explicit assumptions that there are forms of experience that cannot be attained by the means of a certain technique.

Though it is possible to postulate a certain affinity between the nature of the techniques and the content of the experience induced, the nexus between them is not always organic, and unexpected experiences can be incited. In other words, a particular theology is considered, by those scholars whom I propose to see as belonging to the 'Hegelian' approach, to be the representative of a specific religion, and to be a closed system, and to have the nexus between it and the experience determined by an intrinsic logic. However, if we assume a significant affinity between mystical experiences and techniques, we may then speak about a form of relationship that is much more open ended, and then attempt to offer categorizations that will take into consideration the different types of mystical technique. Such a proposal has, perhaps, its strengths, but also its limitations, and the latter are worth emphasizing.

Indeed, the kinds of mystical experience that may be correlated to a certain type of theology, even if a general one, are much more numerous than those that may be related to specific mystical techniques. The reason for this is simple: a scholar will be quite hesitant to reconstruct a mystical technique without solid evidence, but will more easily adventure in creating an affinity between a mystical experience and a theological stance, even if the latter is not mentioned explicitly by the mystic himself. Moreover, there are good reasons to assume that not all mystical experiences are related to mystical techniques.

21 See Moore 1978; Werblowsky 1962:46–8, 50–2, 55, 68. On a vision of philosophy as a path to spiritual experiences, see Hadot 1975:25–70, 1993, 1995; Merlan 1963; Wallis 1976:122 and 143n1; for the pertinent bibliography, see Morgan 1990.

What impresses when reading the exercises of St Ignatius, Sufi mystical treatises, hesychastic exercises, or some kabbalistic writings, is not just the existence of fascinating theologies that allow deep mystical transformations of the personality, but, primarily, in my opinion, the existence of detailed and sophisticated treatments of mystical techniques that are supposed to induce these mystical changes. Likewise, it seems that the specific *regula* of a certain order may bear evidence of its mystical character, much more than the more general theology shared by all the Christian orders do. It is in the *principium individuationis* of each of these religious structures, not only in their theologies, that clues for an understanding of the specifics of mystical experiences should be sought.

On the other hand, mystical experiences are not only a matter of recondite interpretation of sacred texts by resorting to a certain type of nomenclature, but may be conditioned by a sustained praxis of techniques and rituals. Strong affinities exist between the details of the rites and techniques used to trigger a certain experience, and the nature of that experience. Most of the details of these techniques stem from Jewish sources, some of which can be documented in late antiquity. Therefore, the description of these experiences in medieval Judaism should take into consideration both the speculative heritage stemming from the Greek and Hellenistic sources as mediated by translations in Arabic, basically Neoplatonic and Hermetic, and sometimes also Sufi and even Hindu elements, on the one hand; and the contribution of indigenous elements that predated the nascent phases of Kabbalah, on the other.

Another aspect of the 'upward' approach, which studies first the more concrete aspects, puts into relief the greater importance of technique (more than the nature of the divinity). The resort to the term 'ecstasy' comes late in the history of mysticism, and is related to a divestment of the body that implies much more connection to human experience than to divine inspiration or a prophetic illumination. The main approach that describes the experience as a reflection of the supernal presence within man, in order to disclose some form of sublime theological information, is less concerned with ecstasy. A focus on this term does not reduce the religious experience to a psychosomatic event, but rather puts the emphasis upon those elements that are more available to the scholar, while keeping a more neutral position regarding the external elements – divine, angelic or others – that may or may not participate in the experience.

Rituals and theurgy in Kabbalah

As mentioned above, the main layers of Jewish literature are concerned with detailed instructions dealing with the minutiae of religious performances, designated by the term 'Halacha'. The Halachic modes of writing and behaving are quintessential components of many major forms of Judaism, and they constitute the nomos of rabbinism. The attention paid to the minutiae of the performance of commandments throughout the history of Jewish literature, is paralleled by the special attention paid to those modes of action in the mystical literatures, even to modes of action which are not nomian, but which nevertheless enter into the detail of precise performances. The 'technical' nature of Judaism in most of its classical forms, which stresses the centrality of punctilious performance of commandments, invited a technical mode also in the mystical interpretations of these forms.

In general, the techniques developed in medieval Kabbalah relied on the scale of value informing rabbinic Judaism: practices relating to the sanctity of the divine name, the study of the Torah, performance of commandments and loud prayer. Those practices should be understood as forms of rituals, which may be defined by their 'apartness', namely, their distinctness from ordinary activities, and their 'scriptedness', namely, their ordered sequence of actions, which makes them recognizable. When performed as linguistic rituals, namely loudly, they were not only performed in Hebrew, a language that is not the vernacular of most of the authors to be discussed below, but they were quite fixed and their activation broke the course of the ordinary life because of the sanctity attributed to their performance.

If this distinctness is obvious in most forms of Judaism, it is even more intensified in Jewish mystical literatures, which emphasized their religious efficacy, and thus put a special emphasis on punctilious performance. A religion, or a certain type of mysticism, may involve extreme experiences and expressions – like those referring to mystical union – not only because particular phrases are used (though they are indubitably an important factor), but also because circumstantial factors are contrived to ensure their occurrence. It would seem the recurrence of techniques for particular purposes, such as returning from an extreme mystical experience (Idel 1995b:127–33), or of descriptions of bodily symptoms related to a certain experience, are at least as important as theological criteria in accessing unitive experiences.

The difference between the theological and the technical approaches to mysticism extends beyond the methods for dealing with, often times, imponderable experiences, which form part of the more general understanding of a certain form of mysticism. It assumes other dynamics are formative of religious experience, especially in the case of mysticism. Less dependent upon the nature of a reigning theology or authority, or on abstract ideas, a form of mysticism will be conceived as reaching its peak if it can develop specific ways of reiterating ideal experiences and transmitting them as spiritual principles.

I can imagine that a mystic who has undergone extreme mystical experiences will be readier to write about techniques to retrieve these experiences, and because of it the esoteric nature of his lore becomes less important, as he attempts to impart his strong formative experience to others.

Thus, investigation of different forms of mysticism should not only proceed via examination of the theological claims that were available and acceptable in a certain environment; but also, and mainly, via semiotic, literary, anthropological, psychological and neurological explication of their abstract tenets. This requires a certain restructuring of the corpora of mystical literature focused upon by scholars. So, for example, in lieu of expatiating upon the nature of divine attributes or upon emanative processes, scholars of mysticism should inspect the large, albeit incomplete, literature (some is extant only in manuscript) dealing with mystical rationales for the commandments or handbooks dealing with techniques to achieve mystical experiences in Judaism, on hesychastic practices in Orthodox Christianity, and on the practice of *dhikr* and *sama'* in Islam. 'Eastern' forms of mysticism refer to special paths, designated as *via*, *tarīqa* or *derekh*, that are imagined to be conducive to extraordinary experiences. The affinity, or affinities, between the nature of mystical techniques and the ideal of mystical union will clarify the status of the ideal in a certain mystical network, in a way that may be different for network where the mystical techniques to reach such an experience are absent. Not less important are the detailed and complex speculations on the special nature of language and letters in Islamic mysticism, especially in the Shi'ia sect of Hurufiya, and in Kabbalah, and which have few parallels within Christian mysticism.

Such a 'technical' approach, understanding Jewish mysticism as reflecting a deep structure reflected in most important phases of Judaism, should invite a resort to other methodologies that are less oriented towards theology, and which take into account much more linguistics and psychology.

Let me present a passage from a classical legalistic codex, *'Arba'ah Turim*, written by an Ashkenazi author, Rabbi Jacob, the son of the great legalistic authority, Rabbi Asher ben Yehiel (known as ha-Rosh), active in Toledo, early in the fourteenth century:

> It is incumbent to direct one's thought because for Him thought is tantamount to speech… and the pious ones and the men of [good] deeds were concentrating their thought and directing their prayer to such an extent that they reached a [state of] divestment of their corporeality and the strengthening of their intellective spirit so that they verged to the state of prophecy.
>
> (*Tur*, *'Orah Hayyim*, par. 98)

This tractate does not deal at all with theology, mystical or not. The 'state of prophecy' refers to an ecstatic experience – a totally marginal topic in the codex – conceived of as being attainable during the time of regular prayer by means of mental concentration. Whether concentration, directing the prayer and divestment that precede the experience, should be understood as an articulated technique may be a matter of debate. However, what is nevertheless evident, is that mystical aspects of Halakhic way of life are documented in legalistic codices, and the above passage recurs verbatim also in the next most important codex, R. Joseph Karo's *Shulhan 'Arukh.*[22] In other words, a major Jewish ritual was transformed into a technique.

Let me turn now to examples of transforming rabbinic commandments into rituals having theurgical valences, whose performance depends upon detailed acquaintance with the complex supernal structure of divine powers. A central role of the human body, its emergence and growth, plays a pivotal role in kabbalistic symbology, given the centrality of the commandments that are performed by the body, and the complex systems of symmetries between the human organs, the commandments, and the supernal worlds, divine and angelic. This is what I call a comprehensive symbol, and in my opinion, the most important one in theosophical-theurgical Kabbalah.[23]

In a commentary on the rationales of the rabbinic commandments, written by a kabbalist known as R. Joseph of Hamadan, who was active in the second part of the thirteenth century in Castile, we learn about the precise correspondences between divine powers, commandments and human limbs:

> Happy is he, and blessed is his lot, who knows how to direct a limb which corresponds to a limb, and a form which corresponds to a form in the Holy and Pure Chain,[24] Blessed be His Name. Since the Torah is His form, Blessed be He, we were ordered to study the Torah, in order to know that archetype of the Supernal Form, as some kabbalists have said: 'Cursed be he that does hold up all the words of this Torah' – to the congregation… so

22 See the sixteenth-century expansion of this codex known as *Shulhan 'Arukh, ad locum.* Also, see Kaplan 1985:283–4 (where are pointed out some sources and influences of this passage) and Idel 1989:163–4n.136.

23 See, for example, Idel 2002:298–9. See, however, Scholem (1969:35–6, 1972:165, 1974b:14, 1987:449) for his assumption that images of light and letters are the two most important descriptions of the *sefirot*, and following him, Wolfson 2005:3–4. See, also, however, Scholem 1974b:268–9.

24 Like the 'supernal form' this is a technical term for the structure of ten divine *sefirot.*

> that they will see the image of the Supernal Form, moreover, the person who studies the Torah, that he sees the supernal secrets[25] and he sees the Glory of God, literally.[26]

The kabbalistic dictum that 'one limbs sustains – or strengthens – another [supernal] limb', namely a divine power, became a widespread statement from the end of the thirteenth century (Felix 2005:37–143), and in some instances phrases like 'the limb in the Merkavah' or the 'limb of the Shekhinah' also occur in his writings.[27] The limb here is the human one that performs the commandment, while directing the thought to the supreme limb, which is part of the supernal anthropomorphic structure. The source is already found in early Kabbalah, where the assumption is that the 613 commandments correspond not only to the limbs of the human body, but also to the divine chariot, namely the structure of ten *sefirot*, or the divine Glory (see, for example, Meir ibn Gabbai 1950 vol. II:16, fo. 35c; Recanati 1961:fo. 23c).

Here, the human limb is neither a symbol of a lower shadow, in the Platonic sense, nor does it serve some katabatic function, but is the active agent par excellence, the deeds of which impact upon the divine realm, or a part of it, and may even sustain it, performing in an anabatic way. The divine shape is imagined to be also the shape of the Torah, namely the very scroll of the Pentateuch, whose graphic aspect should be shown to the congregation after the ritual reading of the weekly pericope in the synagogue. Thus, there are several types of correspondences between anthropomorphic structures: the divine one, the Torah, the commandments and, finally, the human body. The affinities between these structures are not a matter of symbolism aiding the intuiting the supernal limb, conceived of as ineffable, as Scholem claims in the passages adduced above, but of seeing the supernal world. In my opinion, the two structures are considered to be known to the kabbalist, and their knowledge is imagined to be necessary in order to perform the commandments in the best manner. This is part of a quite technical understanding that allocates to each divine attribute a certain limb and a specific commandment. All this said, kabbalists never created a cult of the

---

25 The Hebrew is '*sodot ha-'elyonot*', a phrase that in its context hardly means mysteries.

26 *Perush le-Ta'amei ha-Mitzvot*, MS Jerusalem, NLI 8° 3925, fo. 110b. For the fuller version of the passage see Idel 2002:69–74 and esp. 73, 298–9, and 1981:65. On this treatise and its real author, see Altmann 1965:256–7. For more on the correspondence of commandments to the supernal Merkavah, namely to the theosophical plane, see the discussions in Idel 2019a:II, ch. 12 (Hebrew).

27 Ibid.:78. The history of the concept of the 'limbs of the Shekhinah' requires a separate discussion. See Idel 2020c.

human body per se, which was solely instrumental for the ritual performance. It should also be mentioned that several important cases of Neoplatonic approaches that depreciate the body are found in Kabbalah, but in other contexts, those that privileged the status of the soul in comparison to the body. This attitude fits the assumption that someone can see the divine form, without resorting to any apophatic epithets.

A much more theurgical understanding of the performance of commandments is found in the writings of a sixteenth-century kabbalist, R. Meir ibn Gabbai:

> For by the performance of the commandments here below, they will be done above, and they will stir their archetypes to complete by their deeds the supernal glory; and whoever does so, is regarded as if he made Him, literally… This is the way of making the name attributed to David, as it is written: 'and David made a name'[28] and that refers to the completion of the glory, the secret of the glorious name,[29] which was completed and unified by his study of the Torah and the performance of its commandments, and by his worship, which he was continuously worshiping, without interruption. For all this causes the making of the name and its completion,[30] which is the supernal will and volition and the intention of the Creation.
>
> (Meir ibn Gabbai 1950, vol. II:1, fo. 25d)

The ritual performance is conceived of as constituting the divine realm – the divine glory – or in other cases, as completing it. The assumption is that 'on high' there are corresponding commandments, and the lower performance stirs or triggers the supernal one. This is quite a kataphatic type of theosophy, the dynamics of which depend on the ritual, not vice versa. These views comprise part what I describe as a process of comprehensive ritualization of the divine world (Idel 2005b:215–20). But this is not an extraordinary passage in theosophical-theurgical Kabbalah, and it is possible to adduce many parallels (Idel 1988a:184–91; Mopsik 1993).

The late fifteenth-century Spanish kabbalist expellee R. Yehudah Hayyat, wrote in his *Minhat Yehudah* (a commentary composed in Mantua on the anonymous early fourteenth-century classic of kabbalistic literature, *Ma'arekhet ha-'Elohut*):

28 II Samuel 8:13. In Hebrew, 'name' may also refer to God.

29 A term for the entire divine pleroma.

30 Namely the *sefirotic* world.

> Man makes a strong impression [*roshem*] on high by each and every step that he takes here below, either by a good or a bad deed. This happens because he is created from the supernal entities in the image of God, and this image connects him with his God like an iron chain which descends from above downward, as when the lowest rung is moved here below, also the highest among them will be moved. And the commandments stem from the ten *sefirot* and when someone performs a commandment below, it is as if he causes the emanation of power on the supernal form on high by means of the pipes of thought[31] onto that attribute, namely *sefirah* that points to that commandment, and then the supernal entities will be blessed because of the lower ones.[32]
>
> (Hayyat 1555:fo. 161b-162a)

The blessing of the higher entities means that the divine powers receive influx from higher levels of divinity, because of the theurgical activities of the humans. Blessing is not an oral formula, but a descending power, as in the Semitic understanding of *berakhah*, as not just a verbal activity but as a cosmic energetic stream.

Here, the correspondence of the higher and lower commandments or limbs is explicated by means of a great chain of being that connects the two realms and allows the impact of the lower upon the higher. Again, we may speak about a technical approach that is grounded in an acquaintance with the details of supernal realm, envisioned as a dynamic map that is a prerequisite for the proper kabbalistic performance of the 613 rabbinic commandments. In this case also, the anthropomorphism is evident.

According to those examples, which can easily be multiplied, the human dependence on the divine, *à la* Schleiermacher, is far from evident, nor is the symbolic type of affinity so central as he surmised.[33] Neither is the 'holy' strictly transcendental, as Rudolph Otto believes, but often times it is generated by human ritual acts, understood in a theurgical manner. Though the divine realm is the ultimate aim of the rituals, these turn into techniques for the kabbalists, depicted as stirring of the chain from below.

---

31 *Tzinorot ha-Mahashavah*, namely the pipes descending from the *sefirah* of Keter to the other divine powers.

32 On theurgy in Hayyat, see Mopsik 1993:341–5, also 350–2 for a French translation and analysis of this passage. See also Idel 2005b:47.

33 As to my views about symbolism in Kabbalah, which emphasizes both the concepts of symmetry and dynamism, see, for example, Idel 2002:272–312, 2015b. For another important discussion of symbols in Kabbalah, see Liebes 1995.

Similar theurgical theories are found in Lurianic Kabbalah (Fine 2003:194, 218–19, 235–48, 255–8; Idel 2011; Kallus 2002). The performance of commandments, and in his views also of a variety of additional customs (Faierstein 2013; Hallamish 2000; Scholem 1969:146–9), have been conceived of as intended to unify the components of the complex theosophical structure, and to reconstruct the shattered structure of the supernal anthropos, by elevating the fallen divine sparks to their primeval place in its structure (Scholem 1974a:268, 274, 278–80). This latter theurgical operation is reminiscent of a series of ancient Hindu-European myths, as was insightfully pointed out by Martin Buber (1988:121–2; see also Idel 1995b:297n263; Lincoln 1986 on this widespread myth in Hindu-European cultures). It is in this kabbalistic school that the assumption that many entities in the supernal world, as well as the soul, also comprise of 613 components, has flowered as part of a more comprehensive view of polypsychism, namely the concomitant presence of many souls or sparks within the same body (Idel 2006b).

Visualization of colours and a kabbalistic mandala

Kabbalists resorted to a variety of techniques in order to reach specific forms of experience (Idel 1980a, 1987:13–72, 1988a:74–111, 2020b).[34] As noted in the previous section, prayer is one such technique. I assume that a variety of Sufi and Hindu techniques were also known by kabbalists, and even some of these influenced them. So, for example, Patanjali's *Yogasutra* was translated into Arabic,[35] and was thus available, at least in principle, to some Jewish authors. In my opinion, Abraham Abulafia has been influenced by the tripartite breathing theory found in yoga practices (Idel 1987:24–6). On the other hand, it is quite probable that a mandala type of visualization was adopted by late thirteenth-century kabbalists, as part of their new understanding of the effects of prayer (Idel 2015c, 2016a). These are techniques in which colours that correspond to divine powers during prayer were visualized, probably as an impact of Tibetan practices related to mandala (Garb 2004:187–200; Idel 1988b:103–11, 1988c:3, 17–27, 1990:119–26, 1994a, 1995:147–8). Elsewhere (Idel 2015c, 2016a), I have analysed in detail a diagram that forms a mandala (Figure 4.1), and belonged to R. David ben Yehudah he-Hasid, a late thirteenth-century kabbalist (ms Milano-Ambrosiana 62, fo. 4a). In the context of R. David's thought, this configuration is manifestly anthropomorphic – the fact that the concepts of

---

34 Most of those analyses deal with anomian techniques, which will not be discussed in the present study, which deals with the transformation of nomian rituals into techniques.

35 For instance, by the famous eleventh-century author al-Biruni. See Pines and Gelblum 1966, 1977, 1983, 1989.

the 'long face' (*'arikh 'anppin*) and the 'small face' (*ze'yir 'anppin*) that appear in the diagram differ from their Zoharic meaning, does not change this. If the understanding proposed above is correct, then the process of visualization not only includes the shapes of the letters of the divine names, colours and circles, but also anthropomorphic configurations of colours that symbolize an aspect of the divine realm.[36]

The traditions discussed above do not assume the contemplation of a static scheme, but the energetic performance of visualizations so as to generate certain shapes in colours, which change from one blessing during prayer to another. Though intended towards an objective divine world, the main type of operation generates effects that stem from human imaginative powers. This dynamic is quintessential for understanding kabbalistic theosophies in general, and has little to do with what is regularly called contemplation (Idel 1988a:229–33).[37] It is obvious that some kabbalists intended to express the idea of the macrocosmos, which is envisioned as been included within the divine macroanthropos. Such a macrocosmic approach is also hinted at in another tradition, that of R. David (MS Cambridge University, Add. 505, fo. 8b).[38] However, this is not just a 'cosmogram', a diagram that was intended to offer in a short manner the structure of the cosmos, as it was intended to help a ritual performance – prayers – accompanied by the visualization of colours and shapes of letters of divine names, which are related to divine powers, the *sefirot.*

The phenomenological affinities between this diagram and the Hindu mandala are indeed interesting.[39] The two practices share the processes of visualization and of imaginary representation of divine forces and colours, and in both cases the circle also has a macrocosmic aspect (Coulianou 1984; Eliade

36 For the importance of the image of man within the highest divine realm, the infinite, according to R. David, see Garb 1999:279–80; Idel 2009a.

37 However, the connection between *kavvanah* and divine names, and the concept of *hamshakhah* in that period scarcely confirms a contemplative type of reading (Idel 1994b; also Afterman 2004:98–104). What are called the contemplative and unitive elements, should be understood as part of a broader structure, be it connected to theurgy or to magic, and as the second phase of a wider model that modifies the nature of the act described by scholars as contemplation in the connection of prayer.

38 Compare also to ms Milano-Ambrosiana, 62, fo. 4b, in the table occurring immediately after the diagram, where a more cosmic propensity can be discerned, as mentioned above.

39 For the resort to the term mandala in the case of the circles found in the treatises of the mid-sixteenth-century Jerusalemite kabbalist R. Joseph ibn Sayyah, see also Garb 1997, 1999:296n259. For techniques of active visualization in modern Jewish mysticism, see Garb 2014:112–13; Persico 2016; Reiser 2014, 2018; Wachs 2010.

1958:219–27; Tucci 1961:vii; Zimmer 1984:65–180).[40] Moreover, while the mandala may be a psychogram, which is at the same time also a cosmogram, it is possible to discern some hints in kabbalistic literature of the existence of a theory of the tree of the *sefirot* imagined to be found within man, occurring in both a text of R. Joseph Ashkenazi, and again in a probably later kabbalistic treatise written in Ashkenaz (Idel 1995a:151–2, n. 84). If the understanding proposed above is correct, then the process of visualization includes not only divine names, colours and circles, but also an anthropomorphic configuration of colours, symbolizing an important aspect of the divine realm (see also, Garb 1999:279–80).

However, there are also clear differences: the kabbalistic diagram is graphically different from the forms of mandalas I have seen; their details are conspicuously unrelated. While the construction of a mandala in the objective world is accompanied by a special liturgy, the visualization of the content of the kabbalistic diagram in someone's mind accompanies Jewish ritualistic prayer serially. These differences notwithstanding, one cannot underrate the possibility that Hindu traditions infiltrated into Kabbalah, perhaps via the intermediacy of Sufi material. R. David lived for a certain period of time in Acre, a fact which may be a clue to explaining the penetration of an alien mystical technique into a Jewish milieu (Scholem 1998, I:141; Zacut 1857:88).[41] R. Joseph was certainly aware of Arabic culture, as he mentions Arabic words

40 It should be mentioned that in some mandalas there are also signs of the zodiac and categories of ten, as in Figure 4.1. For Persian Sufi discussions of seeing colors and circles as part of the *dikhr*, see the contemporary of R. David (Landolt 1986:60–7, 107–8n159), but there is no reference there to an act of visualization to be initiated by the mystic.

41 It should be pointed out that another visitor of Acre in the thirteenth century, R. Abraham Abulafia, less than twenty years after his visit in 1260, designed a macrocosmic diagram as part of a revelation (Idel 1987:109–16). Though the technique of the mandalas differs from one school to another, and it is hard to show specific example's affinities with the diagram, it is interesting that the two kabbalists who visited Acre reflect some form of influence from techniques stemming from the Indian territories. Also, interestingly, Abulafia resorted to many circles in his handbooks in which techniques to reach ecstatic experiences are described, especially in his 1280 book *Hayyei ha-'Olam ha-Ba'* (1989).

and Arabian customs (Ashkenazi 1985:249–50).[42] In any case some views that are characteristic of R. Joseph Ashkenazi, may stem from Ismaili circles.[43]

In my opinion, the visualization of colours reflects the impact of a Sufi view of Hindu origin on R. David, or his source. It should be mentioned that the resort to sources that were found outside Judaism with regards to the experiential aspects of the visualization of colours, is motivated by the claim of R. Joseph Ashkenazi as to the origin of his discussion of colours and prophecy, among 'the wise men of the philosophers' (Ashkenazi 1985:223; Idel 1984–8:23, 1988a:107–8, 111, 2005b:228–32).

Divine descent, ritual and isomorphism

Let me address another instance of isomorphism, found already at the end of thirteenth century,[44] and in a more explicit manner in the mid-sixteenth-century R. Moshe Cordovero's classic of Kabbalah.[45] This is based on the assumption that a lower structure may serve as the receptacle of a higher, corresponding structure, and that this is the case for the Israelite temples, the tabernacle, and the human body (Mottolese 2007). In my opinion, it is not just the symmetry of the structures that induces the descent of the higher power upon the lower one, but also the operations connected to the lower structure, namely the performance of the rituals. This is a Hermetic principle that assumes that through certain acts, supernal powers can be drawn downwards, and it has been adopted by some kabbalists.[46] However, this Hermetic principle has been coupled with the performance of the regular commandments in the Middle Ages:

---

42 A parallel discussion is found in the anonymous *Commentary on Shir ha-Yiḥud*, written in Germany, MS Frankfurt a/M 121, fo. 12b–13a. On an aspect of the Muslim practice R. Joseph mentions, see the earlier Jewish treatments discussed in Septimus 1981. See also in Ashkenazi 1985:157, 159, 229.

43 See Pines 1980:245–7, who exemplified the affinities using later kabbalistic texts that were actually influenced by the specific kabbalistic views of R. Joseph Ashkenazi.

44 See Gikatilla 1994:8: 'Since God wanted to favour us He created the human body with revealed and concealed organs which reflect the constellation of the Divine emanation. If a person succeeds in purifying one of his limb or organs, the same limb or organ will become a throne for the celestial entity, which bears the same name either it will be an eye, a hand and any other limb.' See also Idel 1995b:91; 364 n. 109; 1998b:317–9, and Fishbane 2009:385–418.

45 See Idel 2022.

46 For the impact of Hermetism on Jewish mysticism, see Idel 1988a:166–70, 1988b, 2004b.

> It is well known that the desire of the supernal entities to cleave to the lower ones is in accordance with the preparation of the latter. A great proof for it is found in the construction of the tabernacle [*Mishkan*][47] since its members as a whole and in their details correspond to the supernal matters, namely to the supernal chariots.[48] This is the reason why the [supernal] worlds and those chariots are drawn to and pour the influx upon those materials. And since those materials were dead, from their actions there is a hint that the supernal was drawn upon them, and this is the reason why the *Shekhinah* was dwelling onto them, and the Glory of God was filling the palace.[49] This is the matter of the [human] body that is similar to the spiritual, and it is incumbent upon the spiritual to adhere to the material out of the strength of its desire to it. And the reason is that the lower entities constitute the substratum of the supernal ones.
>
> (Cordovero 1962, II: fo. 75cd)[50]

Becoming the substratum is also the result of the nature of activities, the lower entity, including humans, performs. Again, this is a cataphatic understanding of the divine, feminine, power, which requires a material place to dwell on. A combination of theurgy and Hermetic magic, can be discerned in another passage of Moshe Cordovero, which deals with the possible effects of kabbalistic way of prayer:

> The man whom his Creator has bestowed with the grace of entering the innerness of the occult lore[51] and who knows and understands that by reciting *Barekh 'Aleinu* and *Refa'enu*[52] the intention is to draw down the blessing and the influx by each and every blessing to a certain *sefirah*, and

47 It should be mentioned that in many other cases this term, which in biblical Hebrew means tabernacle, in Cordovero's work also means 'substratum'. See also the next passage quoted from this kabbalist.

48 'Chariots' may point here to the divine powers.

49 Cf. Isaiah 6:1.

50 For a fuller context and analysis of this passage, see Idel, 2005c:190–1. See also Cordovero 1962:fo. 75a: 'Since the [human] body is similar to the spiritual, it is incumbent upon the latter, despite its spirituality, to cleave to the material out of its great desire for it, because the lower [entities] are the tabernacles of the higher ones. And just as the *causatum* desires to ascend to its *causa*, so it is the desire of the *causa* to have the *causatum* near to itself.'

51 Namely Kabbalah. This penetration does not allow an understanding of this passage as dealing with mysteries.

52 Those are the incipit of two blessings of the most important prayer in Judaism, the Eighteen Benedictions.

> the blessing of *Refa'enu* to a certain *sefirah*, as it is known to us, behold, this man is worshiping the Holy One, blessed be Hze, and his *Shekhinah*, as a son and a servant standing before his master, by means of a perfect worship, out of love, without deriving any benefit or reward because of that worship... because the soul of a wise man by the quality of the [mystical] intention that he intends during his prayer, his soul will be elevated by his [spiritual] arousal from one degree to another, from one entity to another until she arrives and is welcome and comes in the presence of the Creator, and cleaves to her source, to the source of life;[53] and then a great influx will be emanated upon her from there, and he will become a vessel and a place and foundation for [that] influx,[54] and from him it will be distributed to all the world... until the *Shekhinah* will cleave to him... and you will be a seat to Her and [then] the influx will descend onto you... because you are in lieu of the great pipe instead of the *Tzaddiq*,[55] the foundation of the world.[56]

The theurgical aspect of the Jewish liturgy is quite conspicuous, despite the presentation of the worship as service: divine influx is brought down from the higher to the lower attributes by specific parts of the prayer. However, the circuit of energy is imagined to descend from the intra-divine realm and to be distributed then to the infra-divine world, an aspect that I call magical, even if the person who prays is depicted as not to benefit himself from it. The descent of the divine power onto the kabbalist assumes some form of erotic encounter between divine feminine power and human righteous, in a manner reminiscent of the desire of the higher for the lower in the first passage adduced above. In our understanding of this passage, some of the more emotional dimensions can be presumed. The technical details, including the theurgical and the magical aspects of prayer, are developed in the very last chapter of Cordovero's influential *chef-d'oeuvre Pardes Rimmonim* (1962), which is considered to be the peak of his very lengthy and detailed theosophical treatment of Kabbalah. It should be emphasized again. that performative as the approaches in the above texts are, they are not devoid of emotional dimensions, such as that which is designated as 'worship out of love'. Finally, in *Pardes Rimmonim*, as in his voluminous commentary on the prayer book, *Tefillah le-Moshe*, I found

53 This is a kabbalistic version of the Platonic *reversio*.

54 See also, for example, Cordovero 1976: 77, 1986:12 (commentary on the *Zohar*).

55 Namely the Righteous, corresponding to the ninth *sefirah*, *Yesod*, a phallic entity according to kabbalistic nomenclature.

56 This is a passage of Cordovero as formulated by his disciple R. Abraham Azulai 1986:fo. 3a. On the context of this passage see Idel 1995b:100–1.

only a peripheral role for elements that constitute the 'Western' attitude to religion, as articulated by scholars of Jewish mysticism mentioned above.

'Mystery', 'wholly other' and other 'Western' concepts

The above 'cataphatic' passages, which I see as being much more representative of the theosophical-theurgical kabbalistic schools than other, scholarly, 'apophatic' views, are scarcely dealing with the unknown, the ineffable, the numinous, or the 'wholly other'. The theosophical world is described in many details in most of the kabbalistic treatises, some of them quite voluminous, while the commandments and the customs were also well known by kabbalists, let alone the limbs of their bodies. The 'secrets' subsist in the revelation of the specifics of the relationship between those three planes. However, they are scarcely mysteries, as they can be explicated in a detailed manner, and in most of the cases they actually are. This is the reason why the large-scale and unqualified resort to the concept of mystery in scholarship of Kabbalah is at least misleading, if not distorting, most of the discussions of kabbalists, understood as they are by scholars in a 'Western' manner (Scholem 1974a:6, 26, 28–31, 41, 44, 57, 268; also Buber 1988:121). An increased awareness of scholars as to the kabbalists' acquaintance with the precise details of techniques, which is a desideratum, can contribute to a de-'mysterization' of this literature and to a better understanding of its gist, which is related to precise types of performance, be they rituals or techniques.

While theosophies changed in time, even in the case of writings authored by the same kabbalist, there was much less change in the more canonical status of commandments and customs. The correlations between the two realms, namely the precise correspondences between a specific ritual and the corresponding divine power, constitute the 'secret', namely the hidden meaning of the biblical and rabbinic texts which describe the details of the performance. This means that the plain sense of the texts and the ritual performances, are seen now as fraught with the spiritual 'surplus', namely the theurgical valences of their ritual behaviour. The awareness of the recently invented significance of the performance, what most of the kabbalists call their 'intention', loaded with fateful consequences, constitutes in my opinion an intensification that transforms the ritual into a technique, because of the integration of the rituals within broader and complex theosophical schemes, and the expectations of the precise effects of one's acts on high, first, and then on low.

Little space is left in such an approach for the intervention of divine grace, for the role of 'mysteries' or for what is normally called contemplation. The extent to which we may speak here about the schematization of mystery, as Buber put it, is a matter of taste, as his assumption as to the very existence of such a mystery is an ontological presupposition, and it is hard to operate with such an assumption is a scholarly way.[57] Though a kabbalist would not consider his approach as anthropomorphic, but theomorphic, as Franz Rosenzweig would put it (Idel 2010:159–67), corporeal isomorphism is an important component of the perception of a ritual as corresponding to a higher divine realm. It should be emphasized that according to several kabbalists, even at the historical beginnings of Kabbalah in late twelfth century, the commandments also have some sort of ontological existence in the higher, divine world, mainly after they have been fulfilled on low, thereby allowing for some form of interaction between the human and divine realms via nomian types of performance.[58]

The intensification of – corporeal, but especially mental – activities changes the psychosomatic system and may induce forms of experience that may have some characteristics in common with other mystical events. These intensifications may de-automatize ordinary behaviour and thus open the consciousness towards other forms of perception or experience. By paying special attention to carefully described patterns of behaviour in a certain society or a small group, and to the ensuing experiences (to the extent they are described), a shift from the predominantly theological orientation of studies of religion and mysticism may be provoked, to one which is much more anthropological and historical. Those rituals that became techniques are initially socially oriented, and less concerned with the spiritual attainments of specific individuals, as are Abraham Abulafia's anomian techniques and of the kabbalists influenced by him.[59] In the history of Kabbalah, especially in the later phases, the anomian techniques become associated with nomian ones, like prayer. This is evident in Cordovero, and this is a tendency different to that described above, of the transformation of a ritual into a technique.

To sum up my proposal: though many mystics belong to specific religious traditions, and should be studied in these contexts, they also intensified their religious activity with a 'surplus', in order to reach stronger experiences than those available in quotidian practice. In cases discussed here, the figure 613 is quintessential, as it is a unifying factor organizing human bodies, commandments and the divine powers in a particularistic manner representative of rabbinic Judaism. This unifying factor stems from the

57 Compare also to Scholem's presupposition as to the existence of what he called a 'mountain', some form of ontological core of reality that he was seeking to discover, or even experience, by means of his scholarly analysis of Kabbalah, cf. Idel 1988a:11–2, 2014:47.

58 See the many examples adduced in Idel 2005b:215–20

59 See Idel 1987.

projections of human types of activities on high, and is part of an upwards type of imagining the supernal worlds. However, the process of intensification related to mental activities is a more universal characteristic, which is nevertheless applied to different particularistic religious behaviours. Some of these intensifications may take the form of accelerated mental activities that may bring about, in some cases, extraordinary mystical experiences, which differ from one religion to another, or even from one individual to another in the same religion (Idel 2009c). If the above interpretation holds water, Kabbalah – Sabbateanism and Frankism aside – was basically nomian, allowing very little space to the anarchic, dissident, or antinomian predilections attributed to mystics by scholarship in the field.

References

Abulafia, A. 1989. *Hayyei ha-'Olam ha-Ba'* (ed. A .Gross, 3rd edn.). Jerusalem.

Afterman, A. 2004. *The Intention of Prayers in Early Ecstatic Kabbalah.* Los Angeles: Cherub Press.

——— 2017. 'And They Shall be One Flesh': On the Language of Mystical Union in Judaism. Leiden: Brill.

Altmann, A. 1965. '*Sefer Ta'amei ha-Mitzwot:* attributed to R. Isaac ibn Farhi and its Author', *Qiryat Sefer* 40: 256–7 (Hebrew).

Ashkenazi, J. 1985. *Commentary on Genesis Rabba'* (ed. M. Hallamish). Jerusalem: Magnes Press (Hebrew).

Azulai, A. 1986. *Commentary on Massekhet 'Avot.* Jerusalem: Moriah Publisher.

Behrens, G. 1988. 'Feeling of absolute dependence or absolute feeling of dependence? (What Schleiermacher really said and why it matters)', *Religious Studies* 34(4):471–81.

Ben Shlomo, J. 1965. *The Mystical Theology of Moses Cordovero.* Jerusalem, Mossad Bialik (Hebrew).

——— 1973. 'Schematism in R. Otto's philosophy of religion', *Iyyun* 24:207–16 (Hebrew).

——— 1974. 'To the question of the uniqueness of religion in the philosophy of Rudolph Otto'. In S. Pines (ed.), *Memorial Volume to Jacob Friedman,* pp. 77–92. Jerusalem: Institute of Jewish Studies, Hebrew University (Hebrew).

——— 1999. 'Afterword'. In R. Otto, *The Idea of the Holy* (tr. M. Ron), pp. 182–203. Jerusalem: Carmel.

Berkovits, E. 2002. 'The concept of holiness'. In D. Hazony (ed.), *Essential Essays on Judaism,* pp. 247–314. Jerusalem: Shalem Press.

Boia, L. 2000. *Pentru o istorie a imaginarului.* Bucharest: Humanitas.

Buber, M. 1966. *Hasidism and Modern Man* (ed. M. Friedman). New York: Horizon Press.

——— 1988. *The Origin and Meaning of Hasidism* (ed. and trans. M. Friedman). Atlantic Highlands: Humanities Press International.

Canetti, L. and Piras, A. 2018. 'Esperienze e tecniche dell'estasi tra tra Oriente e Occidente', *SMSR, Quaderni di Studi e materiali di Storia della religioni* 21.

Cordovero, M. 1962. *Pardes Rimmonim*. Jerusalem: Ahavah we-Shalom.

——— 1976. *'Or Yaqar* , vol. 8. Jerusalem: Ahuzat Israel.

——— 1986. *'Or Yaqar*, vol. 14. Jerusalem: Ahuzat Israel.

Carroll, R.P. 1994. 'Toward a grammar of creation: on Steiner the Theologian'. In N.A. Scott Jr. and R.A. Sharp (eds), *Reading George Steiner*, pp. 262–74. Baltimore: The John Hopkins University Press.

Coulianou, I.P. 1984. 'Le mandala et l'histoire des religions', *Cahiers internationaux de symbolisme* 48–9:53–62.

Delumeau, J. 1990. *Sin and Fear: The Emergence of the Western Guilt Culture, 13th-18th Centuries*. Abingdon: Palgrave McMillan.

Droit, R-J. 1997. *Le Culte de Néant*. Paris: Le Seuil.

Eliade, M. 1958. *Yoga, Immortality and Freedom* (trans. W.R. Trask). Princeton: Princeton/Bollingen Series.

——— 1963. *Aspects du Mythe*. Paris: Payot.

——— 1971. *The Quest, History and Meaning in Religion*. Chicago: The University of Chicago Press.

——— 1974. *Shamanism: Archaic Techniques of Ecstasy* (trans. W.R. Trask). Princeton: Princeton/Bollingen Series.

Elkayam, A. 1990. 'Between referentialism and performativism: two approaches in understanding the Kabbalistic symbol', *Daat* 24:5–40 (Hebrew).

Felix, I. 2005. Theurgy, Magic, and Mysticism in the Kabbalah of R. Joseph of Shushan. Ph.D. thesis, Hebrew University

Faierstein, M. 2013. *Jewish Customs of Kabbalistic Origin: History and Practice*. Boston: Academic Studies Press.

Faivre, A. 1994. *Access to Western Esotericism*. Albany: SUNY Press.

Fine, L. 2003. *Physician of the Soul, Healer of the Cosmos, Isaac Luria and His Kabbalistic Fellowship*. Stanford: Stanford University Press.

Fishbane, E.P. 2009. 'A CHARIOT FOR THE SHEKHINAH, Identity and the ideal life in sixteenth-century Kabbalah', *Journal of Religious Ethics* 37:385–418.

Garb, J. 1997. 'Techniques of Trance in the Jerusalem Kabbalah', *Pe'amim* 70:47–67 (Hebrew).

——— 1999. 'The Kabbalah of R. Joseph ibn Sayyah as a source for the understanding of Safedian Kabbalah', *Kabbalah* 4:255–313 (Hebrew).

——— 2004. *Manifestations of Power from Rabbinic Literature to Safedian Kabbalah*. Jerusalem: Magnes Press (Hebrew).

——— 2011. *Shamanic Trance in Modern Kabbalah*. Chicago: Chicago University Press.

——— 2014. *Kabbalist in the Heart of Storm, R. Moshe Hayyim Luzzatto*. Tel Aviv: Tel Aviv University Press (Hebrew).

Gikatilla, R.J. 1994. *Sha'arei 'Orah*. In *Gates of Light* (trans. A. Weinstein). San Francisco: Harper Collins.

Ginsburg, E. 2006. *Sod ha-Shabbat: The Mystery of Sabbath*. Albany: SUNY Press.

Gruenwald, I. 2003. *Rituals and Ritual Theory in Ancient Israel*. Leiden: Brill.

Hadot, P. 1975. 'Exercices spirituels', Annuaire de la V$^{e}_{e}$ section de l'Ecole pratique des hautes études LXXXIV:25–70.

——— 1993. *Exercices spirituels et philosophie antique*. Paris: Institut d'études augustiniennes.

——— 1995. *Qu'est-ce que la philosophie antique?* Paris: Gallimard.

Hallamish, M. 2000. *Kabbalah, in Liturgy, Halakhah and Customs*. Ramat Gan: Bar Ilan University Press (Hebrew).

Hayyat, Y. 1558. *Ma'arekhet ha-'Elohut*. Mantua.

Hooke, S.H. 1932. 'The myth and ritual pattern in Jewish and Christian apocalyptic'. In S.H. Hooke (ed.), *The Labyrinth: Further Studies in the Relation between Myth and Ritual in the Ancient World*, pp. 213–33. New York: Macmillan.

——— 1953. *Babylonian and Assyrian Religion*. London: Hutchinston's University Library.

Idel, M. 1980a. 'On the metamorphoses of an ancient technique to attain a prophetic vision in the Middle Ages', *Sinai* 86:1–7 (Hebrew).

——— 1980b. 'The image of man above the sefirot: R. David ben Yehudah he-Hasid's doctrine of the supernal sefirot (*Tzahtzahot*) and its evolution', *Daat* 4:41–55 (Hebrew, see 2009a for English version).

——— 1981. 'The concept of the Torah in Heikhalot literature and its metamorphoses in Kabbalah', *Jerusalem Studies in Jewish Thought* 1:23–84 (Hebrew).

--------- 1983. 'Inquiries in the doctrine of *Sefer ha-Meshiv*', *Sefunot* 2:201–26 (Hebrew).

——— 1986. 'The world of angels in human shape'. In J. Dan and J. Hacker (eds), *Jerusalem Studies in Jewish Thought* [= *Studies in Jewish Mysticism, Philosophy and Ethical Literature Presented to Isaiah Tishby*], pp. 1–66. Jerusalem: Hebrew University (Hebrew).

——— 1987. *The Mystical Experiences in Abraham Abulafia* (trans. J. Chipman). Albany: SUNY Press.

——— 1988a. *Kabbalah: New Perspectives*. New Haven: Yale University Press.

——— 1988b. 'Hermeticism and Judaism'. In I. Merkel and A. Debus (eds), *Hermeticism and the Renaissance*, pp. 59–76. New Jersey: Cranbury.

----------1988c. 'Kabbalistic prayer and colors'. In D.R. Blumenthal (ed.), *Approaches to Judaism in Medieval Times*, vol. 3, pp. 17–27. Atlanta: Scholars Press.

——— 1989. *Studies in Ecstatic Kabbalah*. Albany: SUNY Press.

——— 1990. *Golem: Jewish Magical and Mystical Traditions on the Artificial Anthropoid.* Albany: SUNY Press.

——— 1993. 'Some remarks on ritual and mysticism in Geronese Kabbalah', *Journal of Jewish Thought and Philosophy* III:111–30.

——— 1994a. '*Kavvanah* and colors: a neglected kabbalistic responsum'. In M. Idel, D. Dimant and S. Rosenberg (eds), *Tribute to Sara: Studies in Jewish Philosophy and Kabbalah Presented to Professor Sara O. Heller Wilensky*, pp. 1–14. Jerusalem: Magnes Press (Hebrew).

——— 1994b. 'The mystical intention of the eighteen benedictions by R. Isaac Sagi Nahor'. In M. Oron and A. Goldreich (eds), *Massu'ot, Studies in Kabbalistic Literature and Jewish Philosophy in Memory of Prof. Ephraim Gottlieb*, pp. 31–42. Jerusalem: Mossad Bialik (Hebrew).

——— 1995a. 'An anonymous kabbalistic commentary on *Shir ha-Yihud*'. In K.E. Grözinger and J. Dan (eds), *Mysticism, Magic, and Kabbalah in Ashkenazi Judaism*, pp.139–54. Berlin: Walter de Gruyter.

——— 1995b. *Hasidism: Between Ecstasy and Magic.* Albany: SUNY Press.

——— 1998a. 'From structure to performance: on the divine body and human action in the Kabbalah', *Mishqafayim* 32:3–6 (Hebrew).

——— 1998b. *Messianic Mystics.* New Haven: Yale University Press.

——— 2001. 'Torah: between presence and representation of the divine in Jewish mysticism'. In J. Assmann and A.I. Baumgarten (eds), *Representation in Religion, Studies in Honor of Moshe Barasch*, 197–236. Leiden: Brill.

——— 2002. *Absorbing Perfections: Kabbalah and Interpretation.* New Haven: Yale University Press.

——— 2004a. 'On the theologization of Kabbalah in Modern Scholarship'. In Y. Schwartz and V. Krech (eds), *Religious Apologetics: Philosophical Argumentation*, pp. 123–74. Tübingen: Mohr.

——— 2004b. 'Hermeticism and Kabbalah'. In P. Lucentini, I. Parri and V.P. Compagni (eds), *Hermeticism from Late Antiquity to Humanism*, pp. 389–408. Turnhout: Brepols.

——— 2005a. *Ascensions on High in Jewish Mysticism, Pillars, Lines, Ladders.* Budapest: CEU.

——— 2005b. *Enchanted Chains, Techniques and Rituals in Jewish Mysticism.* Los Angeles: Cherub Press.

——— 2005c. *Kabbalah & Eros.* New Haven: Yale University Press.

——— 2006a. '*Ganz Andere*: on Rudolph Otto and concepts of holiness in Jewish mysticism', *Daat* 57–9:xxvi–xxxi.

——— 2006b 'The secret of impregnation as metempsychosis in Kabbalah'. In A. and J. Assmann (eds), *Verwandlungen, Archaeologie der literarischen Communication* IX:341–79. Munich: Fink.

——— 2007. *Ben: Sonship and Jewish Mysticism.* London: Continuum.

——— 2009a. 'The image of man above the *sefirot:* R. David ben Yehuda he-Hasid's theosophy of ten supernal *sahsahot* and its reverberations', *Kabbalah* 20:181–212.

——— 2009b. 'On the performing body in theosophical-theurgical Kabbalah: some preliminary remarks'. In M. Diemling and G. Veltri (eds), *The Jewish Body, Corporeality, Society, and Identity in the Renaissance and Early Modern Period*, pp. 251–71 Leiden-Boston: Brill.

——— 2009c. 'Performance, intensification and experience in Jewish mysticism', *Archaeus* XIII:93–134.

——— 2010. *Old Worlds, New Mirrors, On Jewish Mysticism and Twentieth-Century Thought.* Philadelphia: University of Pennsylvania Press.

——— 2011. 'Ascensions, gender and pillars in Safedian Kabbalah', *Kabbalah* 25:66–86.

——— 2014. *Mircea Eliade, From Magic to Myth*. New York: Peter Lang.

——— 2015a. 'Transfers of categories: the German-Jewish experience and beyond'. In S. Ashheim and V. Liska (eds), *The German-Jewish Experience Revisited*, pp. 15–43. Berlin: De Gruyter.

——— 2015b. 'Symbols and symbolopoiesis in Kabbalah'. In F. Buzzetta and M. Golfetto (eds), *Il Simbolismo. La grammatica del sacro*, pp. 197–247. Palermo: Officina di Studi Medievali.

——— 2015c. 'Visualization of colors, 1: David ben Yehudah he-Hasid's kabbalistic diagram', *Ars Judaica* 11:31–54.

——— 2016a. 'Visualization of colors, 2: implications of David ben Yehudah he-Hasid's diagram for the history of Kabbalah', *Ars Judaica* 12:39–51.

——— 2016b. 'The liturgical turn: from the Spanish Kabbalah, to the Kabbalas of Safed, and to Hasidism'. In U. Erlich (ed.), *Jewish Prayer: New Perspectives*, pp. 9–50. Beer Sheva: Ben Gurion University of the Negev Press (Hebrew).

———2017. ,Early Hasidism and Altaic tribes: between Europe and Asia', *Kabbalah* 39:7–51 (Hebrew).

——— 2019a. *R. Menahem Recanati, the Kabbalist.* Jerusalem: Schocken Books (Hebrew).

——— 2019b. *Vocal Rites and Broken Theologies: Cleaving to Vocables in I. Ba'al Shem Tov's Mysticism.* New York: Crossroad.

——— 2020a. *The Gate of Intention: R. Isaac ben Shmuel of Acre and Its Reception.* Los Angeles: Cherub Press.

——— 2020b. 'Abraham Abulafia: the apotheosis of a medieval heretic in modern Me'ah She'arim'. In R. Goetschel and G. Sharvit (eds), *Canonization and Alterity: Heresy in Jewish History, Thought and Literature*, pp. 125–58. Berlin: W. de Gruyter.

——— 2020c. '"Limbs of the Shekhinah": on ascent of the divine feminine in Kabbalah and her decline in modern scholarship'. In E. Atlan *et al.* (eds), *Die weibliche Seite Gottes, Visuelle Darstellungen einer verdrängten Tradition* [*The Female Side of God: Art and Ritual*], pp. 77–110. Bielefeld: Kerber Verlag.

——— 2022. *"Male and Female": Equality, Female Theurgy, and Procreation: R. Moshe Cordovero's Dual Ontology*. New York: Ktav.

Kallus, M. 2002. The Theurgy of Prayer in the Lurianic Kabbalah. Ph. D. thesis, Hebrew University.

Kaplan, A. 1985. *Meditation and Kabbalah*. York Beach: Weiser.

Kellner, M. 2018. 'Maimonides on holiness'. In A. Mittleman (ed.), *Holiness in Jewish Thought*, pp. 112–36. Oxford: Oxford University Press.

Landolt, H. 1986. *Nuruddin Isfarayini, Le révélateur des mystères: Traité de soufisme*. Lagrasse: Verdier.

Leiser, B. 1971. 'The sanctity of profane: a pharisaic critique of Rudolph Otto', *Judaism* xx:87–93.

Lewis, C.S. 1967. *The Discarded Image*. Cambridge: Cambridge University Press.

Liebes, Y. 1995. 'Myth vs. symbol in the Zohar and Lurianic Kabbalah'. In L. Fine (ed.), *Essential Papers on Kabbalah*, pp. 212–42. New York: New York University Press.

Lincoln, B. 1986. *Myth, Cosmos, and Society*. Cambridge, Mass.: Harvard University Press.

Lorberbaum, Y. 2015. *In God's Image: Myth, Theology and Law in Classical Judaism*. Cambridge: Cambridge University Press.

Lovejoy, A.O. 1976 [1936]. *The Great Chain of Being: A Study of the History of an Idea*. Cambridge, Mass.: Harvard University Press.

Macquarrie, J. 2001. *Twentieth Century Religious Thought*. Harrisburg, PA: Trinity Press International.

Mauss, M. 1950 [1943]. 'Les techniques du corps'. In M. Mauss, *Sociologie et anthropologie*, pp. 365–83. Paris: PUF.

Meir ibn Gabbai, R. 1950. *'Avodat ha-Qodesh*. Jerusalem: Levin-Epstein.

Merlan, P. 1963. *Monopsychism, Mysticism, Metaconsciouness*. The Hague: Martinus Nijhoff.

Moore, P. 1978. 'Mystical experience, mystical doctrine, mystical technique'. In S.T. Katz (ed.), *Mysticism and Philosophical Analysis*, pp. 112–14. New York: Oxford University Press.

Mopsik, C. 1993. *Les Grands Textes de la Cabale. Les rites qui font Dieu*. Lagrasse: Verdier.

Morgan, M. 1990. *Platonic Piety, Philosophy & Ritual in Fourth-Century Athens*. New Haven: Yale University Press.

Mottolese, M. 2007. *Analogy in Midrash and Kabbalah: Interpretive Projections of the Sanctuary and Ritual.* Los Angeles: Cherub Press.

——— 2017. *Bodily Rituals in Jewish Mysticism: The Intensification of Cultic Hand Gestures by Medieval Kabbalists.* Los Angeles: Cherub Press.

——— 2018. 'Between somatics and semiotics – the Lulav ritual gestures and its Kabbalistic re-signification', *Kabbalah* 42:7–61.

Otto, R. 1960. *Mysticism East and West: A Comparative Analysis of the Nature of Mysticism* (trans. B.L. Bracey and R.C. Payne). New York: The Macmillan Company.

——— 1999. *The Idea of the Holy* (tr. M. Ron). Jerusalem: Carmel (Hebrew).

Persico, T. 2016. *Jewish Meditation: The Development of Spiritual Practices in Contemporary Judaism.* Tel Aviv: Tel Aviv University Press (Hebrew).

Pines, S. 1980. 'Shi'ite terms and conceptions in the *Kuzari*', *Jerusalem Studies in Arabic and Islam* 2:165–247.

Pines, S. and Gelblum, T. 1966–89. 'Al-Bīrūnī's Arabic version of Patañjali's "Yogasūtra"', *Bulletin of the School of Oriental and African Studies* 29(2):302–25, 40:522–49, 46:258–304, 52:265–305.

Recanati, M. 1961. *Commentary on the Pentateuch.* Jerusalem: Mordekhai Atiyya.

Reiser, D. 2018 [2014]. *Imagery Techniques in Modern Jewish Mysticism* (trans. E.D. Matanky). Berlin: Walter de Gruyter.

Rotenstreich, N. 1977–8. 'Symbolism and transcendence: on some philosophical aspects of Gershom Scholem's opus', *Review of Metaphysics* 31:604–14.

Sarbacker, S.R. 'Rudolph Otto and the concept of the numinous', *Oxford Research Encyclopedia of Religion:* oxfordre.com/religion/view/10.1093/acrefore/9780199340378.001.0001/acrefore-9780199340378-e-88 (accessed 3 May 2025).

Scholem, G. 1960. *Jewish Gnosticism, Merkavah Mysticism and Talmudic Tradition.* New York: Jewish Theological Seminary.

——— 1969. *On the Kabbalah and its Symbolism* (trans. R. Manheim). New York: Schocken Books.

——— 1972. 'The name of God and the linguistic of the Kabbala', *Diogenes* 80:164–94.

——— 1974a. *Major Trends in Jewish Mysticism.* New York: Schocken Books.

——— 1974b. *Kabbalah.* New York: Meridian Books.

——— 1987. *Origins of the Kabbalah* (ed. Z.J. Werblowsky; trans. A. Arkush). Philadelphia: Jewish Publication Society.

——— 1997. *On the Possibility of Jewish Mysticism in Our Time and Other Essays* (trans. J. Chipman). Philadelphia: Jewish Publication Society.

——— 1998. *Studies in Kabbalah* (ed. J. Ben-Shlomo and M. Idel). Tel Aviv: 'Am 'Oved.

Séd, N. 1987. 'Le Mystère des couleurs de J. Gikatilla', *Chrysopaeia* 1:2–30.

Segal, R.A. 1998. *The Myth and Ritual Theory.* Malden, MA.: Blackwell.

Septimus, B. 1981. 'Petrus Alfonsi on the cult of Mecca', *Speculum* 56:134–6.

Smith, W.R. 1989. *Lectures on the Religion of the Semites*. Edinburgh: A. and C. Black.

Swartz, M.D. 2011. 'Judaism and the idea of ancient ritual theory'. In R. Boustan (ed.), *Jewish Studies at the Crossroads of Anthropology and History. Authority, Diaspora, Tradition*, pp. 294–317. Philadelphia: University of Pennsylvania Press.

Tishby, I. 1964. *Paths of Faith and Heresy*. Ramat Gan: Massada (Hebrew).

——— 1991. *The Wisdom of the Zohar: An Anthology of Texts* (trans. D. Goldstein). Washington: Littman Library.

Tucci, G. 1961. *The Theory and Practice of the Mandala*. London: Rider & Company.

Turcanu, F. 2003. *Mircea Eliade, Le prisonnier de l'histoire*. Paris: La Découverte.

Underhill, E. 1937. *Worship*. London: Nisbet, & Co.

Wachs, R. 2010. *The Flame and the Holy Fire: Perspectives on the Teachings of Rabbi Kalonymus Kalmish Shapiro of Piaczena*. Alon Shevut: Tevunot (Hebrew).

Wallis, R.T. 1976. 'Nous as experience'. In R.B. Harris, *The Significance of Neoplatonism*, pp. 121–54. New York, SUNY Press.

Werblowsky, J.Z. 1962. *Joseph Karo, Lawyer and Mystic*. Oxford: Oxford University Press.

Wolfson, E.R. 1988a. *Sefer ha-Rimmon, The Book of the Pomegranate* (ed. M. de León). Atlanta: Georgia.

——— 1988b. 'Mystical rationalization of the commandments in *Sefer ha-Rimmon*', *HUCA* LIX:217–51.

——— 1988c 'Mystical-Theurgical dimensions of prayer in *Sefer ha-Rimmon*', *Approaches to Judaism in Medieval Times* III:41–80.

——— 1989 'Anthropomorphic imagery and letter symbolism in the *Zohar*', *Jerusalem Studies in Jewish Thought* 8:147–81 (Hebrew).

——— 1995. *Along the Path*. Albany: SUNY Press

——— 2005a. *Language, Eros, Being*. New York: Fordham University Press.

——— 2005b. '"*Megillat 'Emmet ve-'Emunah*": contemplative visualization and mystical unknowing', *Kabbalah* 5:55–110.

Zacut, A. 1857. *Sefer ha-Yuhasin ha-Shalem* (ed. Z. Filipowski). London: The Hebrew Antiquarian Society.

Zimmer, H. 1984. *Artistic Form and Yoga in the Sacred Images of India* (trans. and ed. G. Chapple and J.B. Lawson). Princeton: Princeton University Press.

5

Contemplative practices in Asian Sufism

Dhikr exercise, the subtle body and their diagramed representations

THIERRY ZARCONE

In memoriam Arthur F. Buehler (1948–2019)

The aim of this chapter is to explore the subtle body in Sufism, and especially in the Naqshbandī lineage, which has developed a quite complex theory regarding it, in which it is composed of subtle points called *laṭīfa* (plural. *laṭā'if*). These points are activated by the Sufi through the practice of the *dhikr*, an exercise composed of litanies, breathing techniques and visualizations. The teaching and the practice of *dhikr* is facilitated by several representations in diagrams of the subtle body, sometimes with directions about the way to perform it in relation to these subtle points. The final stage of the *dhikr* and the height of the mystical experience, called *sulṭān al-adhkār* or 'sultan of the *dhikr*', is represented in some diagrams by a subtle point; more, the practice of the 'sultan of the *dhikr*' is impregnated with gestures borrowed from yoga. Hence, some diagrams embody a hybridization of the Naqshbandī subtle physiology with its yogi counterparts. The same phenomenon is observed among the Chinese Naqshbandī with regard to Taoist subtle physiology and meditation exercises.

Bahā' al-Dīn Naqshband (d. 1389), the eponym of the Naqshbandī Sufi order, received in a dream a spiritual regime composed of eight phrases originated one century before in Central Asia by 'Abd al-Khalīq Ghijdūvānī (d. 1220) a mystic of the same area. Ghijdūvānī may have been inspired by two other rules elaborated previously by two major Sufi figures of Baghdad and Central Asia, namely Abū-l-Qāsim Junayd (d. 911) and Najm al-Dīn Kubra (d. 1221). Junayd's rule is composed of eight phrases dealing with 'ritual purity', 'spiritual withdrawal', 'fasting', 'silence', 'recollecting God' (*dhikr*), 'rejecting stray thoughts', 'binding the heart to the shaykh and non-opposition to God and to the shaykh'. These rules were especially followed during spiritual withdrawal and the practice of recollecting of God (*dhikr*) (Radtke 2005; see also Elias 1995:119–24). A short comment on these rules was printed in Tashkent in 1898 by a shaykh of the Qādiriyya lineage (al-Janūshānī 1898; see Zarcone 2000:315–17); and demonstrates that this method was still of interest for the Sufis of the modern age, one millenary after the death of Junayd. Three centuries after the death of Junayd, Najm al-Dīn Kubra completed the rule of the great shaykh of Baghdad with two phrases: 'sleeping only when overcome by fatigue' and 'avoiding excessive eatings and drinking'. The influence of Junayd and Najm al-Dīn Kubra's rules upon Ghijdūvānī and Bahā' al-Dīn Naqshband is obvious. The rule elaborated by the latter comprehends eleven phrases (three new phrases are from Naqshband himself). This rule, named 'Sacred Principles' (*Kalimāt-i Kudsiyya*) by the Naqshbandī Sufis, is, writes Hamid Algar (1990:9), 'a general statement' of the character and spiritual method of this Sufi lineage.

The eleven sacred phrases encourage an ascetic life: some of them focus on concepts of 'internal mystical journey' (*safar dar vatan*) or of 'solitude in society' (*khalvat dar anjumān*) that are a part of a general mystical mindset. The other phrases emphasize more technical practices on the mystical path, especially the development of mindfulness and awareness:[1] 'awereness of breath' (*hūsh dar dam*) and 'watching over the steps' (*nazar dar qadam*). In addition, three phrases focus on the mindfulness through the practice of the recollection of God (*dhikr*): 'awareness of time' (*vuqūf-i zamānī*), 'counting of *dhikr* repetition' (*vuqūf-i 'adadī*) and 'keeping the heart constantly attentive to God' (*vuqūf-i qalbī*).[2] This last phrase, according to the Kurdish Sufi, Mavlānā Khālid (d. 1827), a leading figure of the Naqshbandiyya in the Ottoman lands in nineteenth century, is epitomized by a verse of the Quran: 'there are signs for men possessed of minds who remember God, standing and sitting and on their sides, and reflect upon the creation of the heavens and the earth…' (3:191; Baghdadī 1987:45). The general spirit of the way Naqshbandī Sufis practice *dhikr* is that it must be an exercise performed in an isolate place but

1 I borrow this term from Francisco Varela *et al.* 1991:23.

2 Annemarie Schimmel interprets the principle *bāz gard* as 'restraining one's thought', though Arthur Buehler translates it as 'returning to the world after performing *dhikr*'. Also, Schimmel translates the principle *nigāh dāsht* as 'to watch one's thought', while Buehler writes 'guarding one's spiritual progress' (Buehler 1998:234; Schimmel 1975:364). On these eleven sacred phrases, see also Papas 2010:215–23; Tosun 2002:334–8; Zarcone 1996:301–15.

inside society, as Islam prohibits monachism and the abandonment of the world (*tark-i dunyā*), contrary to some other Sufi groups and individuals (for example the members of the Qalandariyya lineage, see Zarcone 1997:21–9). Such practice fits with the principle of 'solitude in society', one of the eleven phrases.

Further, the eleven sacred phrases, especially those which concern the *dhikr*, must be understood as the elements of a physical and spiritual practice aiming, among other goals, to activate a subtle body consisting of several subtle centres called *laṭīfa* (plural, *laṭā'if*). In addition to the teaching of a living Sufi master, the Naqshbandī treatises provides some diagrams which point to the localization of the subtle centres in the body, and show, in some cases, the movements of the *dhikr*, which is mentally conveyed from one centre to another.

The subtle body and its centres (*laṭā'if*) in the Naqshbandiyya

One of the major specificities of the Naqshbandī Sufi order is the concept of a non-physical, spiritual or more precisely 'subtle body',[3] structured around five, six or seven subtle points or centres. These centres, which are all located in general in the upper abdomen, have two main significations. Firstly, they form part of a Sufi cosmological interpretation of the universe, which is both physical and subtle, and each of these centres shows the successive stages of the spiritual development of the Sufi. Secondly, and more importantly for our purpose here, these centres are benchmarks of progress in realizing the subtle body; they can be activated through the *dhikr* exercise, leading the practitioner to higher states of consciousness.

The Quranic source for these subtle centres is a hadith of the prophet Muḥammad describing the body of the descendants of Adam, the first man, and its major elements, which are linked more or less with the subtle centres of the Sufi body in the Naqshbandiyya:

> Surely in the body of the sons of Adam there is flesh (*madgha*), and in this flesh is the heart, and in the heart is the inner heart, and in the inner heart is a most inner heart, and in the most inner heart is a secret, and in the secret is the hidden and in the hidden is a light (*nûr*)... (*inna fī jasad ibn Adam al-maghdat wa fī'l-maghdat qalb wa fī'l-qalb fu'ād wa fī'l-fu'ād zamīr wa fī'l-zamīr sirr wa fī'l-sirr khafī wa fī'l-khafī nūr...*)[4]

3 'Subtle' is used in Indian philosophy and yoga, also in Neoplatonism; it characterizes some elements of the body that cannot be perceived by the senses.

4 I use here the Arabic text of this hadith quoted in a treatise of the Ottoman sufi Emīn-i Tokādī (eighteenth century), edited and translated from the Arabic to

The subtle points here are five: heart (*qalb*), inner heart (*fu'ād*), most inner heart (*zamīr*), secret (*sirr*) and the hidden (*khafī*). However, the same hadith, quoted by the Indian Ḥājjī Imdād Al lāh (d. 1899) in his Sufi manual *Ḍiyā al-qulūb* (1865–6:12), shows some differences with the version presented above. The most inner heart (*zamīr*) is replaced by the soul (*rūḥ*), and the hidden (*khafī*) has disappeared. There is still a great uncertainty concerning the veracity of this hadith, which is nevertheless quoted by Sufi authors, though in various ways. For instance, the Ottoman Emīn-i Tokādī (d. 1708), a member of the Ottoman Naqshbandiyya, mentioned this hadith in a little book on the spiritual path that comprises of a commentary of the subtle centres mentioned above and of the eleven phrases.[5]

The Naqshbandī lineage has synthezised previous writings on these subtle centres, the oldest being made, as mentioned above, by the mystic Junayd (d. 910) in tenth century (Buehler 1998:106–7). First of all, the subtle centres have a cosmological characteristic and represent the scale of the spiritual progress, from the 'world of creation' to the 'world of divine command' – as well demonstrated, for example, by the Indian Naqshbandī Shāh Walīullāh (d. 1763) (Hermansen 1988:1–25; Ventura 1991, vol. 1:475–85). The five, six, or seven centres are interpretated as different grades of being experienced by the Sufi when performing the *dhikr*, that is travelling to God. The lower stages are composed of the four elements (fire, air, earth and water), while the higher stages consisted of the subtle centres (five here): heart (below left breast), spirit (below right breast), mystery (above left breast) inner (above righ breast) and innermost (sternum). Aḥmad Sirhindī (d. 1624), eponym of the Mujaddidī branch of the Naqshbandiyya lineage, which has replaced almost all the other branches of this lineage in India, Turkey and the Middle East, adopted a system composed of five subtle centres, *qalb*, *rūḥ*, *sirr*, *khafī* and *akhfa*, that has become the standard since this time (Buehler 1998:105–6).

In addition, some Sufis in the Indian subcontinent, under the influence of yogic and Tantric practices, have given new places to some subtle centres, almost identical with the *cakra* that are the subtle centres in yoga, although there is in general no correspondence between the yogic and Sufi subtle physiology (Bhattacharya 2003: 94–5). Mir Muḥammad Nu'mān (d. 1648), a disciple of Sirhindī, writes for example that the subtle centre 'mystery' is located between the breasts, the 'inner' centre in the forehead, and the 'innermost' centre at the top of the skull (Tosun 2005a:58; see also Imdād Allāh 1865–6:20). These locations are the same as those of the Anāhata, Ajnā and Sahasrāra *cakra* of the Tantric physiology (though the number of *cakra*

Turkish by Şimşek 2005:143–4, 153.

5 'Risāla fī ḥakkī sulūk,' in Şimşek, 2005:143–4, 153.

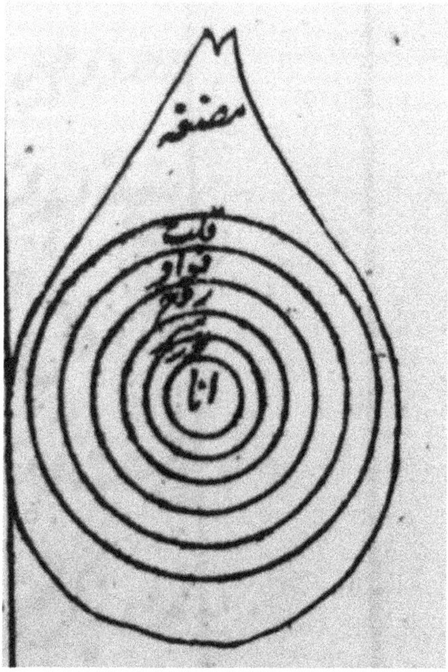

maḍgha (flesh)

qalb (heart)
fu'ād (inner heart)
rūḥ (soul)
sirr (secret)
nūr (light)
ānā (I)

Figure 5.1 Indian representation of the subtle centres (Imdād Allāh 1865–6:12).

and their location vary depending on the texts). Many Sufis think nevertheless that the subtle centres are neither physical organs nor subtle organs, and that their location in the body is purely conventional (Tosun 2005a:58–9). There is a notable difference here with the Indian *cakra*, which are regarded on the contrary as 'real' subtle elements in the body.

Besides, there exist diagramed representations of the subtle body with indications of its centres; such diagrams illustrate books to make the written text clearer, but they are available also in the format of portable sheets. Some of them teach more than the location of the subtle centres; they can indicate which are the specific movements made by the mind during the *dhikr* when moving from one subtle point to the other, and also which colours and names of the prophets are attached to the centres (Figures 5.1 and 5.2). These diagrams are found in almost all the areas the Naqshbandiyya was introduced into.[6]

I have collected some of these diagrams from libraries and private archives in Xinjiang, India, Iran and Turkey. One diagram I found at Yarkand, in Xinjiang, in the hands of a Naqshandī shaykh, is particularly interesting. It

6 Different authors and shaykhs stipulate different colours. A. Buehler (1998:110) suggests that each shaykh who has experienced the activation of the subtle centres, described what was revealed to him.

akhfa (innermost)

pitān (breast) *pitān*

khafī (hidden) *sirr*

rūḥ *qalb*

sadr (breast)

Figure 5.2 Indian representation of the subtle centres with indication about their location. From the Manāhīj al-sayyr va madarīj al-khayr of Abū'l-Ḥasan Zayd Mujaddidī Fārūqī (d. 1993, Delhi) printed in Delhi by the Dargāh-i Haḍrat-i Shāh Abū'l-Khayr; Abū'l-Ḥasan Zayd Mujaddidī Fārūqī 1956–7:17.

is integrated into a large sheet (1.4 m) that contains some abstracted texts of Naqshbandī teaching. It includes, for example, a listing of the eleven phrases accompanied with short commentaries, a brief presentation of the *dhikr* and a text on Sufi ethics. The diagram of the five subtle centres is situated in the central part of the sheet (Figures 5.3a and 5.3b).[7] The major teachings of the Naqshbandī lineage that a Sufi must know are actually all grouped on this sheet: it is clearly a perfect vade mecum of this order and a portable manual.

Diagrams of the activation of the subtle body through the *dhikr* exercise

The Naqshbandī *dhikr* practice can be quite simple; it involves a silent and mental repetition of the Muslim profession of faith, 'there is no god but God', '*la ilāh illā Allāh*', while holding the breath (*habs-i nafs*, prison of the breath) according to a particular method. This *dhikr* is called *dhikr nafy va ithbāt*, i.e. *dhikr* of 'negation' ('there is no God') and then of 'affirmation' ('but God'). Some contemporary Naqshbandī shaykhs in Turkey and in India – who are certainly not alone – advocate that, according to a tradition attributed to the Sufi Junayd (d. 911), the practice of the contemplation can be learn from the observation of a cat sitting and waiting to pounce on a mouse. The cat, explains Junayd, 'was totally consumed in this activity to the point that not even a hair moved on him'.[8]

7 On this document see Zarcone 2010:150.

8 Abū'l-Ḥasan Zayd Mujaddidī Fārūqī 1956–7:56; 'Abdullāh Shāh (d. 1964, Hyderabad), 'Sulūk-i mujaddidiyya' in Buehler 2015:341–2; Mehmed Zahid Kotku (d. 1981, Istanbul) in Kotku *c.*1980, vol. 2:250.

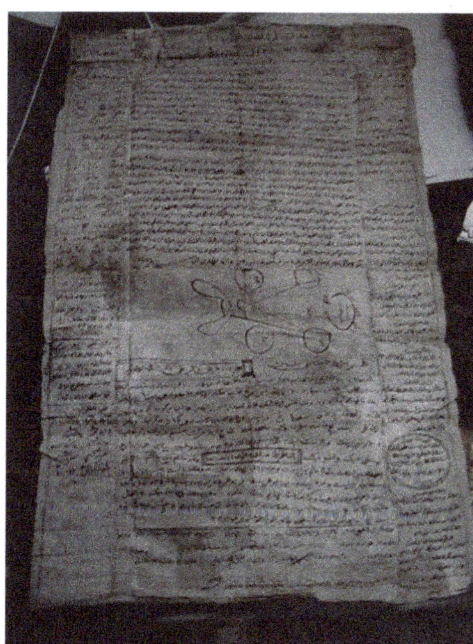

Figure 5.3a Naqshbandī portable vade mecum, Yarkand, 1945.
Figure 5.3b Diagram of the subtle centres in a Naqshbandī portable vade mecum, Yarkand, 1945.

There are in general two ways to perform this *dhikr*. The first one implements one or two subtle centres only, contrary to the second, which activates all of them. Both methods are sometimes represented in the Naqshbandī treatises in the form of diagramed representations that help the practitioner.

The first method consists of a 'three-blow' (*ḍarb*), actually a three-movement, exercise. The first movement is to hold the breath below the navel, and then mentally to bring up the word '*lā*' from below the navel to the middle of the forehead. The second movement is to convey mentally the word '*ilāh*' from the middle of the forehead to the right shoulder, ending with the final forceful mental motion 'hitting' (*ḍarb*) the heart from the right shoulder with '*illā Allāh*' (Buehler 1998:128–9; Mavlānā Khālid Baghdadī 1987:51). While doing this, the practitioner has to count how many times he repeats the sentence '*lā ilāh illā Allāh*' in one breath. This practice fits here with one of the eleven phrases: 'counting of *dhikr* repetition', *vuqūf-i 'adadī*.

The second method of *dhikr* is based also on the sentence '*lā ilāh illā Allāh*', but with the *dhikr* moving through the subtle centres. However, there are many variants of this method, especially regarding the role of the centres and the order of succession. Some variants, as shown in an Indonesian drawing (Figure 5.4), involve performing the *dhikr* upon the first centre, i.e. the heart, and then moving to the second centre, i.e. the spirit, and so on, up to the last centre, the innermost. Another more complex variant performed in Xinjiang and probably elsewhere, is to start the recitation of the *dhikr* at the navel and to move through the 'most secret' centre to the top of the head, called 'throne' (*'arsh*), and then to move back through the secret, mystery and spirit centres (pers. comm. Khalīfa 'Abd al-Raḥmān Qarī in Urumchi, Xinjiang, in 1998; see also Ayyūb Qārī 1953–4:36–7, n.d.:42–3).

During a Naqshbandī initiation I observed in Tashkent in 1996, the new disciple shook hands with his master (who was Shaykh Qurbān 'Alī, a major shaykh of the Naqshbandiyya-Mujadiddiyya in Uzbekistan and a representative of Shaykh Ibrāhīmjān, d. 2009) before receiving instructions about the *dhikr* practice, that is to the places of the subtle centres in the body and how to hold the breath during the *dhikr*. I observed the same ceremonial at Taybad, in southern Khurasan (Iran), in 2017, during a ceremony directed by a local Naqshbandī shaykh trained in Pakistan by a well-known figure of this lineage, Mavlānā 'Umar Sarbāzī (d. 2007). These two ceremonies followed scrupulously the written treatises and the diagramed representations of the first method exposed above. It is through an initiation ritual operated by a living spiritual master, when accepting a new disciple, that such teaching can be transmitted.

The 'sulṭān of the dhikr' (sulṭān al-adhkār): technique and/or spiritual state

According to some Naqshbandī shaykhs, the final stage of the *dhikr*, and the height of the mystical experience, whatever the method adopted, is characterized by the fact that the entire body of the Sufi, and not only some

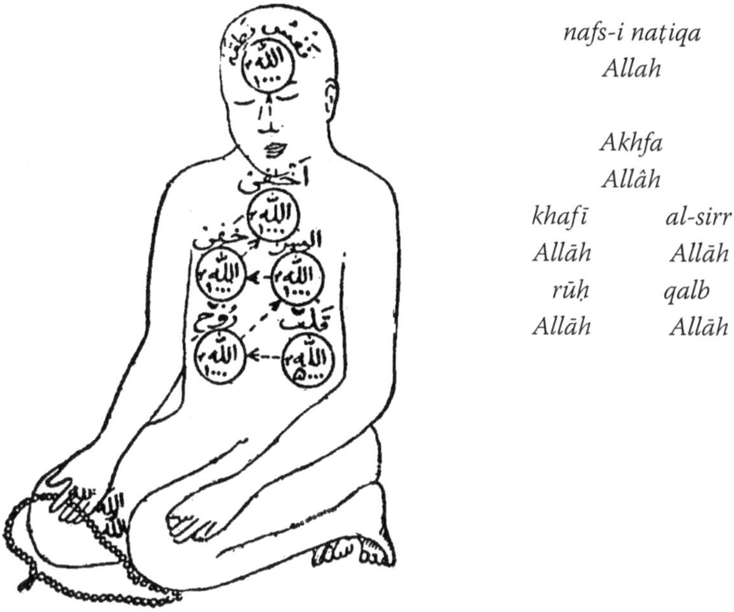

Figure 5.4 Indonesian Representation of the subtle centres from Dr. Al-Shaykh Haji Jalaluddin. 1961. Rahasia Mutiara ath-Thariqat an-Naqsyabandiyah. Jakarta. Picture republished in van Bruinessen 2007:250.

subtle centres, is possessed by the *dhikr*, 'from hairs to feet', according to the expression used by Imdād Allāh (1865–6:38) in India and Mavlānā Khālid Baghdadī (1987:49) in the Ottoman Empire. This state is named *sulṭān al-adhkār, dhikr-i sulṭānī, sulṭān al-dhikr* or, more simply, *sulṭān*, meaning 'the number one among the *dhikr*'. Many Naqshbandī shaykhs have highly praised it. The Indian Mīr Dard (d. 1785), for instance, wrote that 'when man reaches perfect recollectedness and peace – this is the *dhikr-i sulṭānī*' (Schimmel 1976:131). We agree here with the interpretation of A. Buehler (1998:112, 128–9), that 'a subtle body has been formed when one can perform *sulṭān al-dhikr*'.

The concept of *dhikr-i sulṭānī* or *sulṭān al-adhkār* is actually borrowed from Indian Sufism, especially from the Chishtiyya and Qādiriyya lineages, who have adopted it since at least the sixteenth century. Two major figures of these orders, 'Abd al-Quddus Gangūhī and Dārā Shīkūh refer to it (Digby 1975:21–2; Rizvi 1986: vol. 2, 137–8). In the eyes of Gangūhī (d. 1537), the '*sulṭān* of the *dhikr*' is a higher spiritual state of consciousness (Digby 1975:21–2). In a seminal article about the life and teaching of this Sufi, Simon Digby wrote that "Abd al-Quddus used to say that in the early years of his spiritual life, when *sulṭān-i dhikr* often overcame him and gave him no respite; he feared that he was about to lose his reason and that he would lapse into a permanent state of madness (*junūniyat*).' (ibid.:22). In Gangūhī's eyes the phenomenon of *sulṭān-i dhikr* is equated with the prophetic inspiration (*vahy*). He wrote:

> I was in *namaz-i ma'kus* [devotions performed upside down while hanging suspended by a rope tied to the heels] when the *sulṭān-i dhikr* manifested itself and put to flight my external existence. A state of obliteration (*mahviyat*) came to pass and there was no consciousness apart from my consciousness of myself. In that state I had to pass beyond this consciousness of myself and reach the annihilation of annihilation (*fanā' al-fanā'*). By God's grace this came to pass and the world of eternality (*baqā'*) was revealed.
>
> (Digby 1975:21–2)

By way of parenthesis, it can be said that usually, when performing this *dhikr*, Gangūhī was also executing an astonishing posture inspired from yoga that is called *namāz-i ma'kūs* or 'inversed prayer'. It is performed upside down while hanging suspended by a rope tied to the heels (Digby 1975:22; see also Kugle 2012:240–52). This yogic posture is not unknown to Sufism, and is even mentioned in a Persian translation of a yoga treatise.[9] It was also performed by some other Persian and Indian Sufis (Digby 1975:20–1).

One of the leading figures of the Indian Qādiriyya, Dārā Shīkūh (d. 1659), who was very well informed about Hindu religion and yoga, emphasized one particular aspect of the practice of the *sulṭān al-adhkār*: it must be performed in a secluded place and the body technique adopted comes from yoga (though different from that mentioned above) combined with the control of breathing and the recitation of the *dhikr lā ilaha/illa allāh* ('there is no god but God') in two periods of time. Another particularity of this exercise is the apparition of many subtle sounds.

> Sit in a secluded spot (*khalvat*) in the posture in which the holy Prophet – may God grant him blessings and peace – used to sit (on one's knees as for prayer), but do not place the hands upon the knees. Rather, place each elbow on the knees and reach up with the hands, and with the thumb close the hole of each ear so that no air may pass out of them. With the index fingers shuts both eyes in such a way that the upper eyelid may remain firmly presseed against the lower eyelid, but without the fingers pressing on

9 Named *Baḥr al-Ḥayat* (Ocean of Life), this text is a compilation by the Sufi Shaykh Muḥammad Ghavth Gvaliyārī around 1551. There is one manuscript with an illustration of an inversed posture in a manuscript dated 1602. See Ernst 2018.

> the eyeballs. Place the ring finger and pinkie of each hand on the upper and lower lips, so as to close the mouth and not permit breath to pass through it. Place the two middle fingers on the sides of the nose, the right middle finger on the right nostril, and the left middle finger on the left nostril.[10]

Two very similar hand gestures (*mudra*) are practised by Hindu ascetics: the *sanmukhi mudra* and the *yoni mudra*. The first one refers to the six (*shan*) holes/mouth that need to be sealed in order to progress in the spiritual quest: the ears are closed with the thumbs, the two eyes with the two index fingers, the nostrils with the middle fingers, and the mouth with the other fingers (Figures 5.5a and 5.5b). The yogi, when practising the *sanmukhi mudra*, adopts an alternative nasal breathing (Brosse 1976:20–1).

Then, to continue with Dārā Shīkūh, one of the consequence of the *dhikr* is that the Sufi can hear a voice, sometimes accompanied by subtle sounds that resemble those of a big cauldron boiling, or the buzzing sound of a nest of bees, or even of drums and kettledrums, though these sounds are 'boundless and eternal without any cause or means' (Dārā Shikūh 1956:9–10 and Kugle 2012:144–5). There are many parallels between this description and some writings of the Central Asian Najm al-Dīn Kubra, who mentions also subtle sounds, especially those of bees.[11] Moreover, Dārā Shikūh indicates that these subtle sounds are proof that the Sufi has entered the state of *sulṭān al-adhkār*. He links this tradition to 'Abd al-Qādir al-Jīlānī (d. 1165) the eponym founder of the Qādiriyya Sufi lineage, and to his own Indian master the Qādirī Miyān Mīr (d. 1635). However, Dārā Shikūh adds that originally the first to hear such subtle sounds was the prophet Muḥammad, when he was praying in the cave of the Hira Mount at Mecca (Dārā Shikūh 1956:12; Kugle 2012:151–2).

> Hearing this sound, it will gradually grow more powerful and overwhelming, so much so that will seem to come from all sides of you and there will be no place or no time when this sound will not manifest. This sound, which takes you away and beyond yourself, is a drop from the ocean of eternal resonance. So you can guess its vastness.
>
> [...]
>
> When you perfect this subtle and noble practice, this primordial sound will overpower the sounds of drums (*daf*), even kettledrums (*naqāra*) or the loudest sounds which instruments can generate.

10 *Risāla-i Ḥaqq-numā*, written in 1645, see Dārā Shikūh 1956. I rely here on the English translation, 'The compass of truth', by Kugle 2012:144–5.

11 In his *Fawātiḥ al-jamāl wa fawā'iḥ al-jalāl*, translated to French by Ballanfat, see Najm al-Dīn Kubra 2001:150–6.

Figure 5.5a A yogi practising the sanmukhi mudra (seventeenth or eighteenth century). Image from Baker 2012:253.

> [...]
>
> Congratulations and blessings, my friend, if you become capable of this practice called the 'Prime Recitation' (*sulṭān al-adhkār*). For then the subtle world (*'ālam-i laṭāfat*) becomes apparent to you, and also an absolute being that is constant and eternal. If you perform this subtle practice (*shughul-i laṭīf*), it will cause you to become more subtle in your very being, and plunge you into the ocean of subtelety and absolute being, free of conditions and qualities...
>
> (Dārā Shikūh 1956:12–3; Kugle 2012:152–3)

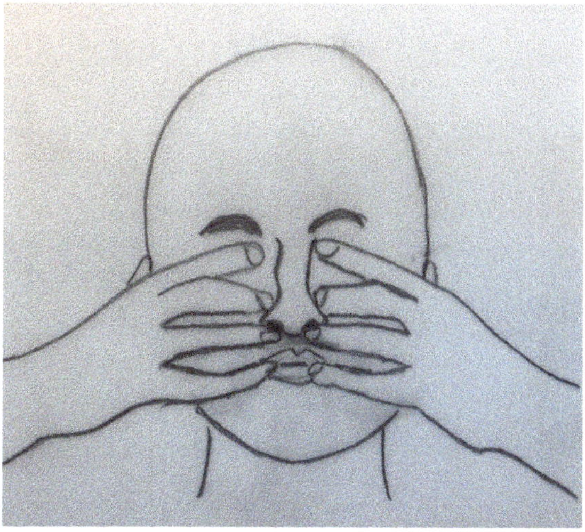

Figure 5.5b Detail of the sanmukhi mudra.

About two centuries after the death of Dārā Shikūh, Imdād Allāh (d. 1899), a member of the Chishtiyya Ṣābiriyya lineage, wrote some commentaries about the *sulṭān al-adhkār* in his well-known *Ḍiyā al-Qulūb*, a manual on Sufi rituals, and especially on the *dhikr* performed by the Sufis (see Kugle 2003:42–60). There is a great likelihood that Imdād Allāh read Shikūh's *Risāla-i Ḥaqq-numā*.

> The practice of the *sulṭān* of the *dhikr* requires that the disciple sit in a narrow room in order to be far form the noises and tumult. Then, he will read the *istighfār*, the *a'vadh* and the *bismillāh* in front of his heart, and he will therefore read three times this prayer in presence of his heart (*qalb*). 'O Allāh, grant me light, and make for me a light, and magnify for me light, and make me a light.' Therefore, he will sit down or stand straight or lie or stay in any way that he wants. He leaves his body powerless and without will, and contemplates himself as if he is dead (*mithl-i marda*). Then, he will meditate with all his strength on the hairs of his body, from his head to the feet. After breathing in while saying the name of the Essence, i.e. 'Allāh', he will exhale and visualize the 'He' (*Hū*). So, while the breath comes in and out, all his hairs, from their roots, experience '*Allāh*' and '*Hū*'. He will be occupied with this exercise to such an extant that he will be immersed (*mustaghraq*) and lose consciousness...
>
> (Imdād Allāh 1865–6:20, 38)

The second aspect of the *sulṭān al-adhkār* method taught by Imdād Allāh reminds one of the yogic hand gesture *sanmukhi mudra* mentioned above, as the Sufi must refrain using his five senses. He will close his ears, mouth and eyes with his fingers or with cotton, and start performing the *dhikr*. The consequences are that he will listen to a subtle voice and be surrounded by subtle lights while feeling an indescribable pleasure (ibid.:20–1, 38). This voice (*āvāz*) is interpreted as the 'voice of the Unity' (*āvāz-i aḥadiyyat*) or the 'eternal voice' (*āvāz-i sarmadī*). This is, he writes, the voice which brings inspiration (*ilhām*) to the saints. Besides, in some cases – and here Imdād Allāh draw upon Gangūhī – he writes that when the *sulṭān dhikr* occurs, there is a roaring as of thunder and the sounds of flashes of lightening, and a trembling happens through the whole body. Then the Sufi enters the state of annihilation (*maḥviyyat*) and of no-self (*bī-khūdī*); at this moment, he is surrounded by lights that resembles those of flashes of lightening, of stars, moon and sun (Digby 1975:22–3, and n. in margin of p. 21). Thus, lights and sounds are the main elements which accompany the *sulṭān al-adhkār* when considered as a state of higher consciousness.

The *sulṭān al-adhkār* is mentioned by several other Indian Sufis. For example, by Muhammad Anamul Ḥaq, in Bengal, who unfortunately doesn't indicate his source. The practice he relates closely resembles Dārā Shikūh's method and relies also on the *sanmukhi mudra* yogic hand gesture:

> Either at the dead of night, the '*sālik*' should retire to a dark closet (*ḥujrah*), or during the day time, he should repair to a lonely place (e. g. a jungle) far away from human habitation, where he should sit in a squatting posture, placing the two elbows on the two corresponding knees, shutting up completely the two orifices of ears by the tips of two thumbs, drawing the four forefingers near the eyelids, completely shutting the eyes and stopping the mouth by the little and ring fingers of the two hands, so that no breath can come out through the mouth; after this he should shut the left nostril first by the middle finger and draw the breath through the right nostril in accompaniment with the recitation '*lā ilāha*', and then shut the right nostril first by the middle finger of the right hand. Protracting the breath by this method he should practice '*dhikr*' continuously till he lets out the protacted breath together with the recitation of '*illāllāh*'.
>
> (Anamul Haq 1975:106–7)

While in Ahmadabad, Gujarat, in 1995, I met the Naqshbandī-Mujaddidī Shaykh al-Ḥājj 'Abd al-Bakrī (aged approximatively 65 or 70 at this time), who was also initiated into the Qādiriyya through a local shaykh. 'Abd al-Bakrī. The imam of a little mosque named Sunnari, near to the General Post Office of the city, 'Abd al-Bakrī, was a well-educated person and had a private library, he directed *dhikr* assemblies and teach several forms of *dhikr*: *dhikr jahr*, *dhikr khāfī-bāṭin* and *dhikr sulṭān al-adhkār*. He agreed to show me how he was practising this last *dhikr*, that is in a way almost similar to the description of Dārā Shikūh: he closed his ears, eyes, mouth and nose with his fingers, and executed longer and longer suspensions of his breathing. This was proof that this particular yoga-inspired method of the closing of the six openings was still going on among some contemporary Sufis in India. 'Abd al-Bakrī told me that he was taught this method ten years before by a certain Sayyid Ḥusayn Naqshbandī. Then, during our conversation, he mentions the *Mi'yār al-sulūk*, a book where, he said, I'll find more details about this *dhikr*. This book is actually a Naqshbandī manual authored by Shāh Muḥammad Hidāyat 'Alī Naqshbandī Mujaddidī Jaipūrī (the complete title is *Mi'yār al-sulūk va dāfi' al-avhām va al-shukūk*) that was printed in Kanpur in 1927, and does indeed contain a little chapter about the *dhikr sulṭān al-adhkār* (Shāh Muḥammad Hidāyat 'Alī Naqshbandī Mujaddidī Jaipūrī 1927:102–9).

There is also another extant Sufi manual printed at Ahmadabad by a local branch of the Naqshbandiyya (linked to the Mujaddidiyya of Delhi) that gives some details on the *sulṭān al-adhkār*. There are few differences with the presentation by Imdād Allāh and many sentences from the *Ḍiyā ul-Qulūb* are reproduced in it ('Abd al-Raḥīm Khān n.d.:25).

The sulṭān al-adhkār in the Naqshbandiyya and its representations in diagrams

I write briefly above that the representation of a subtle body constitued of five centres was first systematized in seventeenth century by Aḥmad Sirhindī, the major figure of the Naqshbandiyya in Asia. We do know, however, of some other systems of the subtle body that existed before him in Central Asian Sufism, with five or seven, sometimes more, subtle centres, since at least the time of Junayd (Buehler 1998:105–10). For instance, Baqībillāh (d. 1603), Sirhindī's master, developed a sevenfold system.[12] But neither the term *sulṭ ān al-adhkār* nor *dhikr-i sulṭānī* are found in Sirhindī's writings,[13] although – and it is quite surprising – these terms are mentioned in many Sufi manuals authored by Sirhindī's sons, disciples and successors, from India to Mecca, and from Istanbul to Chinese Turkestan and north-west China.

The *Mabdā ū Ma'ād* of Sirhindī contains a description of the spiritual state that occurs when the Sufi has activated the higher subtle centres: Sirhindī writes that 'when the six subtle centres [*qalb*/heart, *rūḥ*/spirit, *sirr*/

12 In his *Kulliyāt-i Baqībillāh ya'nī Majmu'a-yi kelām ve rasā'il va malfūẓāt va maktūbāt*; see Baqībillāh n.d.:111.

13 I found no mention of these terms in the index of the *Maktūbāt* made by Buehler 2001.

secret, *khafī*/inner, *akhfa*/innermost, *nafs*/soul] have arrived at the end of the process, they all fly to the sacred world. After this, another subtle centre, *qālib*, which represents the body, remains empty.' According to Sirhindī, the consequence for the Sufi is a 'death before death' (*mavtī ka pīsh al-mavt*). He explains later that the subtle centres will return to the body (*qālib*), although they have been transformed through this experience, and that the Sufi is now in a state of extinction (*fanā*) similar to death (*ḥukm-i mayyit*). Moreover, the centres are illuminated (*tajallī*) and go across to a kind of new life (*sar ḥayāt*), being now permanently in the neighbourhood of God.[14] These conditions are actually those of the state of *sulṭān al-adhkār*. The likelihood is that Sirhindī avoided the use of this expression because of its connection to yoga practice. Nor did he recommend the hand posture *sanmukhi mudra*.

After Sirhindī, the Naqshbandiyya openly integrated the *sulṭān al-adhkār* or *dhikr-i sulṭānī* into its own system of thought and practices, both as a spiritual state and a technique, and also, though rarely, as a new subtle centre (see below). According to some Naqshbandī treatises and from my own observations in India and in Central Asia, it is clear that only experienced Sufis, if they are authorized by their master, can perform the method called '*sulṭān* of the *dhikr*', and that a particular preparation is required to do it. Muḥammad Ma'ṣūm (d. 1668), the third son of Sirhindī, reports that the *sulṭān al-adhkār* starts when the *dhikr* 'spread throughout the entire body' (Muḥammad Ma'ṣūm 1962: vol 2, letter 13). Meḥmed Emīn-i Tokādī (d. 1745), a famous Ottoman Mujaddidī, refers also to the *sulṭānī zikri* (Şimşek 2004:261, 2007:269).

Later, in nineteenth century, one leading figure of the Indian Naqshbandiyya, the Indian Shāh Ghulām 'Alī Dihlavī (d. 1824), mentions the *sulṭān al-adhkār* in his *Makātib-i sharīf* (1962[1915–16]:letters 66, 73). He is the shaykh who initiated the Kurdish Mavlānā Khālid, eponym of the Naqshbandiyya-Khālidiyya, the lineage that has replaced the Mujaddidiyya in the Ottoman Empire. It is no surprise that Mavlānā Khālid refers to the *sulṭān al-adhkār* in his teaching concerning the subtle centres. He mentions the centres *qalb*, *rūḥ*, *sirr*, *khafī*, *akhfa* and a new one, *nafs* (soul), located between the two eyes. He writes that when the *dhikr* is performed upon the whole body, and not upon one centre only, the consequence is a state of spiritual awareness (*yaqaza*) called *sulṭān-i ezkār* (Mavlānā Khālid Baghdadī 1890:61, 1987:48–9).

Let us mention the Naqshbandī-Mujaddidī family based at the *khānaqāh* (Sufi lodge) of Delhi, who was forced to fly India in 1870, and set up a famous convent and a madrasa in Medina, where many Muslims from around the

---

14 Giordani 2004, French translation, 184–6, facsimile, 288–90. See also the translation in Turkish of this text by Tosun 2005b:101–3.

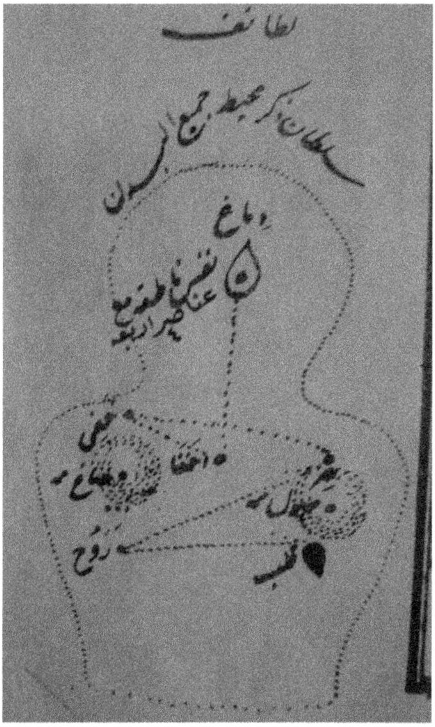

Figure 5.6 Ottoman diagram (Muḥammed Rüstem Reşīd, 1857).

world were taught the Mujaddidī doctrines and practices. Its most renowned shaykh, Muḥammad Maẓhar (d. 1883), authored a little manual for the novices entitled *Risāla-yi ṭārīqat*. In a copy of this text Shaykh Maẓhar gave to one of his disciples living in Tashkent, we read a clear reference to the *sulṭān al-adhkār* (*tsar' zikrov*, in Russian as this manual is accessible in a Russian translation only).[15]

To my knowledge, one of the oldest diagrams of the subtle body, dated 1857, was drawn by the Ottoman Muḥammed Rüstem Reşīd, probably a Naqshbandī a member of the Khālidī branch of the Naqshbandiyya (Figure 5.6). In this diagram, the *sulṭān al-adhkār* is not interpreted as a subtle centre but as a spiritual state that impregnates the entire body. The following sentence appears at the top of the drawing, which has a human form: 'the *sulṭān* of the *dhikr* comprehend the entire body' (*sulṭān-i zikr muḥīṭ-i cami' ül-beden*). The diagram shows also the five subtle centres; in addition, we read the following indication near the brain (*dimāğ*): 'human reason and the four elements'

15 The translation of this manual, originally in Arabic and dated 1870, was made by Nil Sergeevish Lykoshin in 1899; see Muḥammad Maẓhar 1899: vol. vii, 140.

(*nefes-i natıqa ma' 'anāṣır-i erba'*). In order to help the Sufi who performs this *dhikr*, the diagram indicates where are the right (*sağ*) and the left (*sol*).

The *sulṭān al-adhkār* is mentioned in several Sufi books written by Khalidī Naqshbandī up to the present day. For example, 'Abdülḥamīd Futuḥī writes in his *Adāb ül-zakirīn necāt ül-salikīn* that the state of *sülṭān ül-ezkār* appears when the Sufi has finished performing the *dhikr* upon the five subtle centres, and as soon as these centres are united with the body ('Abdülḥamīd Futuḥī 1852:7). This view is confirmed by the contemporary Kurdish shaykh Osman Sıraceddin ('Uthmān Sirāj al-Dīn), who described the state of *sulṭān al-adhkār* as a permanent *dhikr* that pervades almost all the body of the practitioner. For Sıraceddin, only talented Sufis can reach such a mystical stage, which requires a strong asceticism. We do know that another Kurdish shaykh brought one of his disciples, who was ill, to the state of *sulṭān al-adhkār*, and as soon he experienced it, he was cured (Muḥammed Osman Sıraceddin en-Nakşibendi el-Kadiri 1991:85–6).

The sultān al-adhkār as a subtle centre

In a few sources, the *sulṭān al-Adhkār* is regarded as a subtle centre (*laṭīfa*) similar to the five or six others centres, and it is represented, in this way, in some diagrams used by Naqshbandī shaykhs. It is situated in a specific place in the subtle body, either at the top of the head or between the two eyes. From this, we must understand that the state of *sulṭān* or *sulṭān al-adhkār* is reached when the subtle centre bearing this name is activated. Its localization is probably inspired by the two subtle centres (*cakra*) of yoga or Tantrism, namely the *ajnā* and *sahasrāra cakra*, the latter being depicted as 'the apex of yogic meditation' and the 'seat of the Absolute' (Khanna 2003–4:232). Interpreting the *sulṭān al-adhkār* as a *laṭīfa* is an innovation that appears, to my knowledge, in Central Asia, Xinjiang and Turkish diagrams only, and seems to be absent in India. As there are few explanations in the written documents about this point, the origin may be oral. I was told, for exemple, in 1995, at Tashkent (Uzbekistan), by the Naqshbandī shaykh Qurbān 'Alī, that the *laṭīfa* named '*sulṭān*' is situated between the two eyes.

In some other cases, instead of a *laṭīfa* named *sulṭān al-adhkār*, the diagrams mention the name of the particular exercise which brings the state of *sulṭān al-adhkār*; hence, it is named either *dhikr-i sulṭān* or *sulṭān dhikr*, sometimes only *sulṭān*, and it is usually situated in the skull. These mentions appears in diagrams from Yarkand, Xinjiang (Figure 5.7); Karamut, Kazakhistan (Figure 5.8a, 8b); Turkey (Figure 5.6); and Ferghana Valley, Uzbekistan (Figure 5.9). The diagrams provide also, in some cases, several indications about the colours of the centres, with the names of the prophets linked to each centres. Also, we find the names of the elements that compose the world and the

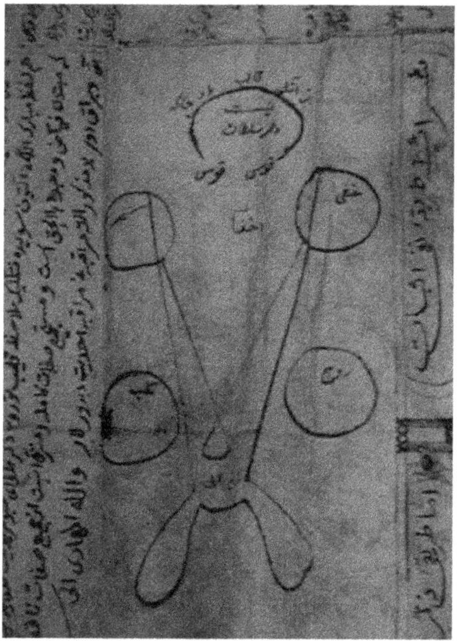

khāq su qālib ātesh āb
nīst
dhikr-i sulṭān

sirr akhfa khafī

qalb rūḥ

zīr-i nāf
(under the navel)

Figure 5.7 Central Asian diagram, detail from Figure 5.3 (Yarkand, 1945).

physical body: earth (*khâq*), water (*su*), body (*qālib*), fire (*ātash*) and water (*āb*) – for example, in the *Manaqib-i Dukchi Ishan*, Ferghana Valley, 2004.

Hybridization of the Naqshbandī diagrams with yoga and Taoism

There is a quite rare diagram that shows an unusual hybridization of the Naqshbandī and yogic subtle bodies (Figure 5.10). It is found at the end of the *Divān* (n.d.) of the Central Asian Naqshbandī Salāḥ al-Dīn Ushī alias Thāqib (d. 1910) who lived at Ush, in Ferghana, and set up the Thāqibiyya branch of the Naqshbandiyya (active today in Xinjiang only). The first particularity of this diagram is that there are seven subtle centres, including the *laṭīfa sulṭān al-adhkār* situated at the top of the head, as the *sahasrāra cakra* in yoga. Some indications are given for each *laṭīfa* (its colour, planet, religion, element etc.), and about the *sulṭān al-adhkār* it is written: 'The seventh [subtle centre] is the *laṭīfa sulṭān al-adhkār* / Its element is the air / Its planet is Saturn / Its religion is Solomonic / Its foundation is the soul.' (Salāḥ al-Dīn Ushī n.d.:192).

Second, this diagram welcomes the two subtle channels (*nādī*) of the yogic physiology (*idā* and *pingalā*), which are usually transliterated as *hingāla* and *bingāla* in Persian (Ernst 2006; Kugle 2012:167–92) (as is the case in this diagram). These two channels, which distribute the vital energy, are located on either side of the spinal chord. Between these two channels, in the spine, a point named *sangamana* is mentioned: its signification is 'to unite or join, to move together', it is actually a 'point of convergence' (Monier Williams 1872:1104).

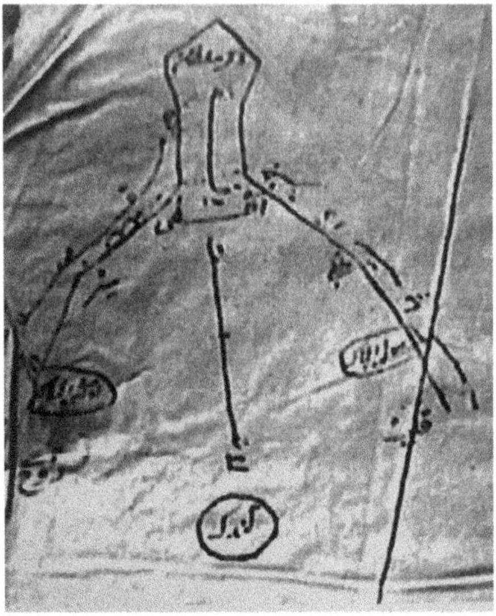

Figure 5.8a *Central Asian diagram (n.d.), Museum of Karamut, Karamut, Kazakhistan.*

Figure 5.8b *Detail of the diagram in Figure 5.8a.*

Unfortunately, there is no explanation in the *Divān* about the presence of these three elements borrowed from the yoga physiology. In a treatise on the Naqshbandī spiritual path written by Khvāja Faḍl Aḥmad, better known as Ṣāḥibzāda, in early nineteenth century, it is indicated that these yogic elements come from the Chishtiyya Sufi lineage, many of whose teachings and practices were absorbed by the Naqshbandiyya-Mujaddidiyya in sixteenth century, as were those of two other orders, Qādiriyya and Suhrawardiyya

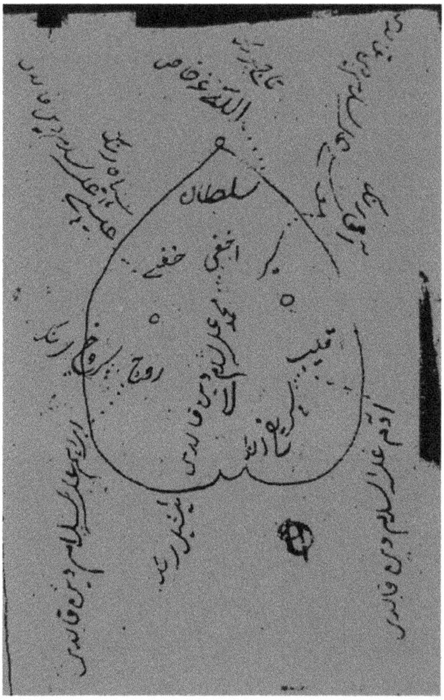

Figure 5.9 Central Asian diagram – Andijan, 1898 (Dukchi Ishan 2004: plates section).

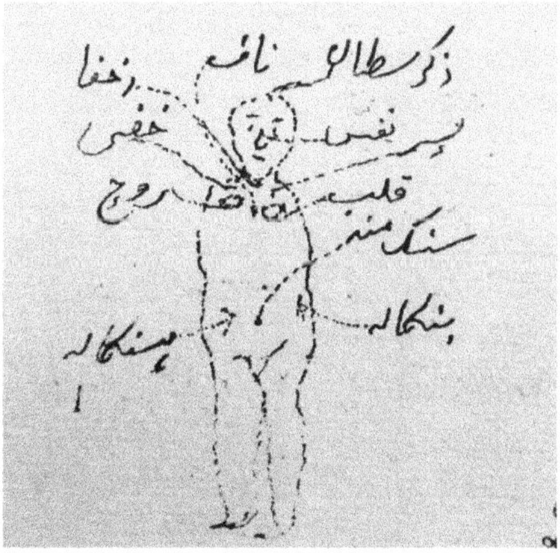

Figure 5.10 Central Asian diagram, Osh, Kirghizistan, early twentieth century (Salāh. al-Dīn Ushī n.d.:199).

(Aḥmad Sirhindī was initiated into these four Sufi orders). Ṣāḥibzāda reports that *hingāla*, *bingāla* and *sangamana* are no more than the three *laṭīfa* adopted by the Chishtiyya, all situated under the navel, with the *sangamana* between the two others (Khvāja Faḍl Aḥmad [Ṣāḥibzāda] 1959:318). It is however quite unusual to see in the same diagram such hybridization of the components of the Naqshbandī and yogic subtle physiologies. Ṣāḥibzāda was originally from Peshawar, in India, where he met Chishtī Sufis, before to travel to Central Asia, Caucasus and the Ottoman Empire in early nineteenth century. He was probably taught some yogic techniques when living at Peshawar.[16]

The *sulṭān al-adhkār* is associated with Taoist concepts in the practice of a Chinese Qādirī Sufi branch based at Lanzhou (Gansu province) and named Wenquantang Menhuan after its founder Ma Wenquan or Muḥammad Ibrāhīm Ayyūb al-Ṣīnī (d. 1882). This shaykh was initiated into the Qādiriyya order by a Javanese shaykh in Mecca. A diagram of the *laṭā'if* including the *sulṭān al-adhkār* appears in a guidebook for meditation published in 2005 by the Wenquantang *menhuan* (Wenquantangyatou 2005).[17] It is mentioned that the knowledge provided by this book must be taught only by a master in this Sufi path (*wusidaji*) and by no one else. The *sulṭān al-adhkār* – presented here as one among the other *laṭā'if* – is named *sulitani* in Chinese (from *sulṭān*) in several diagrams; one of these diagram is called 'diagram/image of the elements of the human body' (*renti weifen tushi*) (ibid.:5). The subtle centre *sulṭān* is the upper *laṭīfa* located at the top of the skull (Figure 5.11). The other *laṭā'if* are, from the bottom: *muḥīt* (under the navel), *qalb*, *rūḥ*, *sirr*, *khafī*, *akhfa* (all above the navel), *nafas*, *sulṭān* (all above the neck). It is unusual to find *muḥīt* – one of the names of God – among the subtle centres. The inspiration may come from Ibn 'Arabī, who wrote that *muḥīt* is that which surrounds, encircles or embraces. *Muḥīt* may also means the nature which exists at the periphery, while the inside is the inner nature of the things. In these diagrams, *muḥīt* can represent the lower state of the being (Chittick 1998:224).

One interesting fact, however, is that the subtle centre *sulṭān* is mentioned in another diagram (Figure 5.12) in this manual, which illustrates the practice of a particular *dhikr* called '*dhikr* of the *yin* and *yang*' (*yinyang zike'er*), also named *xihuerqi zike'er* ('*dhikr* of the two breathing inspiration-expiration') (ibid.:18). We understand from this diagram that this *dhikr* is composed of two movements; the first movement is mentally conveying upward the sound 'i' (*xi* in Taoism) from the point *muḥīt* or *yin* (inspiration), at the bottom of the

---

16 Ernst (1998:183–4) mentions a nineteenth-century diagram of a 'justaposition of yogic (*cakra*) and Sufi physiologies', though it not clearly based on the *laṭā'if* and doesn't give any place to the *sulṭān al-adhkār*. See also Speziale 2007:137–55.

17 I am indebted to Alexandre Papas who gives me a copy of this book he found in the hands of a Salar member of the Wenquantang *menhuan* in the Salar autonomous district in Gansu (see Papas and Ma Wei 2015). Paul Miaza (Paris) helped me to read the section in this book that interests me.

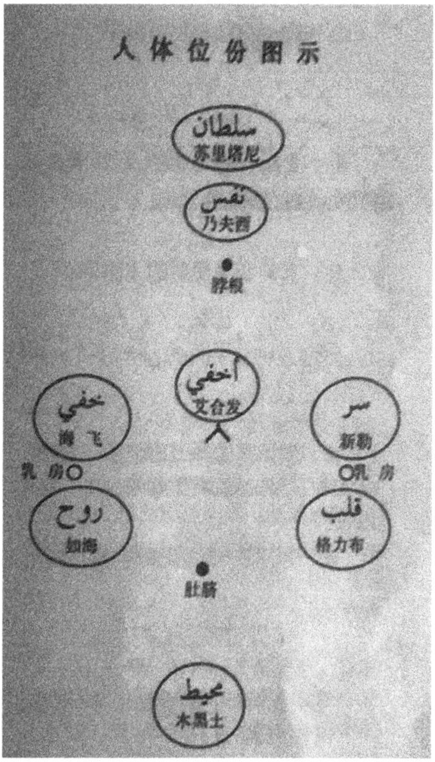

Figure 5.11 Chinese diagram (Wenquantangyatou 2005:5).

body, to the point *sulṭān* or *yang* (expiration), in the skull, and then conveying backward the sound 'u' (*hu* in Taoism) to the *muḥīt*. This *dhikr* reminds one of the Taoist technique that aims to 'unify the *yin* and *yang*' in order to 'feed the vital principle' (Maspero 1971:485).

Conclusion

Sufis diagrams representing the subtle body are quite rare, if not unknown, except in the Naqshbandiyya Sufi order after the seventeenth century. Such diagrams are composed of figurative image (a body), geometrical figures (circle, triangle) and lines, all mixed with text. So, this is an intermediary genre between literature and drawing. Diagrams give researchers a particular insight into Sufis' visual approaches to their subtle anatomy, linked to their mystical practice, and also into their teaching through figures and images.

Actually, the diagrams have two functions. The first is to teach the cosmological order of the universe, as understood by the Naqshbandī, from the physical world to the Essence, considering the subtle centres as intermediary levels of consciousness between them, and showing the correspondances between the microcosm (the body) and the macrocosm

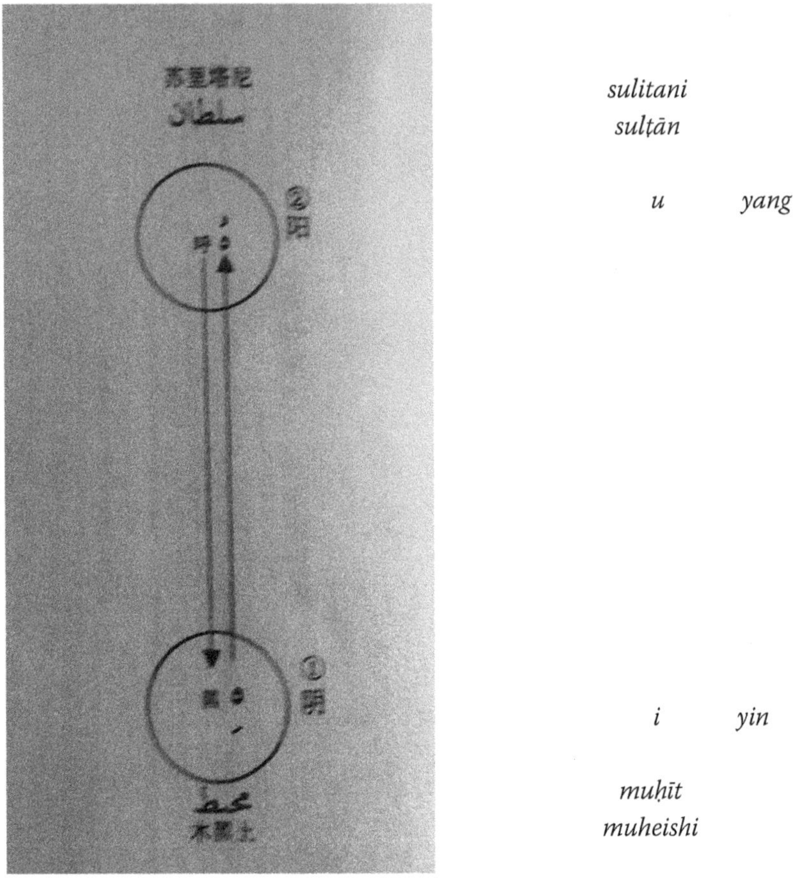

Figure 5.12 Chinese diagram of the dhikr of the yin and yang (Wenquantangyatou 2005:18).

(the world and the Essence) formed by a 'network of relations'. Looking at the diagrams, one can immediately situate the position of the man in the universe and his links with the Essence. The subtle points, disposed at precise places, resemble the different steps of a path between earth and the sky. Jean-Claude Schmitt, who investigates religious diagrams in medieval Christianity reports that 'the drawing of a figure is the creation of an abstraction which is not a representation of the reality but aims to visualize its dynamic principles' (Schmitt 2019:15). But, above all, the diagrams help the Sufi to memorize the elements of the subtle body for the practice of *dhikr*. In sum, the diagram is not far from the figure of the art of memory of the medieval and Renaissance period.

The second function of the diagram is gnostic; it teachs the technique of the *dhikr*, the motion of the breath from one centre to another, sometimes as indicated by geometrical lines, and of the words spoken at each stage.

As this technique is complex, such a diagram can be a significant help and complementary to oral teaching by a shaykh.

Finally, the fact that few diagrams in Central Asia and in China have combined the subtle body, breathing and contemplative exercices of the Naqshbandiyya with those of yoga and Taoism, may seem surprising. The hybridization of the Naqshbandī *dhikr* with Taoist ideas through the yin-yang paradigm can be understood if we consider the attempts by the Hui Sufis to harmonize the Muslim faith with their Chinese culture. However, this is not the case among the Naqshbandī of India and Central Asia, who were strongly opposed to Indian culture and never tried to harmonize it with their own. Some Indian Sufis, however, among the Chishtī, Shaṭṭārī and Qādirī lineages, did not remain insensitive to the wealth of knowledge of the yoga (though criticizing it); and saw aspects in common with Sufism, and thus borrowed some elements of its subtle physiology and contemplative techniques. Such commonalities were also the case with Indonesia Sufism and Tantrism and yoga (Braginsky 2004).

References

Primary

Anon. 1945. 'Naqshbandī portable vade mecum'. Manuscript, Archives of the Naqshbandī khānaqāh of Mullā Niyāz Ishān, Yarkand, Xinjiang, Popular Republic of China.

Abū'l-Ḥasan Zayd Mujaddidī Fārūqī. 1956–7. *Manāhīj al-sayyr va madarīj al-khayr.* Delhi: Dargāh-i Haḍrat-i Shāh Abū'-Khayr.

'Abd al-Raḥīm Khān n.d. *Silsila-i sharīf-i khānadān-i Huḍarā-i Naqshbandiyya.* Ahmadabad: n. ed.

Ayyūb Qārī, Ḍiyā al-Dīn Yarkandī. 1953–4. *Manba' al-Asrār* [1938]. Manuscript copied by Ibrāhīm al-Qarāqāshī (thumm al-Shahyārī) in 1953–4, private collection Kashgar.

— — — n.d. *Ḥusn al-anẓar fī Manba' al-Asrār.* [Xinjiang].

Baqībillāh. n.d. *Kulliyāt-i Baqībillāh ya'nī Majmu'a-yi kelām ve rasā'il va malfūẓāt va maktūbāt.* Lahore: Din Muhammad and sons.

Dārā Shikūh. 1956. *Risāla-i Ḥaqq-numā* [1645] (ed. S.M.R. Jalālī Nāīnī. *Muntakhabāt-i athār*). Tehran: n.ed.

Dukchi Ishan. 2004. *Manaqib-i Dukchi Ishan: Heal of the Uprising of Andijan in 1898* (ed. B. Babadjanov). Tashkent-Bern-Almaty: Institute of Oriental Studies and University of Bern.

'Futuḥī, Abdülḥamīd. 1852. *Adāb ül-zakirīn necāt ül-salikīn.* Istanbul: n.ed.

Ghulām 'Alī Dihlavī, Shāh. 1992. *Makātib-i sharīf* [1915–16]. Istanbul: Hakikât Kitabevi.

Imdād Allāh, Ḥājjī. 1865–6. *Ḍiyā al-Qulūb*. Delhi: Mujaba'i Press.

Kamāl al-Dīn Shaykh al-Janūshānī. 1898. *Hasht ādāb-i dhikr.* In *Manāqib Ḥaḍrat-i Gawth al-aẓam*. Namangan: Litografija Ishkakija.

Khvāja Faḍl Aḥmad (Ṣāḥibzāda). 1959. 'Risāla-yi murādān athar-i Khvāja Faḍl Aḥmad al-mushtahir ba-Ṣāḥibzāda' (ed. M. Molé). 'Quelques traités naqshbandis', *Farhang-i Irān-i Zamīn* 6:308–18.

Kotku, M.Z. *c.*1980. *Tasavvufî Ahlak*. Istanbul: Seha Neşriyat.

Mavlānā Khālid Baghdadī 1890. *Tercüme-i adāb-ı ṭarīkat-ı 'aliye-i Nakşibendiye-i Hālidiye risālesī* (trans. Ş. Aḥmed b. 'Alī). Istanbul: n.ed.

— — — 1987. *Halidiye Risalesi* (ed. Y. Çicek). Istanbul: Umran.

Muḥammad Maẓhar, Shaykh. 1899. 'Risāla-yi ṭārīqat' (ed. and trans. N.S. Lykoshin). In *Sbornik materialov dlja statistiki Syr-dar'inskoj oblast* vol. vii:137–50. Tashkent: Syr-Dar'inskij Oblastnoj Statistieskij Komitet.

Muḥammad Ma'ṣūm. 1962. *Maktūbāt-i Ma'ṣūmiyya*. Karachi.

Muḥammad Osman Sıraceddin en-Nakşibendi, el-Kadiri, Şeyh. 1991. *Sirac ül-Kulûb*. Istanbul: n. ed.

Muḥammed Rüstem Raşīd. 1857. 'Tercüme-i silsiletü'l neseb-i li Şeyh Muḥammed el-Buharī'. Manuscript, İstanbul Araştırmaları Enstitüsü, Istanbul.

Najm al-Dīn Kubra. 2001. *Les Éclosions de la beauté et les parfums de la majesté, Fawātih al-jamāl wa fawā'ih al-jalāl* (trans. P. Ballanfat). Nîmes: Éditions de l'Éclat.

Salaḥ al-Dīn Ushī. n.d. *Divān*. Manuscript in the private collection of Muhammad Kulīm Qadhī Tahar Khān, Osh, Kirghizistan; n.d. Completed by a text dated 1353/1936–7.

Shāh Muḥammad Hidāyat 'Alī Naqshbandī Mujaddidī Jaipūrī. 1927. *Mi'yār al-sulūk va dāfi' al-avhām va'l-shukūk*. Kanpur. Maṭba'-i Intiẓāmī.

Wenquantangyatou. 2005. *Chuji gongxiu zhinan*. n. ed.

Secondary

Algar, H. 1990. 'A brief history of the Naqshbandi order'. In M. Gaborieau, A. Popovic and T. Zarcone (eds), *Naqshbandis: Historical Development and Present Situation of a Muslim Mystical Order*, pp. 3–44. Istanbul: Isis Press.

Anamul Haq, M. 1975. *A History of Sufism in Bengal*. Dacca: Asiatic Society of Bangladesh.

Baker, I.A. 2012. 'Enbodying enlightenment: physical culture in Dzogchen as reveal in Tibet's Lukhang murals', *Asian Medicine* 7:225–64.

Braginsky, V. 2004. 'The Science of women and the jewel: the synthesis of Tantrism and Sufism in a corpus of mystical textes from Aceh', *Indonesia and the Malay World* 32:93 (July):141–75.

Bhattacharya, F. 2003. 'Un texte du Bengale médiéval: le yoga du kalandar (*Yoga-Kalandar*)', *Bulletin de l'École française d'Extrême-Orient* 90(1):69–99.

Brosse, T. 1976. *Études Instrumentales des Techniques du Yoga: Expérimentation Psychosomatique*. Paris: École Française d'Extrême-Orient.

Buehler, A. 1998. *Sufi Heirs of the Prophet: The Indian Naqshbandiyya and the Rise of the Mediating Sufi Shaykh*. Columbia: University of South Carolina Press.

— — — 2001. *Analytical Indexes for the Collected Letters of Ahmad Sirhindī*. Lahore: Iqbal academy Pakistan.

— — — 2015. 'Sufi contemplation. Abdullâh Shāh's Sulūk-i mujaddidiyya'. In Louis Komjathy (ed.), *Contemplative Literature: A Comparative Sourcebook on Meditation and Contemplative Prayer*, pp. 307–57. New York: Suny Press.

Chittick, W. 1998. *The Self-Disclosure of God: Principles of Ibn 'Arabī Cosmology*. New York: State University of New York Press.

Digby, S. 1975. "Abd al-Quddus Gangohi (1456–1537 A.D.): the personality and attitudes of a medieval Indian Sufi)'. In *Medieval India* vol. III:1–66. Aligarh: Centre of Advanced Study Department of History Aligarh Muslim Univ.

Elias, J.J. 1995. *The Throne Carrier of God: The Life and Thought of 'Alā' ad-Dawla As-Simnānī*. New York: State University of New York Press.

Ernst, C.W. 1998. 'The psychophysiology of ecstacy in Sufism and Yoga', *North Carolina Medical Journal* 59(3):182–4.

— — — 2006. 'Two versions of a Persian text on yoga and cosmology attributed to Shaykh Mu'in al-Din Chisti', *Elixir* 2:69–125.

— — — 2018. 'Chishtī meditation practices of the later Mughal period'. In L. Lewisohn and D. Morgan (eds), *The Heritage of Sufism: Late Classical Persianate Sufism (1501–1750)*, vol. 3, pp. 344–57. Oxford: Oneworld Publications.

Giordani, D. 2004. Expériences mystiques d'un soufi indien du XVIIe siècle. Le Mabdâ' o Ma'âd de Shaykh Aḥmad Sirhindī. PhD, Paris: École des hautes études en sciences Sociales.

Hermansen, M.K. 1988. 'Shāh Walī Allāh theory of the subtle spiritual centers (*latā'if*): a sufi model of personhood and self-transformation', *Journal of the Near Eastern Studies* 47(1):1–25.

Khanna, M. 2003–4. 'A journey into cosmic consciousness: kundalini Shakti', *Indian International Centre Quaterly* 30(3–4):224–38.

Kugle, S.A. 2003. 'The heart of ritual is the body: anatomy of an islamic devotional manual of the nineteenth century (1)', *Journal of Ritual Studies* 17(1):42–60.

— — — ed. 2012. *Sufi Meditation and Contemplation: Timeless Wisdom from Mughal India*. New York: Sulûk Press.

Maspéro, H. 1971. 'Les Procédés de nourrir le principe vital dans la religion taoïste ancienne', [*Journal asiatique*, 1937]. In H. Maspéro (re-edited), *Le Taoïsme et les religions chinoises*, pp. 481–589. Paris: Gallimard.

Monier Williams, M.A. 1872. *A Sanskrit English Dictionary*, Oxford: Clarendon Press.

Papas A. 2010. *Mystiques et Vagabonds en Islam: Portraits de Trois Soufis Qalandars.* Paris: Cerf.

Papas, A. and Ma Wei. 2015. 'Sufi lineages among the Salar; An overwiew'. In M.-P. Hille, B. Horlemann and P.K. Nietupski (eds), *Muslim in Amdo Tibetan Society: Multidisciplinary Approaches*, pp. 109–34. Lanham, Maryland: Lexington Books.

Radtke, B. 2005. 'The eight rules of Junayd: a general overview of the genesis and development of Islamic dervish orders'. In T. Lawson (ed.), *Reason and Inspiration in Islam: Theology, Philosophy and Mysticism in Muslim Thought: Essays in Honour of Hermann Landolt*, pp. 490–502. London: I.B. Tauris.

Rizvi, S.A.A. 1986. *A History of Sufism in India*, 2 vols. Delhi: Munshiran Manoharlal Publishers.

Schimmel, A. 1975. *Mystical Dimension of Islam.* Chapel Hill, NC: University of North Carolina Press.

——— 1976. *Pain and Grace: A Study of Two Mustical Writers of Eighteenth-Century Muslim India.* Leiden: Brill.

Schmitt, J.-C. 2019. *Penser par figure: Du Compas Divin aux Diagrammes Magiques.* N.p.: Arkhe.

Şimşek, H.İ. 2004. *Osmanlı'da Müceddidîlik XII/XVIII Yüzyıl.* Ankara: Sûf Yay.

——— 2005. *Mehmed Emîn-i Tokâdî.* Istanbul: İnsan Y.

——— 2007. 'Mehmed Emin Tokadî'nin *Tuhfetüt-Tullâb li Hidâyeti'l-Ahbâb* Risalesinin Karşılaştırmalı neşri', *İlmî ve Akademik Araştırma Dergisi* 18:263–75.

Speziale, Fo. 2007. 'Istruzioni sullo dhikr nei centri sottili in alcuni trattati in urdu sulla via mistica', *Mediaeval Sophia* 1:137–55.

Tosun, N. 2002. *Bahâeddîn Nakşbend.* Istanbul: İnsan Y.

— — — 2005a. *İmam-i Rabbânî Ahmed Sirhindî.* Istanbul: İnsan Y.

— — — 2005b. *Rabbânî İlhamlar, Mebde' ve Mead.* Istanbul: Sufi Kitap.

van Bruinessen, M. 2007. 'After the days of Abû Qubays: Indonesian tranformations of the Naqshbandiyya-Khâlidiyya', *Journal of the History of Sufism* 5:225–51.

Varela, F.J., Thompson, E. and Rosch, E. 1991. *The Embodied Mind: Cognitive Science and Human Experience.* Cambridge: MIT Press.

Ventura, A. 1991. 'L'Invocazione del cuore'. In B. Scarcia, A. Rostagno and L. Rostagno (eds), *Yād-Nāma in memoria di Alessandro Bausani*, vol. 1, 475–85. Roma: Bardi Editore.

Zarcone, T. 1996. 'Le 'Voyage dans la patrie' (*safar dar watan*) chez les soufis de l'ordre *naqshbandī*'. In M.A. Amir-Moezzi (ed.), *Le Voyage Initiatique en Terre d'Islam. Ascensions Célestes et Itinéraires Spirituels*, pp. 301–15. Louvain: Peeters.

— — — 1997. 'Pour ou contre le monde: une approche des sociabilités mystiques musulmanes dans l'Empire ottoman.' In F. Georgeon and P. Dumont (eds), *Vivre dans l'Empire ottoman. Sociabilités et Relations intercommunautaires, XVIIIe-XXe siècle*, pp. 21–9. Paris: L'Harmattan.

— — — 2000. 'La Qâdiriyya en Asie centrale et au Turkestan oriental.' *Journal of the History of Sufism* 1–2:295–338.

— — — 2010. 'Sufi families private archives: about some unknown sources for the intellectual history of Sufi lineages in 20th century Xinjiang.' In J. Millward, Y. Shinmen, and M. Sawada (eds), *Studies on Xinjiang Historical Sources in 17–20th Centuries*, pp. 140–61. Tokyo: The Toyo Bunko.

III

PSYCHOSOMATIC TECHNIQUES

6

Numinous disorder and self-transformation in Central Asian shamanism

PATRICK GARRONE

This work aims to establish that Central Asian *baksylyk* belongs to the shamanic sphere and that its officiant, the *bakshi*, must be considered as a true shaman.[1] To do so, it is necessary to highlight the common elements between *baksylyk* and Siberian shamanism. However, the diversity of techniques used by the *bakshi*s, as well as the differences with those of the Siberian shamanism, show the two institutions to be of different natures. The search for a common denominator for *baksylyk* and Siberian shamanism leads to the numinous disorder that appears at the beginning of the shamanic path. This disorder is an indication of a spiritual process of transformation implemented in and by supranature, most importantly that of a layman into a shaman. All other techniques used by Central Asian or Siberian officiants gain their legitimacy and their effectiveness in this initial process. The similarity in way the shaman accedes to the status of intercessor with supranature in both cases, implies that the Central Asian *bakshi* must be considered, beyond its Muslim veneer, as a true shaman, and *baksylyk* itself as an Islamized shamanism.

Nowadays, the very notion of shamanism is strongly criticized. In talking about this subject, some scholars even mention a 'scientific illusion' (Rydving

1 *Bakshi* is the most widespread local term for a 'shaman', though *baksha* is used when it is a female officiant. In the current work, when referring to the Central Asian shamans, male or female, I shall use the term *bakshi* for convenience. *Baksylyk* is a term often used to designate Central Asian Islamized shamanism, deriving from *bakshi* and the *-lyk* substantive suffix, and could be translated as 'the *bakshi* path'.

2011). Yet, even in 1935, Shirokogoroff declared that using the term 'shamanism' outside the Tungus (Siberian) context revealed a Western tendency towards generalization (Shirokogoroff 1999:268). Still, according to Shirokogoroff, this generalization did not give an account of the diversity of the phenomena today classified as belonging to the category 'shamanism'.

The concept of shamanism varies a lot in usage, depending on the scholar. One can thus point out several ways of interpreting shamanism: evolutionist; historical and/or geographic; or based on the officiant's skills. In defining who is a shaman and what shamanism is, the last approach considers the specific techniques used in the institution. This point of view has been particularly illustrated by Mircea Eliade. Despite the confusion that the generalized use of terms like 'shaman' and 'shamanism' can bring, from geographical, historical or cultural points of view, Eliade's definition excessively widens their meaning by focusing much more on the means used ('ecstatic techniques') than on the goals to be achieved (1968:24). Recent works have caused these established conceptions of shamanism to evolve. For instance, Roberte Hamayon defines shamanism as a set of mental perceptions and observances: being based on gifts and counter-gifts involving the supernatural; or aiming to obtain assets not supposed to be only produced by natural means, such as rain, fertility, success or luck (Hamayon 2015:10).

With regard to Siberian shamanism, moreover, Roberte Hamayon also distinguishes between that of the earlier hunter societies (Lot-Falck 1953) and that of later pastoral societies. For the first, the shamanic institution is central, in the second, it is peripheral.

Islamized shamanism in Central Asia

Central Asian Shamanism can also be designated as peripheral. This for two reasons: one, because it is not based on a hunting economy; two, because, as a result of syncretism with Islam, this type of shamanism differs significantly from the historical version.

Given the criticisms regarding the generalization of the concept of shamanism, one can wonder what allows one to propose that Central Asia is precisely harbouring a different type of shamanism. A clear rationale cannot be expected from the corpus of Central Asian shamanic beliefs, which have been structured by Islam for a long time now, with all voiced opinions having to be orthodox from a Muslim point of view. This is particularly the case in urbanized and old areas of settled life. To establish elements that would usually designated as belonging to authentic Central Asian shamanism, it is necessary to consider the practices and the techniques implemented by the *bakshi*.

Spiritual techniques and Central Asian shamanism

Generally speaking, a technique is a process used to obtain a determined result. Spiritual techniques involve an altered state of consciousness, whether momentary or permanent, and from that are indicative of a change of status. From this point, I use the term 'technique' with the sense of 'spiritual technique'. In surveying the field of Central Asian shamanism, I shall only consider the techniques involving an altered state of consciousness, and consequently a change of status. Actually, in the case of a successful shamanic cure, patients can be considered as transformed due to the recovery of their former state of health; it is not to be taken, therefore, that they would necessarily thereby have reached a fundamentally new status from a cognitive or spiritual point of view.

Furthermore, this essay will not touch on neuro-phenomenological perspectives on spiritual techniques themselves. I shall only look for the local meanings and the implications of techniques used by the *bakshi*: that is to say, for their prevailing logic within the shamanic institution. The very spiritual techniques, the really transforming ones, are those which, according to the opinion of the community and of the protagonists of shamanism, qualify someone as a shaman; that is to say, these techniques grant a shamanic status. In fact, whether the shamanism in Siberian or Central Asian shamanism, the use of a shamanic ritual does not 'make' a shaman and performing a shamanic rite is not sufficient to deserve this status: 'One can engage in shamanic practice without being a shaman and the whole ritual life is imbued with shamanic principles.' (Hamayon 1990:67).

In the Islamized shamanism of Central Asia, as in the shamanism of previous eras, techniques can generally be observed during public rituals, and thus almost everyone can repeat them, without necessarily themselves being a shaman. There is even a 'domestic' shamanism, whose officiant can be any member of the community following an actual shaman's instructions. Nevertheless, important shamanic sessions require shamans to perform them. I shall attempt to highlight, among the techniques used by the *bakshis*, the ones which might fulfil the following criteria: being widely practised in the Central Asian area; making the one who uses them be considered a shaman by the community; being also present in Siberian shamanism, thus 'authenticating' the shamanic status of the Central Asian *bakshis*.

Techniques of Islamized shamanism in Central Asia

The Central Asian shaman no longer intercedes on behalf of his community, nor does he appear any more as a master of elements, as a helper in the quest for good fortune, or a vital strength regulator[2] between the Spirit of the Forest and a hunting community, like his Siberian counterparts. Consequently, it is among the healing rituals that I shall look for techniques shared with earlier shamanism. Actually, in Central Asia, healing rituals are almost the only field in which shaman skills still remain (Basilov 1992).

The problem is that in these healing rituals, no technique emerges as characteristic of the whole Central Asian area. Thus, in areas of ancient sedentary lifestyles, there are wide local variations in rituals invoking protective or helpful spirits, or Sufi saints, use of different musical instruments (drums in the majority of the cases), cross-legged posture and simplified *dhikr*s (recollections of God borrowed from Sufism). Generally, these sessions are well ordered, with an absence of excess, and do not give the impression that their officiants are undergoing personality changes, even when these shamans, *bakshi*s, claim to see what no one else can, and pretend to exert an influence on what is far beyond the reach of anyone in the community. Admittedly, the recurrent use of the drum in this type of *baksylyk* suggests that the rhythmic stimuli could eventually cause altered states of consciousness. This kind of phenomenon has been documented in the field of neuro-phenomenological research (Aldridge and Fachner 2006). However, one does not know for certain that it is the case here. It is the same situation with regard to the effects of the music and postures.

On the other hand, in remote areas of Central Asia the power of Islam, although present, is not so pronounced among the local communities. In these areas of ancient nomadic ways of life, shamanism – still using invocations to the spirits, postures, singing and, eventually, musical instruments (such *kobuz*, a bowed instrument) – appears much more unleashed, violent and dramatic. According to the ethnographical data, *bakshi*s there do sometimes use techniques likely to produce physiological effects, if not altered states of consciousness. Thus, in the early twentieth century Malov (1918:6) records a *bakshi* in Xinjiang grabbing the rope of a *tugh* (pole in the centre of a yurt) with one hand, and spinning himself around it at high speed, thus causing fatigue and exhaustion leading to changes of state of consciousness. Furthermore, in these areas the *bakshi* is supposed to perform incredible feats (touching

2 In Siberian hunter societies the core of the shamanic function is to carry out a symmetrical and reciprocal exchange (gift and counter-gift) between humans and the spirit of animal species (the Spirit of the Forest being the archetype). Just as humans feed on game, so the spirits of wild species feed on the 'vital force' found in the flesh and blood of men. The purpose of the great shamanic rituals is to establish this exchange and to regulate it, aiming to lengthen the lifespan of humans as much as possible. (see Hamayon 2015:77).

Figure 6.1 *A Kazakh bakshi playing the kobuz (postcard c.1915, priv. coll.). The postcard mentions 'Kirghiz' because at the time the current Kazakh were named Kirghiz. On the other hand, the current Kirghiz were named Kara-Kirghiz.*

red-hot iron, swallowing blades etc.) without resorting to specific techniques, except spirits invocations, postures and singing. States of catalepsy more or less suggesting the shamanic journey in 'supranature'[3] are still mentioned in the area (Basilov 1991:18; Chekaninskij 1929:81; Divaev 1899: 188; Levshin 1832:63), as well as behaviours mimicking wild animals. These are obviously reminiscent manifestations of the original Siberian shamanism.

However, in Central Asia, be it in 'sedentary' areas or in 'nomadic' ones, altered states of consciousness or personality, real or presented as such to the community, do not result from the use of specific and codified techniques. Nothing there is as precise as the spiritual techniques that can be found in the religious trends elsewhere that are codified in writing. There is not in Islamized shamanism a technical codex shared by the whole shamanic institution, or, at least, by an important part of it. At first sight, Islamized shamanism is deprived of a technique which might link it to the Siberian model (Stepanoff and Zarcone 2013). Great variations in the details of the rites are quite usual.

Therefore the presence of spiritual techniques involving altered states of consciousness or changes of status cannot be asserted in Islamized shamanism,

3 Supranature is my attempt to translate a French neologism already used in this field: '*surnature*'. As a noun, *surnature* design a place 'above' nature, bound to it, and acting as a matrix (a mould) for it.

Figure 6.2 A Uyghur bakshi during a ritual with the tugh (photograph of Liang Bin Han, Tuyuq, Turfan, 2003).

for the following reasons: 1) the lack of experimental research carried out on the *bakshi*s themselves (EEG etc.); 2) the impossibility of studying techniques neither openly mentioned nor reported in writings (in contrast to the case in the main religious trends); and 3) the lack of obvious consequences that the implementation of such techniques should have on shamans, i.e., clairvoyance, extrasensory perceptions and especially superhuman feats and other skills of this kind. During my field research in Central Asia, the lack of these kind of extraordinary feats were explained by informants as due to the well-known 'decline of shamanism.' The locals have systematically sent back the fabulous exploits ascribed to shamans to *in illo tempore.*

Islamized shamanism as a system of symbolic representations

Therefore, should we consider Islamized shamanism, and perhaps the whole shamanism itself, as a symbolic system having no other effects than the ones it claims and the ones it is credited with? Thus, as with officiants in other religious contexts, some scholars have expressed the opinion that the performance of the shaman could be a role played honestly (Hamayon 2015:42).

If we consider shamanism as a symbolic system, an additional dimension has then to be brought in. So far, we only have taken into account the appearances of Islamized shamanism that could be observed in reality, that is to say in nature. Considering now the whole symbolic system, supranature is involved, and that widens the prospect. This raises the following questions:

- Is there in shamanism a fundamental and spiritual technique that appears only, or particularly, when taking supranature into account?
- If such a fundamental technique does appear, can it be found also in the Siberian model, thus connecting the Central Asian institution to the shamanic sphere?

Before attempting to highlight the existence of a spiritual technique common to the various forms of shamanism, it is necessary to first consider an important shamanic concept, that of 'initiatory sickness'.

A widespread pattern in shamanism: the so-called 'initiatory sickness'

Siberian and Central Asian shamanisms have in common the so-called 'initiatory sickness' which signifies the call to the shamanic function and which should be apprehended more like a disturbance, even a 'disorder', appearing in the life. so far normal, of the chosen one. This disorder can cover a wide range of manifestations from physical or mental illness to sleep with significant dreams or may even include a particular accident or a strange encounter with a spirit. It is widely accepted that this disorder affects all shamans, whether they belong to the Siberian shamanism of hunting societies, the more peripheral one of pastoral communities, or, at the extreme periphery, the different forms of Central Asian Islamized shamanism. Though nowadays, the expression 'initiatory sickness' is criticized, with the objection that the stage in which this affliction is experienced is neither pathological nor initiatory (Basilov 1997:6–9, 26–8; Hamayon 2015:37) for the following reasons:

- It is believed to result from contact with supranatural entities. The idea that the shaman could be an already mentally ill person who in assuming their function overcame this sickness is no longer seen as plausible.[4]

4 For instance, as early as 1919 Shirokogoroff disagreed with the idea of a mentally ill shaman. On the other hand, Basilov (1995 :11) underlines that among Uzbeks the manifestations of the 'shamanic disease' depends on the culture and the traditions of the community. Moreover, he also mentions that at the beginning of the twentieth century, under the influence of Islam, this 'shamanic disease' became very rare among Tadjik and Uzbek male shamans – thus showing that overcoming it to so as be able to practise shamanism was not necessary.

- This stage is not initiatory itself, and is neither a process or a technique. It has only an elective value, without any implication that due to it alone a simple layman could obtain the status of shaman. This is evident from the fact that in many cases this stage has a coercive function, forcing the 'chosen one' to become a shaman afterwards, by accepting the call he at first resisted.

For these reasons, in referring this episode of a shaman's life, I shall use the expression 'numinous disorder' instead of 'initiatory sickness'. The term 'numinous' corresponds much more to what happens in this phase, which is a contact with a supranature, in the form of a 'call' from it.[5] 'Initiatory', etymologically, refers to a beginning, which would imply the possession of shamanic status from this moment, and that is not the case. As for the term 'disorder', it seems to me to better reflect the range of disturbances that ethnographic literature mentions as manifesting in this phase (paralysis, unusual accident, melancholy, sleep, supranatural meeting and so forth – Garrone 2000:102–10), whose diversity greatly exceeds that of sickness. These events disturb the normal order of things, and are not limited to sickness per se. If the 'numinous disorder' does not itself make a shaman, nevertheless, it is closely connected to the spiritual process qualifying the chosen one as such. Actually, this numinous disorder appears at the beginning of the crucial period that results in the transformation of a layman into a shaman.

Disorder and its declensions as a token of contact with supranature

As noted above, several types of disorder, of alteration of the natural state, are present in Central Asian Islamized shamanism, as well as in the Siberian one. One of the most obvious, involving the most total break with the natural order, is of course death. As part of the process of transforming a layman into a shaman, death appears symbolically: the one who undergoes it has to access a new status that is still part of the living world. Even if any disorder endured by future shamans can be interpreted as a symbolic death, the real, definitive and physiological death is excluded in favour of other variations circumscribed by this life. At the forefront of these is disease. For shamanic peoples, disease is considered to be a state of dissociation of soul and body. This dissociation expresses itself in several forms along a continuum, from the most insignificant to the most dramatic: 'Temporaries absences, without danger for the survival of the body in the case of simple sleep or drunkenness; absence, the seriousness of which depends of its duration in case of illness

5 Numinous, from the Latin *numen*, refers to the idea of divine power (Otto 1923).

(above all mental one); definitive absence, expressed by death.' (Hamayon 1990:329).

The other types of numinous disorder, such as paralysis, melancholy, singular accident, are based on the same pattern of dissociation or separation of the soul and the body. Even though the numinous disorder may take on a less aggressive aspect, as in the case of a supernatural encounter, a nuisance or disturbance, it can still be perceived as an alteration of the soul/body bond. Thus, Garry-Hodzha defeated the Padishah of the jinns encountered at the top of the mountain of Geztepe, and this subsequently allowed him to accede to the shamanic role. It has been said that he defeated her thanks to his good knowledge of prayers, but the trace, even attenuated, of nuisance, of disturbance still appears in the anecdote. Indeed, the Padishah of the jinn admitted Garry-Hodzha could rule the jinns because she had already 'tested' him (Garrone 2000:103). Ovez-Hodzha had the same kind of experience, when he was granted the power to command the spirits by a mysterious young woman who also admitted to having already 'tested' him (ibid.:115).

These numinous disorders, more or less clearly expressed, are present in both Siberian shamanism and the Central Asian Islamized one. The journey of the soul into the supranature is a fundamental skill of shamanism. By its escape from the body as a result of an affliction, the soul of the Chosen One comes into contact with the supranature. The entities which reside there then reveal to him his destiny, and give him the means to fulfil it. These 'elective states' show that the process, the spiritual technique of 'making' the shaman, brings into play the supernatural sphere. These elective states, resulting from numinous disorders in our world, in nature, are indeed experienced and felt as proof of a supernatural connection. Therefore, it implies that the process, the spiritual technique of 'making' the shaman, itself takes place in the supranature.

From numinous disorder to shamanic alliance

The numinous disorder opens the phase in which supranature and the future shaman form an alliance. In some cases, this alliance can be concluded during the brief period between the beginning of the numinous disorder and its ending. It is during this period that the following steps generally occur: appearance of one or several spirits; call of the chosen one by supranature by means of a numinous disorder; presentation of the alliance between supranature and the future shaman; acceptance of the shamanic status by the chosen one; and sometimes the offering of shamanic paraphernalia, for instance a belt allowing the rule of spirits

In other cases, contracting an alliance can take much more time. In these, the numinous disorder is lasting because it is being used by supranature in a coercive way to force the reluctant Chosen One to accept their calling. Those who have undergone this kind of experience sometimes describe this alliance as taking the form of a mystical wedding, uniting the *bakshi*, the shaman, with a protective entity who can provide spiritual aid. For other types of accession to the shamanic status, the relationship of alliance grants the ability to gain helping spirits for shamanic purposes only. Consequently, supranatural alliance appears as the central spiritual process in accession to shamanism, and the only one able to turn a layman into a shaman. This raises the following question: as there is such a process, who uses it; that is say, who is the 'technician'?

Supranature as a 'technician'

The alliance uniting supranature and the shamans is not egalitarian. It is based on a hierarchy between the two contracting parties, in which each receives benefit, but in which one party is subjugated to the other: of course, it is supranature that is superior to the shaman. To have a more precise idea of this balance of power, let us examine the details of the alliances established according to the different declensions of body and soul separation.

Death

Scenarios of death and resurrection are mentioned in Siberian shamanism. It seems that during them the layman is much more undergoing his accession to his new status, than really wanting it. 'Torn apart', the future shamans are pieced together according to the will and the plans of the supranatural entities (Eliade 1968:46–7).

Sickness

Sickness, as a kind of disorder, is widespread in the Islamized shamanism of Central Asia. Even if the *bakshi* more or less openly accepts the alliance, he obviously suffers during this episode. This type of disorder appears as much a sign of the choice made as a tool of coercion.

Sleep or intoxication

These types of scenario are special because they allow a voluntary quest for shamanic status. Using these options, a layman, not having been called, can nevertheless get in touch with supranature. Eliade mentions the taking of cannabis, under Iranian influence, in Finno-Ugrian shamanism (ibid.:310–15). However, the 'intoxication scenario' (alcohol, drugs etc.) is not used in the Central Asian area, where Islam and its prohibitions prevail. Or perhaps should I say 'not anymore used', for one of the Central Asian characters connected with the figure of the archetypal shaman, Burh (also known as

Figure 6.3 *Ruins of Khorkhut's tomb on the anks of the Syr Daria river (from Kaufman 1871–2:pl. 1).*

Figure 6.4 *Retreat hall (chillakhāna) of the mausoleum of Zayn al-Dīn Bābā / Zayniddin Bobo, sixteenth century, Tashkent, 2007 (photograph T. Zarcone).*

Khorkhut, Burkut, Korkut), was called *Burh Sarmastveli*, 'Burh the intoxicated saint.'

On the other hand, the 'sleep scenario' is used in Central Asian shamanism. Shamans acquiring their status through a voluntary quest are considered weaker than those coming to shamanic powers by other means. Thus, in Uzbekistan in 1995 I met a *bakshi* who spent a night in the *mazār* (mausoleum) of a local saint, because he had not, by that point, been called by spirits.

The transformation

Whatever the scenario for the supranatural contact, only it can grant shamanic status. Most of the time, supranature choses someone, creating a de facto obligation. Voluntary quests are another route to shamanism, but they are just a way to get in touch with supranature, to whom the last word always belongs.

Regarding the transformation of a layman into a shaman, we can say that:

- only supranature appears as a maker, that is to say, a technician;
- supranature always has the final decision on whether an alliance is formed;
- only supranature owns the power, and possesses the technique (which is therefore a spiritual one) of creating a shaman;
- future performances of the shaman, and the techniques he will use in them, will only be effective according to the prior spiritual function of supranature.

Without this supranaturely induced transformation, there would be no shamans. I mentioned above that one could engage in shamanic practice without being a shaman. Therefore, practising ritual appears not to be sufficient to access a shamanic status, and likely does not even generate altered states of consciousness.

The shaman is then, the one who:

- subscribes to the symbolic system of shamanism;
- has been chosen by supranature;
- has formed an alliance with supranature;
- perceives himself as a shaman;
- and is perceived as such by his community.

The shamanic alliance

The alliance between the shaman and the supranature is hierarchical, with the shaman occupying the lower status. The evidence for this, is that while the shaman can expect to receive help from the supranature in his attempts to act in his shamanic capacity, this is not always guaranteed, and he must in fulfil a certain number of obligations in return.

For example, sometimes:

- they must reserve a place in their home for their helping spirits, feed them or allow them to rest;
- ritual sacrifices are systematically directed to the helping spirits;
- the mystical union of the shaman with his protecting spirit is subject to conditions and holds him in a thrall: 'I will be your wife ... you will have a spirit to help you, but you will be cursed if you betray me because I shall kill you.' (Lot-Falck 1956:379–80).

However, this hierarchy, involving the vassalage of the shaman, is also based on gift and counter-gift. As already mentioned, shamanism aims to ensure that which cannot be produced by human activity: rain, health, luck, fertility etc. (Hamayon 2015:68). According to this alliance, which has been carried out on its sole initiative, supranature thus allows the shaman to tend asymptotically towards the coincidence of opposites: certifying the uncertain.

Conclusion

The present work aims to establish that in Central Asian *baksylyk*, just as in the earlier Siberian shamanism:

- Accessing the status of shaman (*bakshi*) via a numinous disorder implies the intervention of supranature.
- This intervention takes the form of a hierarchical alliance, through which supranature grants the shamanic status.
- The commonality of an alliance with supranature between the Central Asian *bakshis* and the earlier Siberian shamans, confirms the *bakshis*' shamanic status, despite the Muslim veneer of their practices.
- This creation of a shaman is the major spiritual technique of transformation present in the shamanic system. In fact, it is only by reference to this process, this initial technique that constitutes a shaman, that his subsequent practices gain their full meaning and efficacy.

References

Aldridge, D. and Fachner, J. 2006. *Music and Altered States: Consciousness, Transcendence, Therapy and Addiction*. London: Jessica Kingsley Publishers.

Basílov, V. N. 1984. *Izbranniki duhov*. Moskva: Politizdat.

— — — 1990. 'Dva varianta sredneaziatskogo shamanstva'. *Sovetskaja Ètnografija* (4) jul'-avgust. Moskva: Nauka, 64–76.

— — — 1991. *Izlamizirovannoe shamanstvo narodov Srednej Azii i Kazahstana*. Istoriko-etnograficheskoe issledovanie. Avtoreferat dissertacii na soiskanie uchenoj stepeni doktora istoricheskih nauk. Moskva.

— — — 1992. *Shamanstvo u narodov Srednej Azii i Kasahstana*. Moskva: Nauka.

— — — 1995. 'The shamanic disease in Uzbek folk beliefs', *Shaman* 1(Spring). Budapest.

— — — 1997. 'Chosen by the spirits'. In M.M. Balzer (ed.), *Shamanic Worlds, Ritual and Lore of Siberia and Central Asia*, pp. 3–48. Armonk, New York: North Castle Books.

Chekaninskij, I.A. 1929. '"Baksylyk": Sledy drevnih verovanij kazakov', *Otdel'nnyi ottisk I-go toma Zapisok Otdela Obshchestva*, pp. 75–87. Semipalatinsk.

Divaev, A.A. 1899. 'Baksy v zhizni kirgiza', *Izv. À-va Arh., Ist. i Étn. Pri Imp. Kazanskom Univ.* 15(3):187–90.

Eliade, M. 1968. *Le Chamanisme et les techniques archaïques de l'extase*. Paris: Payot.

Garrone, P. 2000. *Chamanisme et islam en Asie centrale*. Paris: Librairie d'Amérique et d'Orient, Jean Maisonneuve succ.

Hamayon, R. 1990. *La Chasse à l'âme: esquisse d'une théorie du chamanisme sibérien*. Nanterre: Société d'ethnologie.

— — — 2015. *Le Chamanisme: fondements et pratiques d'une forme religieuse d'hier et d'aujourd'hui*. Paris: Eyrolles.

Kaufman (Von), K. (ed.) 1871–2. *Turkestanskij al'bom*. Tashkent?

Levshin, A. 1832. *Opisanie Kirgiz"-Kazach'ih" ili kirgiz"-kajsakskih" ord" i stepej*. St Petersburg.

Lot-Falck, E. 1953. *Les Rites de chasse chez les peuples sibériens*. Paris: Gallimard.

— — — 1956. 'Eroticism and shamanism', *Sexology Magazine* (January):378–83.

Malov, S.E. 1918. 'Shamanstvo u sartov Vostochnago Turkestana'. In *Ko dnju 80-tiletija akademika Vasilija Vasil'evicha Radlova (1837–1917 gg.)*, pp. 1–16 (Sbornik Muzeja Antropologii i Ètnografii Imeni Imperatora Petra Velikago Pri Rossiskoj. 5, pub. 1). Petrograd: Akademii Nauk.

Otto, R. 1923. *The Idea of the Holy*. Oxford: University Press.

Rydving, H. 2011. 'Le chamanisme aujourd'hui: constructions et déconstructions d'une illusion scientifique', *Études mongoles et sibériennes, centrasiatiques et tibétaines* 42.

Shirokogoroff, S.M. 1919. 'Opyt issledovaniia osnov shamanstva u tungusov', *Uchenye zapiski istoriko-filologicheskogo fakul'teta v g. Vladivostoke*, vol. 1. Vladivostok.

——— 1999. *Psychomental Complex of the Tungus*. Berlin: Reinhold Schletzer Verlag.

Somfai Kara, D. and Sarközi, I.G. 2013. 'Legitimization of the shamanic calling among the Sibe', *Shaman* 21:67–78.

Stepanoff, C. and Zarcone, T. 2013. *Le Chamanisme de Sibérie et d'Asie centrale*. Paris: Gallimard.

7

Spiritual techniques among late imperial Chinese literati

VINCENT GOOSSAERT

The elites of late imperial China – the Ming (1368–1644) and Qing (1644–1911) dynasties – have long been considered as, by and large, Confucian, rationalist and religiously sceptical. This bias, deeply rooted in the intellectual history of Sinology, is now being thoroughly and critically examined by new scholarship that looks at the religious world-views, practice and knowledge of these elites. At the same time, the very definition of elite is also being revisited, to include not only the gentry (an English term conventionally used to render an imperial Chinese legal status, defined as those who have passed at least the first degree of the official examinations), but also cultural, economic and clerical power-holders. I have in a separate publication discussed the analytical frameworks available for discussing religion among the elites, largely putting aside the blunt and largely irrelevant concept of 'belief' for more useful tools such as religiosity and religious culture, which allow us to develop a finer-grained image of both collective (social class, family, intellectual currents) and individual choices in a complex, very diverse and yet highly regulated religious landscape (Goossaert 2017b; see also Katz and Goossaert 2021).

In this chapter, I would like to pursue this line of enquiry by looking specifically at the elites' learning and use of various spiritual techniques, defined here as purposeful and codified manipulation of one's and other spirits. By this definition, spiritual techniques include an important ritual component; as we will see, many of the techniques discussed here can be deployed in ritual as well as non-ritual settings. By the same token, they do not include divination, even though such a distinction is eminently arbitrary. The closest Chinese terms for these techniques are *shu* 術 (methods, skills, also including divination and the sciences), *fa* 法 (best translated as ritual technique) and also their compound, *fashu* 法術. These terms are fraught with value judgments throughout the sources available for our study. Elite writers, who define themselves as morally superior to the ordinary person, constantly remind themselves and their readers that techniques may be useful, but that, in terms of self-cultivation and religious attainment, they are no match for sincerity or rectitude, *cheng* 誠, described as interiorized virtue, or habitus. Be it praying for rain,[1] meditating, painting or otherwise, the morally superior man, who abides in perfect sincerity, will accomplish much more than any person merely skilful in specific techniques. The oft-quoted saying *xie busheng zheng* 邪不勝正, 'evil cannot overcome rightfulness', says it cogently: there is no need to master elaborate ritual techniques to protect oneself against harm if one is an upright man.[2]

And yet, many sources shed light on the fact that despite this culturally dominant rhetoric against spiritual techniques, literati did resort to them frequently, and for a vast array of purposes. They did so for reasons that included, but are not limited to, dealing with hostility (demons and other malevolent forces); controlling and enhancing one's bodily energy (*qi* 氣) for good health, but also for performances such as painting and calligraphy; for self-healing (and healing others); for dealing with the threat and imminence of death; and eventually for transforming themselves completely and gaining access to salvation though self-divinization – a goal largely shared by literati during this period (Goossaert 2017a). While some of these goals can be described as quests for spiritual experience, others rather relate to practical needs.

While routinely offering public statements reinforcing the trope of the superiority of the moral man, in their private lives – an admittedly vague concept that covers both really private spaces such as one's own studio, but also family and gatherings of like-minded friends outside official spaces – literati actively sought to learn and practise various techniques, to meet the above goals when just being sincere did not quite seem to suffice. Women were, more than men, held to confine their religious practices to inner, private spaces – the inner courts of elite mansions were dotted with meditation rooms, shrines and other places for the use of devout women (Goossaert 2008; Mann 1997) – but men were also socially constrained to confining

1 See the very good discussion in Snyder-Reinke 2009, of how late imperial elites dealt with rain-making, by complementing an attitude of virtue with elaborate techniques, and the debates that such combinations created.

2 See a discussion of this notion in the writings of the prominent literatus Yu Yue 俞樾 (1821–1906) in Goossaert 2011a:644–5.

certain practices to within walls. To explore this facet of elite's lives – hardly documented in official and public documents – we have to access other types of sources.

The case of Shao Zhilin 邵志琳 (1748–1810)[3]

I would like to start exploring these questions by discussing one case study, that of Shao Zhilin, a man totally unknown to mainstream historiography, who having failed to pass the civil service examinations beyond a certain point (which point exactly is left very vague by our sources), like the vast majority of his peers, never became an official and had to carve himself a place and status in local society – in our case, Jiangnan, the richest and most densely populated part of the Chinese world at the time. Shao was not a prominent literatus (even though he did have interactions with several very prominent persons), but he seems rather typical in terms of certain religious traits shared by the Jiangnan elites of his time, even though he was more committed and religious than the average, and thus these traits were heightened in his case. Shao is however a significant figure because he served as the editor of an influential canon that gathered the revelations of one of the most prominent deities of late imperial China, Patriarch Lü 呂祖 (*Lüzu quanshu* 呂祖全書); the group that supported this project also edited the twin canon of Wenchang 文昌 (*Wendi quanshu* 文帝全書); both were published in 1775.[4] Not only did he compile this large collection of religious texts, he was himself the recipient of one of them, an eschatological scripture (discussed below). Shao, however, would have remained just a name in bibliographical tables – for these two canons tell us very little about him – if he was not also honoured by a lengthier biography in a Daoist hagiographical work, *Jin'gai xindeng* 金蓋心燈 (the mind-lamp of Mt. Jin'gai), compiled in 1821 by Min Yide 閔一得 (1758–1836). The *Jin'gai xindeng* is an extremely rich source on the history of a pious elite community in late eighteenth-century Jiangnan, based at Mt. Jingai, but I will largely limit myself to the case of Shao Zhilin here.

Let us first read my translation of this biography.

> The master was named Shao Zhilin [*zi* Rupei 儒佩, *hao* Qiuyi 秋漪, birth name Tongshan 通善]. His family hailed from Ningbo, and he lived in Zhitou street in Hangzhou. He was an excellent student, but failed several times at the civil service examinations: such was his fate. His birth

---

3 A more detailed study of Shao Zhilin is found in Goossaert forthcoming.

4 These were expanded, second versions of the first such canons, published a generation before in 1744–5 by another group of elite spirit-writing activists (see below, and Goossaert 2015).

was marked by extraordinary signs. Once, when he was six, his mother was putting him to bed after feeding him, when an animal, looking like a very hairy lion with golden eyes, jumped in from behind a curtain, and the surprise induced an enlightenment in him. As he grew up, his intelligence was far above the other boys, but he was mostly fond of sitting in meditation. When aged 15 or 16, he took as his master Cai Laihe 蔡來鶴 from Nanking. [Note: Cai Laihe is an ordination master of the (Daoist) Longmen 龍門 lineage in the 13th generation. In 1782, Cai, together with Wang Yinceng 王寅曾, Guan Huai 關槐 from Hangzhou and Shao went to Jin'gaishan. Cai compiled the *Wendi quanshu* and the *Lüzu quanshu*, and Shao corrected and proofread these editions, which Guan had printed.][5]

Shao later specialized in techniques of mind-fixation leading to deep contemplation (*samādhi*) and visualizations. When already a mature man, he visited the Lü Chunyang [Patriarch Lü] temple at Yunchao [Jin'gaishan], and the god came down for him; He gave Shao a religious name and conferred on him an initiation text.[6] At that time, Shao did not yet have a son; so, he devoted himself to the meritorious work of mediating disputes, so that after a year a son was born.[7] This son is now over twenty and has been studying for several years at the county school.[8]

Later on, Shao made further progress in Buddhist practice, and focused on chanting the incantation of great compassion (*Dabeizhou* 大悲咒). He soon obtained the corresponding *samādhi*, which he continued to cultivate without any pause for over twenty years. On top of that, he engaged in meritorious and charitable practices. He set up a free ferry over Qiantang river, and gave some thirty ox carts, with their animals [to pull the ferry]. He regularly set up soup-kitchens and distributions of free medicinal tea, which still operate today. He also gave away large numbers of coffins for the poor, arranged for the burial of abandoned bodies, and distributed free clothes and medicine. He set up charitable halls for collecting and respectful

5 The *Jin'gai xindeng* has numerous such notes by Min Yide, in which he adds biographical details to the data he had collected elsewhere.

6 *Shouji* 授記. The term (which appears often in *Jin'gai xindeng*) means, in Buddhist contexts, the prediction of one's future Buddhahood, but it likely refers here to a text Patriarch Lü reveals personally to the accepted living disciple.

7 Helping people settling disputes and avoiding going to court was considered a highly meritorious act, and therefore one that bought divine blessings, such as obtaining a son.

8 There is another editorial note here, irrelevant to Shao's life story, which I do not translate.

burning of written paper,[9] releasing of animals about to be butchered, succouring the needy, the widows and the orphans, in over ten different places. He also repeatedly petitioned the authorities asking for special help and tax relief for victims of disasters. All this was accomplished on the initiative and under the management of master Shao, who collected the required funds. He was always personally in charge, always out in summer heat or winter cold, in wind, rain, snow or frost, without ever excusing himself. He accepted complaints and criticism, and never took any personal benefit.

Yet, in the middle of these pressing tasks, he continued to practise chanting the incantation of great compassion. He reached the stage when he could chant it several hundreds of thousands of times a day. Not even in remote times could monks reach that level. Hearing that the master could perform this, people sneered – they had no idea that once one has obtained the *samādhi*, one can reach such attainments. This is why it is said that 'The wheel of the law turns by itself': it does not need to be moved to turn. What Shao did, was chanting with the mind, not something that relies on bodily energy to move along. Yin Yuyang 殷玉陽 (note: he hails from Hangzhou, we ignore his name; he came to Jin'gaishan) said that the marvellous results obtained by master Shao in his chanting of the incantation are not related to audible utterance, but to his advanced [technique] of visualization. This technique (*fa* 法) was secretly transmitted to him by Cai Laihe. It allows those who can enter *samādhi* to reach very advanced levels of practice.

Shao once explained to Yin: my technique to practise chanting in a state of *samādhi* consists in first imagining a Pure world within myself. In this world is a resplendent statue of the Buddha. I practise chanting facing this Buddha until gradually all difference between the Buddha statue and me has vanished. Then, in the blink of an eye, this world transforms into ten, the ten worlds into a hundred, the hundred into a thousand, and the thousand into billions of worlds. In each of these worlds, one can see the Buddha and myself, neither merged nor distinct. That is what the Buddha calls 'worlds as numerous as the sand grains (of the Ganges), that all hold within a grain of rice.' But, one can only explain this to someone who is in the way; it is difficult to explain to someone not practising religion.

The master furthermore excelled in performing the ritual of offering food to suffering souls. Yin Yuyang tells how Shao once performed this ritual

9 Written characters (whatever their meaning) are symbols of civilization and therefore sacred: it was considered a sin to defile them. Papers with characters written on them and not used anymore were to be collected, burnt, and the ashes dispersed in rivers.

at Taicheng, in Nanking. At first, the nocturnal scene was lit by lamps and candles, then a heavy smell of rank of meat overtook the place, the candles' light dimmed to a glow not larger than a bean, a cold wind rose and the whole atmosphere in the ritual arena become terribly oppressing. One could see the master in perfectly motionless meditation, emitting light that grew as bright as the moon and slowly rose up to Heaven. Suddenly, the sound of roaring waves came out of his mouth, and then noises of smashing stones, sharp as thunder, of all tones and pitches. At that moment, lamps became bright again, the rank smell of meat and the cold wind had completely disappeared, and the atmosphere had become cool and pure. Then one saw billions of figures wearing crowns [the saved souls] appear; some were as large as a human, others as tiny as an arm, a finger, a bean or even a grain of rice. All came in throngs to bow, and then disappeared. Who could have guessed that the spiritual power (created by) the chanting practice of master Shao could reach that level?

Master Shao was born in 1748; he died in 1810 and thus lived 63 years. His many charitable works are carried on by Guo Xingqiao from Hangzhou.[10]

While there are many other biographies of late imperial elites that mention their religious practices, this one is unusual (even within the *Jin'gai xindeng*) for the extent of its detail. Shao Zhilin's biography is particularly interesting, as it draws the portrait of a man who was extremely active in setting up charities of all kinds, but also a superb ritualist famed for his salvation rituals for the dead – the biography describes him as performing in such a way that the audience could see the myriads saved souls ascending to heaven. And all this was sustained by a very intense devotion focused on reciting the *Dabeizhou*. It is not so frequent that biographies of elites deal so precisely with the technical aspects of spirituality and self-cultivation.

Shao, like many of his peers, was employed by associations set up by members of the gentry to raise funds for and run charities: the biographic story moves between this public life and his own private spiritual practice, and the latter gives him the strength and resilience to excel in the former. We thus get a rare glimpse of the articulation between public life and career, on the one hand, and spiritual techniques on the other. The practices themselves are not unique or even atypical; we see them discussed in many technical manuals. While the self-cultivation literature of the late imperial period remains very little studied, we know that such manuals circulated on a large scale, both in print (for open circulation) and in manuscript (for transmission to initiated

10 *Jin'gai xindeng* 金蓋心燈, 7.50a–52a.

disciples). What is remarkable in Shao Zhilin's story is how these techniques, which we tend to think of as separate from public life, are weaved into one narrative, and how this narrative switches quickly between them.

Biographies, as well as the very numerous anecdotal records (*biji* 筆記) written by literati about themselves or their colleagues, also tell us not just how these techniques worked but also how they were learnt, tried, put in practice, and combined with one another in context. I would thus like to comment on Shao's life by contextualizing and explaining some of the key elements of the specific spiritual techniques he deployed in his career as a religious activist.

Spirit-writing

The first technique that warrants discussion is spirit-writing. This is not only a crucial element in Shao Zhilin's life, it also made it possible for us to read his biography in the first place: he was included in the *Jin'gai xindeng* because he was an active participant in the Jin'gaishan spirit-writing group. Spirit-writing (*fuji* 扶乩, *fuluan* 扶鸞, *feiluan* 飛鸞, *jiangbi* 降筆) emerged during the eleventh and twelfth centuries as a specific technique for producing revelations, opening a new chapter in the middle of a long history in which other techniques (dreams, hallucinatory trances, sometimes induced by drugs) had already long been in use (Boltz 2009:349–88; Goossaert 2022). In spirit-writing, one or two mediums are possessed by a deity who uses their hands to write characters with a specific implement (most often in wood) on sand, ashes or another support; these characters are then noted down by a copyist and sometimes, if necessary, corrected by the deity. This possession is quiet and dignified, by contrast to other types of possession that literati routinely disparage. It can be used to produce very short, ad hoc revelations, as answers to specific questions by devotees or as poems, or to compose long, elaborate texts over many seances. It is organized by groups of adepts (most of whom typically cannot work as mediums themselves), who are individually initiated by the deity as disciples. Such groups can gather in private homes or in small shrines; some of the most successful build their own temples.

Shao Zhilin practised spirit-writing in different places, as was (and is) usual. He and his master Cai Laihe actually operated a spirit-writing shrine, named Guixiangji 桂香集, dedicated to both Wenchang and Patriarch Lü, and a temple to both gods, Tianxiangge 天香閣 (the former was presumably located within the latter). This was located just outside Jingci Monastery 淨慈寺, on the southern shores of the West Lake in Hangzhou.[11] We find

11 See Zhao Jinjian preface, *Lüzu quanshu* (1775). In his postface to the *Wendi quanshu*, Cai Laihe signs as being in Nanping's Guixiangji; Nanping is the hill on which the Jingcisi sits.

surprisingly little external information on this shrine; perhaps it was short-lived. In any case, all the major participants in the editorial work of both *Wendi quanshu* and *Lüzu quanshu* were members of this shrine. Cai is known through a preface of the *Lüzu quanshu*,[12] where he is described as a Hangzhou man, who had been a student in Suzhou, and then returned to settle in his temple in Hangzhou; he is introduced as a noted philanthropist particularly active in cherishing written characters, *xizi* 惜字.

Lai Chi-tim (2013) has shown that one major purpose of the compilation of the 1775 canons, beyond claims that the originals had become rare, was to include newly revealed texts and re-centre them on the Jiangnan region: for Patriarch Lü, he counts 27 new texts revealed at 17 different spirit-writing shrines in Jiangnan, notably at Guixiangji and at Jin'gaishan. The 1775 *Lüzu quanshu* includes a scripture revealed to Shao himself, apparently at his spirit-writing shrine in Hangzhou,[13] which carries an explicitly eschatological title – *Guanghui xiuxin baoming chaojie jing* 廣慧修心保命超劫經 (Scripture on crossing the end of the kalpa and preserving one's life through cultivating one's mind and expanding one's wisdom) – and in which Patriarch Lü is presented as the saviour designated by the whole pantheon to rescue humans from their kalpa predicament.[14] This eschatological preoccupation is confirmed by Shao himself, who wrote that he was reciting an earlier Wenchang apocalyptic scripture, the *Jiujie baojing* 救劫寶經, every day.[15] So we have a literatus who was good at acting as a medium, and as such was writing convincing divine revelations – that Shao himself was a medium is nowhere said explicitly (it hardly ever is in Chinese sources in general), but would seem obvious to the reader. Presumably, most educated men had tried it, and the gifted ones were identified, trained and encouraged from early on. This possession technique was complemented by scholarly knowledge (for editing revealed texts) and daily regimens of learning scriptures by rote and reciting them every day (Goossaert 2019).

Beside their own shrine, Shao and his master Cai were also active and regular participants at another more famous spirit-writing shrine located at Jin'gaishan 金蓋山, a hill just south of Huzhou 湖州, northern Zhejiang. This hill was the location of a very active Patriarch Lü cult and spirit-writing centre: a temple devoted to Patriarch Lü was in operation there since the 1760s and 1770s, and its spirit-writing altar, Yunchaotan 雲巢壇, produced a number

12 Preface by Zhao Jinjian in *Lüzu quanshu* (1775), shou.15a.

13 This scripture, which must have been very important for Shao, was expurgated from later Patriarch Lü canons as unauthentic.

14 On late imperial eschatological texts, see Goossaert 2014.

15 Shao Preface to *Lüzu quanshu* (1775).

of scriptures. A closely associated nearby shrine, the Yiyuntan 怡雲壇, also produced texts. Nine of these texts were included by Shao in the 1775 *Lüzu quanshu*, only one of which (*Jingshi gongguoge* 警世功過格, Ledger of merits and demerits to awaken the world) made it into the *Daozang jiyao* 道藏輯要 (Essentials of the Daoist canon), the famous canon anthologizing elite spirit-writing texts published in Beijing *c.*1806.[16] At this stage, the Jin'gaishan shrines had failed to print most of their own texts, not to mention their own canon; the *Lüzu quanshu* editors note that they obtained most of the Jin'gaishan texts as manuscripts.[17]

During Shao Zhilin's lifetime, the Jin'gaishan site took a new direction with the arrival of a retired official from a prominent local gentry family, Min Yide, who developed it into a regional Daoist centre (Esposito 2013, 2014; Mori 1999). Min gave it an entirely new identity as a site for the Longmen lineage of Quanzhen 全真 Daoism; this came about as the conflation of two distinct traditions, Longmen – in which one member of another prominent local lineage, Shen Yibing 沈一炳 (1708–86), had become a cleric – and the Patriarch Lü spirit-writing cult. Min Yide was healed by Shen Yibing 's master and became his disciple; the Shen and Min lineages were both patrons of the Patriarch Lü cult, and thus Min Yide decided to merge the two traditions into one, at the cost of inventing a new history for Jin'gaishan. This is the background for the role of Cai Laihe in our story – described as a Quanzhen cleric but undocumented elsewhere.[18]

At the core of the temple that he enlarged, the Chunyanggong 純陽宮, Min Yide placed the Yunchaotan at which large numbers of the members of the local gentry families were initiated as disciples of Patriarch Lü, and they received from him (as well as other gods) several other scriptures. Min later edited and published scriptures he had obtained in two collections: *Daozang xubian* 道藏續編 (23 texts) and *Gushu yinlou cangshu* 古書隱樓藏書 (thirty-seven texts, including all twenty-three texts of the *Daozang xubian* and fourteen more). These two collections were published by the Chunyanggong in 1834, shortly before Min Yide's death. By contrast to some less durable groups, it proved to be a very successful organization, and during the late

16 *Jingshi gongguoge* 警世功過格, JY 277. Besides, shorter revelations (poems, short tracts) at Jin'gaishan were included in JY 165 *Lüdi shiji* 呂帝詩集 and JY 168 *Yulu daguan* 語錄大觀. JY notes the text number in the *Daozang jiyao* following the catalog: Lai Chi-tim 2021..

17 *Lüzu quanshu* (1775), prefaces to juan 43, 44.

18 This biography, however, is included in a later section reserved for those who were not affiliated with the Longmen lineage that Min Yide put at the centre of his re-organized Jin'gaishan.

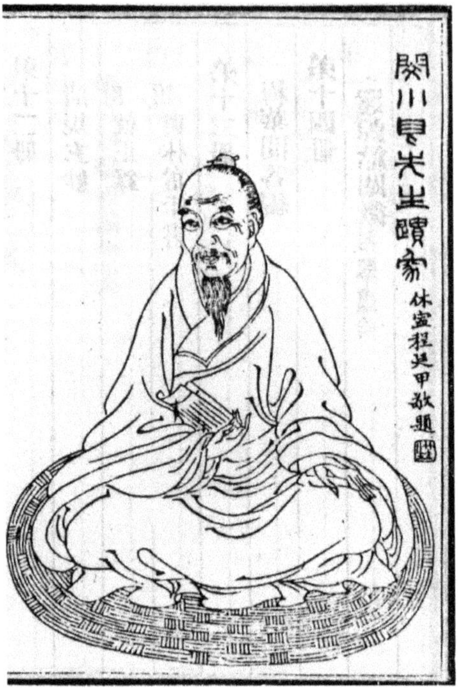

Figure 7.1 Portrait of Min Yide. From Gu Shuyinlou cangshu 古書隱樓藏書.

nineteenth century developed as a network, opening branches throughout the Jiangnan region: there were over seventy such active branches in 1949, which had thousands of disciples, over half of which were women (the massive female participation seems to date from the very last decades of the Qing, even though a few women were active in earlier spirit-writing groups).[19]

Having introduced the historical importance of Jin'gaishan, let us return to our case study. Why would a man like Shao Zhilin become deeply involved in the spirit-writing group at Jin'gaishan when he was busy running (among other things) his own spirit-writing shrine in Hangzhou, some 100 km away? The biography, which suggests he first came in 1782 (years after he had obtained the Jin'gaishan texts and published them) does not offer a straightforward answer, but at least two reasons seem highly plausible. First, the intrinsic interest of the texts revealed there, and a probable desire to have access to more; and second, the fact that it was a unique place to learn spiritual techniques, both from the gods and from human adepts. Indeed, among the texts revealed at Jin'gaishan, we find the same types as produced in other shrines, and anthologized by Shao in the Patriarch Lü and Wenchang canons:

19 The role of women around Min Yide and his network, as both disciples and masters to other scholars, is remarkable: see Liu Xun 2015, 2016.

liturgy, inner alchemy manuals, eschatological, cosmological and doctrinal scriptures, hagiography and morality books. But, we also find dialogues (*yulu* 語錄) between gods and human adepts that record direct divine instructions. While the adepts thus instructed are usually not named (and we do not know whether Shao was directly concerned by the extant instructions), these instructions nonetheless illuminate the kind of teaching that took place at such spirit-writing groups. The 'dialogues' at the Yunchao shrine, besides stories and teachings on moral life, show the deity instructing his adepts in such techniques as daily meditation (*zuogong* 坐功), breathing techniques, sleep regimens, the nurturing of *qi* energy etc.[20]

Spiritual techniques

While spirit-writing is a technique (that naturally requires adepts to be 'sincere', a prerequisite for the gods to descend on them that also necessitates training in skills), it is by no means self-contained; quite the contrary, as the recorded dialogues between the revealing gods and their human disciples show us, it is a medium for the development of a whole host of other spiritual techniques, which we also see put to work in Shao Zhilin's biography. I would thus now like to evoke some of the most important among them.

Incantations and visualizations

The recitation of the *Dabeizhou* is the technique most prominent in the narrative of Shao's life. This incantation, or *dhāraṇī*, runs to eighty-four verses, mostly transliterated from the Sanskrit (and thus unintelligible to almost all Chinese); it has been extremely popular since its appearance in medieval times, and is part of the Buddhist daily monastic office.[21] We should first remark that though it may surprise some readers unfamiliar with Chinese religious culture, a mixing of Buddhism and Daoism (among others) is in fact neither syncretic nor exceptional. A Buddhist spirituality was seen as entirely compatible with a self-proclaimed Confucian identity and the performance of Daoist ritual. This potent *sanjiao* (three teachings) religiosity is the essence of the Patriarch Lü and Wenchang canons that Shao edited. Both Daoism and Buddhism have long traditions of incantations and visualizations, and Guanyin, the Bodhisattva invoked by the *Dabeizhou*, is also a Daoist deity. While advanced practice linked to the *Dabeizhou* tends to be found among self-identified Buddhists, it was also present in popular religious primers as

20 *Yulu daguan* 語錄大觀, JY 168, 39a–57a.

21 Liu Hong (2016) comments on some early modern stories that document its wide popularity.

well as everyday encyclopaedias for literati, and was frequently used by all kinds of people in cases of need or stress.

The practice of the *Dabeizhou* is often encountered in late imperial narratives, especially in situations of danger or crisis, when people are taught to (or spontaneously, which suggests they had learnt it) recite it to secure divine protection. Many examples can be found in eighteenth- and nineteenth-century anecdotes about literati, and indeed it is referred to several times in the *Jin'gai xindeng*. The verb *chi* 持 that I translate as 'to recite', actually means 'to hold' or 'to practise', and refers to more than just enunciation, but also to proper mental and bodily attitudes. What really gave it the quality of an advanced spiritual technique were Shao's elaborate visualizations that allowed for the multiplication of the incantation. While Sinological historiography has mostly paid attention to the very complex visualization techniques described in the texts of the medieval Daoist Shangqing 上清 tradition (Robinet 1979), as well as in medieval Buddhist manuals (often qualified as 'tantric'), accounts such as Shao's document the continued relevance of visualizations much closer to the contemporary period.

Another type of intense recitation prized among literati (and the population at large) was that of the Buddha Amithaba's name, *nianfo* 念佛, the core Pure Land practice. A much simpler incantation than *Dabeizhou*, it also called for highly repetitive routines, and daily regimens of tens of thousands of iterations. By contrast to other incantations such as the *Dabeizhou* or many others found in the Patriarch Lü and Wenchang canons and other spirit-written revelations, the *nianfo* was primarily death-oriented. Its aim was to prepare and ensure the perfect state of mind at the moment of death, and thus rebirth in the Pure Land, where one is sure to become a Buddha. The *nianfo* was part of a larger repertoire of deathbed and *ars moriendi* techniques that late imperial literati read about and, in some cases, actively learnt (Birnbaum 2007; Eskildsen 2006). Indeed, late imperial religious culture is largely one of good death, and advanced practitioners, whether lay or clerical, are very often primarily discussed in terms of how successfully they prepared and performed (typically in public) their death.[22] This dimension is not explicit in the records concerning Shao Zhilin, though it was entirely pervasive in his milieu.

The abundant literature about late imperial lay Buddhists documents the spiritual exercises they engaged in, including *nianfo* and recitations of incantations such as the *Dabeizhou*; in some cases, biographies tell us about advanced visualization techniques not unlike the one that Shao practised. One well-known example is the *Jushizhuan* 居士傳 (Lives of lay Buddhists), the

22 Goossaert 2011a:644. One example of the staging of exemplary death is in *Jin'gai xindeng* 7.77a.

collection of biographies of lay Buddhists compiled by Peng Shaosheng 彭紹升 (1740–96), a prominent member of one of the most famous elite families of the time – his father, the high official Peng Qifeng 彭啟豐 (1701–84) contributed a preface and material to the Wenchang canon that Shao Zhilin co-edited.[23]

Inner alchemy

A second major body of spiritual techniques prominently found in Jin'gaishan texts and the Patriarch Lü canon that Shao edited is inner alchemy (*neidan* 內丹). This tradition formed around the eighth to tenth centuries, by integrating earlier manipulative alchemical practices, now entirely interiorized within the body, as well as cosmological speculations.[24] Its history is built around a tension between contemplative and technical approaches.[25] The former, while rejecting the technicity of certain practices, cannot be equated with mere 'sincerity': it still requires a mastery of speculative cosmology, as well as breathing techniques. Even in its more contemplative forms, inner alchemy relied on charts and diagrams that expressed the structure of both the cosmos and the human body, and that served as a tool for meditation and in some cases, visualizations. Such charts, and I provide an example below, were included in the *Lüzu quanshu*, which Shao Zhilin co-edited (they were already present in the earlier, 1744, edition of this canon and thus were not created by Shao).

The prestige of *neidan* was considerable during the late imperial era, and is reflected not only in the cult of its patriarchs – Patriarch Lü being the most prominent – but also in literature and the arts, where *neidan* imaginary is very pervasive. To what extent and to what degree it was actually practised by literati is still unknown, but the appeal of a spiritual master such as Min Yide largely depended on his teaching inner alchemy to numerous men and women from elite families in Jiangnan.

It is important to note that while the more advanced stages of *neidan* practice aimed at transforming the individual ontologically, to attain transcendence, many lay practitioners started with more mundane aims, the most important of which was self-healing. In a series of important articles, Liu Xun has richly documented the religious lives of several men and women from elite Jiangnan families who had direct connections to Min Yide and Jin'gaishan, and has shown how the connection often started with Min Yide curing them,

---

23 As an example, *Jushizhuan* 48.8a–9b (biography of Cheng Jiqing 程季清, a mid-seventeenth-century scholar) discusses his visualization techniques.

24 See Robinet 1995; and the many publications of Fabrizio Pregadio.

25 Eskildsen (2016) offers a cogent discussion of this tension for earlier (thirteenth century) texts, but his analysis remains valid for later periods.

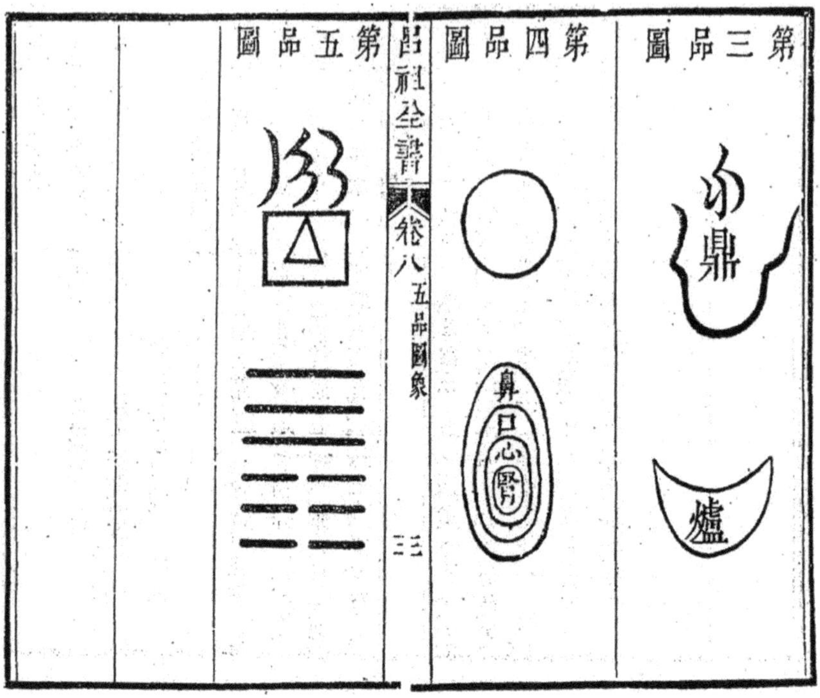

Figure 7.2 Charts for inner alchemical practice, in Wupinjing, Lüzu quanshu (32 juan edition).

and then teaching them preliminary *neidan* practices. The beneficial effects of such practices led these people to read further and to seek instruction from Min and other masters, and also to become assiduous participants in spirit-writing cults that received instructions from Patriarch Lü and other immortals and deities (Liu Xun 2015).

Note that one of the texts most valued by the Jin'gaishan tradition (revealed originally by another spirit-writing group in the early seventeenth century) is a rather esoteric *neidan* manual, 'The Secret of the Golden flower', *Taiyi Jinhua zongzhi* 太乙金華宗旨 (Esposito 2013:pt. 4). This text was translated by Richard Wilhelm (1873–1930), with a foreword by Carl Jung, and found a receptive audience at Eranos and with the people who frequented Monte Verita during the first half of the twentieth century, thus offering a fascinating encounter with the institution that made the present edited volume possible.

Rituals

The purpose of *neidan* techniques was not only to transcend oneself, but also to save others; they inform sublimation rituals whereby one can alchemically transform and save the dead.[26] The last section in Shao's story above shows him performing a ritual for saving the dead – literally, the 'small distribution of (blessed) food to suffering souls', *xiao shishi ke* 小施食科. From the title, we cannot tell whether this was a Buddhist or a Daoist ritual (both traditions use this term), although the former seems more likely. But whether or not Shao used *neidan* in the course of ritually saving untold numbers of dead souls, as an adept of Patriarch Lü he had to engage with both inner alchemy and liturgy.

Dealing with the dead was a major focus of scholars who learnt ritual techniques. This included the benevolent ritual transformation of the dead, whether one's kin or not, and also the protection against and if necessary the exorcism of the malevolent dead – arguably the most common theme in the stories and anecdotes about the religious lives of late imperial literati. Mastering simple techniques to protect oneself against the malevolent dead – what Don Sutton (2000) calls Confucian magic – was first and foremost a question of learning from an expert. Many of these techniques involved the use of talismans, *fu* 符, and talismans for all kinds of purposes can be readily found in everyday encyclopaedias and manuals of the good life – as well as in spirit-written texts, such as the Patriarch Lü and Wenchang canons co-edited by Shao Zhilin. Indeed, spirit-writing groups produced new salvation liturgies (Tao Jin 2013).

Wanfa guizong 萬法歸宗 (The myriad techniques returning to their common origin) was one of several much-distributed collections of talismans and other ritual techniques, including for summoning deities through spirit-writing (Boltz 2009). Yet, drawing a talisman requires learning, for one has to empower it with one's own energy (*qi*). Another type of manual that circulated widely (it still does) in late imperial times was that for ritual medicine, *zhuyou* 祝由 (lit. to conjure the cause [of the illness]), that use talismans, incantations and other rites to heal a whole variety of mental and physical ailments, and which had long been part of the medical curriculum and as such was studied by literati (Fang Ling 2002, 2013).

On the other hand, more advanced ritual techniques (like the salvation performed by Shao Zhilin) also required an ordination (taking vows in the Buddhist context, or obtaining a divine rank through ordination registers, *lu* 籙, in the Daoist context). Many literati underwent lay ordinations, which gave them a rank and a status in the divine world, and thus ensured them divine protection (Goossaert 2017a). Some of them received the ordination register

26 Sublimation (*liandu* 煉度) rituals appear around the twelfth century and represent a new stage in the history of rituals for the dead, whereby the main agent of the salvation of dead souls is the ritual master's own powers of symbolical alchemical transformation.

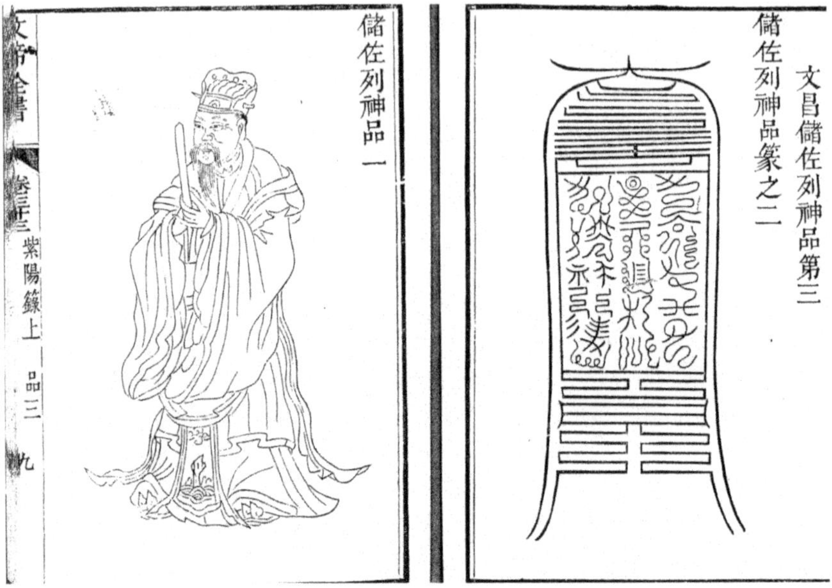

Figure 7.3 Portrait of Lord Wenchang, and talisman, both part of the ordination register to become a member of Wenchang divine administration; Wendi quanshu 1775 edition.

of Wenchang, and thus became, while still alive, officials in Wenchang's divine administration (the Jade Bureau, Yuju 玉局);[27] indeed, the template for this ordination register was included in the Wenchang canon that Shao Zhilin co-edited.

Moral self-cultivation

The world-view of the elites in general, and of active members of spirit-writing groups in particular, was largely based on the notion of moral retribution for human actions, and of the need to reform oneself and others towards a more moral life. This was the topic of the morality books, *shanshu* 善書, produced in massive numbers by spirit-writing groups such as Jin'gaishan, Tianxiangge and others. These books develop a consensual morality drawing from the three teachings, but also an eschatological world-view that threatened, in more or less precise terms, a final apocalypse if humans did not mend their ways.

One particular subgenre of the morality books point more specifically at the techniques deployed towards moral self-cultivation: the registers of merits and demerits (*gongguoge* 功過格) (Brokaw 1991; Goossaert 2012). The ledgers listed, sometimes in great detail, the number of points won or lost for each

27 *Jin'gai xindeng*, 7.30a–b has a case of an adept promoted in the Jade bureau.

good or bad action (give one cash to a poor, +1 point; kill a dog, -100 points etc.) and provided a form that adepts should fill every day, listing their good and bad deeds (including mental acts) and computing the balance of their account. One such ledger, the *Jingshi gongguoge*, was revealed at Jin'gaishan during the same period when Shao Zhilin was visiting and included by him in the *Lüzu quanshu*. While the whole exercise may seem somewhat bookish, it was actually (as one can see in the diaries, *riji* 日記, of some literati) an intense and sustained self-introspection routine that aimed at constantly observing and correcting oneself, a fully-fledged spiritual exercise. This is a case where the categories of spiritual technique, exercise and discipline seem very much to overlap, if not merge.

Correcting any single devious thought thus entailed the use of developed techniques of mental self-control. A particularly important case is sexual self-control. By the eighteenth century, when the whole of Chinese society was undergoing what can aptly be described as a puritan turn, sexual and gender issues became even more prominent than before in morality books, and whole scriptures on the topic were revealed by spirit-writing, or written by activists (Goossaert 2013). This literature, while strongly patriarchal in orientation, also tended to portray women as victims of asymmetrical power relationships, and blamed lack of male self-control for most of the world's sexual disorder. This strongly encouraged the teaching to young men of appropriate mental and physical techniques. Shao Zhilin himself was one of the men who felt highly concerned by the issue: he 'obtained'[28] in 1771 and commented in 1774 a version of Wenchang's divine pronouncements on sexual morality (*Yuhai huikuang baoxun* 慾海迴狂寶訓, Precious instructions on how to stop being foolishly engulfed by desires).[29] In some cases, mental techniques men had to resort to included visualizations (such as viewing women as corpses, or as one's own mother) that originated in ancient Buddhist monastic disciplinary practices.

Another tool for moral self-cultivation was the recitation of litanies of confession, *chan* 懺. This type of liturgical text, very common in both Buddhism and Daoism since the medieval period, did not (by contrast to other liturgies) require an ordained priest – even though it was and is still common to invite one. Spirit-writing groups did reveal large number of such litanies,[30] and the groups practised them, chanting these texts that run through long lists

28 This text was apparently already part of the 1744 Wenchang canon, and is included as part of a series of short tracts in juan 14 of *Wendi quanshu*.

29 *Wendi quanshu*, juan 30.

30 The *Daozang jiyao* has a very large collection of them, JY 247 *Chanfa daguan* 懺法大觀.

of sins (that overlap very much with the ledgers of merits and demerits) and the names of the gods and Buddhas called on to redeem them. Even though the technical element is less prominent here than in self-introspection and moral self-control, it still requires training for the proper chanting – which naturally implied bodily techniques: proper bodily posture, breathing etc. More generally, scripture recitation, either solo or in groups, was an important part of the devotional and spiritual lives of elites, and was conceived as a total exercise of disciplining and refining body and mind.

Meditation

Meditation is a modern, Western category that can encompass different types of spiritual techniques in the Chinese world – an etic perspective that is both illuminating and risky if it totally ignores emic distinctions. I use it here to refer to spiritual techniques that aim at calming the mind, rather than actively creating new mental realities, as in the case of the visualizations (linked to the multiplied recitation of the *Dabeizhou*) or the inner-alchemical transformations of the self evoked above. Traditions of meditation were numerous and taught at various venues in late imperial China. The Buddhist *chan* 禪 meditation was the signature practice of the elite monastic clergy, but advanced lay practitioners (including women) could join monastic *chan* retreats, and some also practised privately, sometimes under the guidance of a master (monastic or lay).[31] Some members of eighteenth-century spirit-writing groups were avid Chan practitioners and inserted relevant texts in the Patriarch Lü canons, which was somewhat controversial, but nonetheless showed that Chan was taught and practised in at least some groups (Lai Chi-tim 2013). Besides, many members of the elites were also engaging in so-called Confucian meditation – quiet sitting, *jingzuo* 靜坐 (Gernet 1981; Taylor 1979). While the differences between Confucian quiet sitting, Chan meditation and Daoist inner-alchemical practices were the topic of enduring debates, and sometimes controversies, the people who practised them overlapped to a very significant extent. Terms best translated as meditation, but not easily ascribed to one specific tradition, e.g. 'silent sitting', *mozuo* 默坐, constitute the most common reference to spiritual techniques in the *Jin'gai xindeng*. Shao's biography tells us that he practised meditation (*fuzuo* 趺坐, lit. sitting cross-legged) already as a child, suggesting that this was a foundation for the more advanced techniques he mastered later in life.

31 The literature on Chan is gigantic; let us just mention here Gregory (1986), which explores Chan as a part of a larger set of Buddhist spiritual techniques, including visualizations and *nianfo* (Gregory uses a larger definition of meditation than I do here).

Learning spiritual techniques

The case study of Shao Zhilin has so far allowed us to look at spiritual techniques not as a mere list of practices that late imperial Chinese people could 'choose' and 'do' if so they fancied, but as interrelated practices that fed into and often reinforced each other. It also sheds some light on the crucial, but also neglected (if, again, one works primarily with normative manuals rather than narrative sources) issue of how one could learn them in the first place. In this regard, one key theme is the question of learning from books vs. oral instructions from a master – a theme that runs all through the second millennium, when intellectuals worried about too much knowledge being seemingly easily accessible without proper study under the qualified guidance of a master. The availability of divine masters (communicating through spirit-writing) substituting for human ones only compounded the problem. As already said, technical manuals for all kinds of spiritual and ritual techniques (handbooks on talisman-making and simple rituals, meditation manuals, *qi*-enhancing, self-healing and life-nurturing *yangsheng* 養生 methods, and inner-alchemy primers etc.) were widely available. Such material (albeit usually in more simplified forms) was also largely present in general-use handbooks and everyday encyclopaedias (almanacs, religious primers and catechisms etc.); the highly developed commercial book market facilitated such a circulation (Goossaert 2011b). Many stories tell us how a person would first read a book, become interested in a technique, and then seek a master for specific instructions.

How did literati find masters, or groups of practitioners? Family and lineage were key loci for training and transmission, and not only from father to son; women in the family could be religious experts and train their male kin in meditation, inner alchemy and visualization. Families were known for specific traditions of practice. Daniel Burton-Rose's (2016) superb case study of the Peng family from Suzhou (we mentioned above two of its prominent members, Peng Qifeng and Peng Shaosheng, who had direct connection with Shao Zhilin) shows how spirit-writing techniques, inner alchemy, Chan meditation, Pure Land practices and more were transmitted within this supposedly typical Confucian family; individual Pengs had differing personal inclinations and even sometimes debated with each other – which only shows that all these techniques were available to them.

Schools and academies were also venues for training in ritual, and hence of certain spiritual techniques particularly linked to ritual. Whereas the historiography so far has largely focused on the intellectual contents of the education provided by these institutions, it is certain that they also trained their students in bodily and mental self-control techniques. Similarly, many members of the elites took a Buddhist or Daoist cleric as their master, and

Figure 7.4 Patriarch Lü 呂祖. *Jueyunxuan Yunxiao xuanpu zhi* 覺雲軒雲霄玄譜志. *Shen Rui* 沈睿. *1939 edition in Zhongguo daoguan zhi congkan, vols 22–3.*

thus visited monasteries and requested personal training in various practices, often including, but not limited to, meditation, as well as personal advice. Shao Zhilin's master Cai Laihe is a good (albeit poorly documented) example.

Finally, as our case study amply confirms, spirit-writing groups where like-minded people came together for the shared goal of transforming themselves and the world were a key locus for learning spiritual techniques; members exchanged their experience and skills (as well as technical manuals and other texts), and the gods both encouraged them and revealed techniques, charts and other documents directly useful for their practice.

Conclusions

Even though we have restricted ourselves to the records directly linked to one person, Shao Zhilin, we found documents, manuals, discussions and descriptions pertaining to a large range of spiritual techniques, which the historiography tends to classify separately as Buddhist, Daoist or Confucian (or medical, popular etc.). This case is exceptional in the level of commitment of the individual concerned, but not by the practices themselves, which we have seen widely disseminated in both normative and narrative sources. Members of the late imperial elites like Shao Zhilin defined themselves in contrast to clerical virtuosi and ascetics – they were active in local society, running charities and other local affairs, holding official positions or engaging in business, and the life and ethos of a reclusive meditator had little allure for them. Yet, they were just as interested in their own salvation, particularly by moving along the path to self-divinization.[32]

Because of this aim of turning themselves into gods, and also in order to deal with all their commitments (staying healthy in the midst of professional pressure, performing efficacious rituals, rising up to the calls of the deities who instructed them through spirit-writing), they were just as keen as clerics and ascetics when it came to learning a whole range of advanced spiritual techniques. While constantly upholding their class-bound claim on moral rectitude and sincerity, they filled their private life with training in, and recourse to, spiritual techniques. As narrative sources allow us a view of these people learning such techniques in different venues and settings, we realize that their practical, immediate (self-healing, performing rituals) and transcendental (salvation) uses were inextricably mixed, just as the various techniques they engaged in were combined in multifarious ways.

References

Primary

Guanghui xiuxin baoming chaojie jing 廣慧修心保命超劫經. In *Lüzu quanshu* 呂祖全書, 1775.

Jin'gai xindeng 金蓋心燈, compiled in 1821 by Min Yide 閔一得 (1758–1836). 1876 edition in *Daojiao wenxian* 道教文獻, vol. 10. Taipei: Danqing tushu, 1983.

Jingshi gongguoge 警世功過格, JY 277.

Jushizhuan 居士傳, by Peng Shaosheng 彭紹升. 1878 edition reprinted by Yangzhou: Jiangsu Guangling guji keyinshe, 1991.

JY: text number in the *Daozang jiyao* following Lai Chi-tim 2021.

Lüdi shiji 呂帝詩集, JY 165.

Lüzu quanshu 呂祖全書, 1775. In *Zhonghua xu Daozang* 中華續道藏, vol. 20. Taipei: Xinwenfeng, 1999.

32 One detailed description of the divinization of a Jin'gaishan adept in *Jin'gai xindeng*, 7.55a–b.

Wendi quanshu 文帝全書, 1775. Original edition at Waseda University Library.
Yulu daguan 語錄大觀, JY 168.

Secondary

Birnbaum, R. 2007. 'The deathbed image of Master Hongyi'. In B.J. Cuevas and J.I. Stone (eds), *The Buddhist Dead: Practices, Discourses, Representations*, pp. 175–207. Honolulu: University of Hawai'i Press.

Boltz, J.M. 2009. 'On the legacy of Zigu and a manual on spirit-writing in her name'. In P. Clart and P. Crowe (eds), *The People and the Dao. New Studies in Chinese Religions in Honour of Daniel L. Overmyer*, pp. 349–88. Sankt Augustin: Monumenta Serica.

Brokaw, C.J. 1991. *The Ledgers of Merit and Demerit. Social Change and Moral Order in Late Imperial China*. Princeton: Princeton University Press.

Burton-Rose, D. 2016. Terrestrial Reward as Divine Recompense. The Self-Fashioned Piety of the Peng Lineage of Suzhou, 1650s–1870s. PhD dissertation, Princeton University.

Eskildsen, S. 2006. 'Emergency death meditation techniques for internal alchemists', *T'oung Pao* 92(4–5):373–409.

— — — 2016. 'Debating what Lü Dongbin practiced: why did the Yuan Daoist Miao Shanshi denounce the Zhong-Lü texts?', *T'oung Pao* 102(4–5):407–47.

Esposito, Monica. 2013. *Creative Daoism*. Wil/Paris: UniversityMedia.

— — — 2014. *Facets of Qing Daoism*. Wil/Paris: UniversityMedia.

Fang Ling. 2002. 'Les médecins laïques contre l'exorcisme sous les Ming. La disparition de l'enseignement de la thérapeutique rituelle dans le cursus de l'Institut impérial de medicine', *Extrême-Orient Extrême-Occident* 24:31–45.

— — — 2013. 'Quanzhen Daoism and ritual medicine: a study of 'Thirteen sections of *Zhuyou* medicine from the Yellow Emperor inscription'. In V. Goossaert and Liu Xun (eds), *Quanzhen Daoists in Chinese Society and Culture, 1500–2010*, pp. 208–32. Berkeley: Institute of East Asian Studies.

Gernet, J. 1981. 'Techniques de recueillement, religion et philosophie: à propos du *jingzuo* 靜坐 néo-confucéen', *Bulletin de l'École Française d'Extrême-Orient* 69:289–305.

Goossaert, V. 2008. 'Irrepressible female piety: late imperial bans on women visiting temples', *Nan Nü. Men, Women and Gender in China* 10(2):212–41.

— — — 2011a. 'Yu Yue (1821–1906) explore l'au-delà: la culture religieuse des élites chinoises à la veille des révolutions'. In R. Hamayon, D. Aigle, I. Charleux and V. Goossaert (eds), *Miscellanea Asiatica*, pp. 623–56. Sankt Augustin: Monumenta Serica.

——— 2011b. 'Daoists in the modern Chinese self-cultivation market: the case of Beijing, 1850–1949'. In D. Palmer and Liu Xun (eds), *Daoism in the 20th Century: Between Eternity and Modernity*, pp. 123–53. Berkeley: University of California Press.

——— (ed.) 2012. *Livres de Morale Révélés par les Dieux*. Paris: Belles-Lettres.

——— 2013. 'La sexualité dans les livres de morale chinois'. In F. Rochefort and M.E. Sanna (eds), *Normes Religieuses et Genre: Mutations, Résistances et Reconfiguration, xixe- xxie siècle*, pp. 37–46. Paris: Armand Colin.

——— 2014. 'Modern Daoist eschatology: spirit-writing and elite soteriology in late imperial China', *Daoism. Religion, History and Society* 6:219–46.

——— 2015. 'Spirit-writing, canonization and the rise of divine saviors: Wenchang, Lüzu, and Guandi, 1700–1858', *Late Imperial China* 36(2):82–125.

——— 2017a. *Bureaucratie et Salut: Devenir un Dieu en Chine*. Geneva: Labor & Fides.

——— 2017b. 'Diversity and elite religiosity in modern China: a model', *Approaching Religion* 7(1):10–20.

——— 2019. 'Late imperial Chinese piety books', *Studies in Chinese Religions* 5(1):38–54.

——— 2021. 'The Jin'gaishan network'. In V. Goossaert and Liu Xun (eds), *Daoism in Modern China. Clerics and Temples in Urban Transformations, 1860–Present*, pp. 83–119. London: Routledge.

——— 2022. *Making the Gods Speak: The Ritual Production of Revelation in Chinese History.* Cambridge: Harvard University Asia Center.

——— forthcoming. 'Shao Zhilin 邵志琳 (1748–1810), a Religious Life. Spirit-writing, Charity, and Rituals in mid-Qing Jiangnan', *Daoism: History, Religion & Society* 道教研究學報 14.

Gregory, P.N. (ed.) 1986. *Traditions of Meditation in Chinese Buddhism*. Honolulu: University of Hawaii Press.

Katz, P.R. and Goossaert, V. 2021. *The Fifty Years that Changed Chinese Religion, 1898–1948*. Ann Arbor: AAS.

Lai Chi-tim 黎志添. 2013. 'Qingdai sizhong *Lüzu quanshu* yu Lüzu fuji daotan de guanxi 清代四種《呂祖全書》與呂祖扶乩道壇的關係', *Zhongguo wenzhe yanjiu jikan* 中國文哲研究集刊 42:183–230.

Lai Chi-tim 黎志添, ed. 2021. *Daozang jiyao tiyao* 道藏輯要提要. Hong Kong: Chinese University Press.

Liu Hong. 2016. 'La pratique de la *Dhâranî de la grande compassion* (大悲咒) dans la Chine du XIIe siècle d'après le *Yijian zhi* (夷堅志, 1198)'. In V. Durand-Dastès (ed.), *Empreintes du tantrisme en Chine et en Asie orientale*, pp. 103–16. Leuven: Peeters.

Liu Xun. 2015. 'Of poems, gods, and spirit-writing altars: the Daoist beliefs and practice of Wang Duan (1793–1839)', *Late Imperial China* 36(2):23–81.

——— 2016. 'An intoning immortal at the West lake: Chen Wenshu and his pursuits in inner alchemy and spirit-writing in late Qing Jiangnan', *Cahiers d'Extrême-Asie* 25:77–111.

Mann, S. 1997. *Precious Records: Women in China's Long Eighteenth Century*. Stanford: Stanford University Press.

Mori Yuria 森由利亞. 1999. 'Ryo Dōhin to Zenshinkyō: Shinchō koshū Kingaisan no jirei o chūshin ni 呂洞賓と全真教–清朝湖州金蓋山の事例を中心に'. In Sunayama Minoru 砂山稔 *et al.* (eds.), *Kōza Dōkyō daiichikan: Dōkyō no kamigami to kyōten* 講座道教弟一巻:道教の神々と経典, pp. 242–64. Tokyo: Yūzan kaku.

Robinet, I. 1979. *Méditation Taoïste*. Paris: Dervy.

——— 1995. *Introduction à l'alchimie Intérieure Taoïste: de l'Unité et de la Multiplicité: Avec une Traduction Commentée des Versets de l'éveil à la Vérité*. Paris: Cerf.

Snyder-Reinke, J. 2009. *Dry Spells: State Rainmaking and Local Governance in Late Imperial China*. Cambridge, Mass.: Harvard University Asia Center.

Sutton, D. 2000. 'From credulity to scorn: Confucians confront the spirit mediums in late imperial China', *Late Imperial China* 21(2):1–39.

Tao Jin 陶金. 2013. 'Suzhou *Dadong wushang jiuji tianxian chuanjie keyi* chutan: Yi ge Qingdai Beijing yu Jiangnan wenren jitan jiaohu yingxiang de anli 蘇州『大洞無上九極天仙傳戒科儀』初探——一個清代北京與江南文人乩壇交互影響的案例', *Daoism: Religion, History and Society* 5:111–41.

Taylor, R.L. 1979. 'Meditation in Ming neo-orthodoxy: Kao P'an-Lung's writing on quiet-sitting', *Journal of Chinese Philosophy* 6(2):149–82.

IV

CORPOREITY

8

An insuperable citadel?

Corporeity and incorporeity in Indian Buddhism[1]

CRISTINA SCHERRER-SCHAUB

Preamble

Ascetism and spiritual praxis are coessential to Indian Buddhism as they are part of a shared tradition of Indian lore. Specific techniques of visualization emphazise the visualized image in such a way that the external representation of the corporeal elements will lead the practitioner to see and know the progressive detachment from and the successive fading away of corporeity. Moving further to incorporeity (i.e. to the 'sphere of mind') the practioner progresses towards the 'insuperable citadel',

The adherence of the putative yogin to different doctrinal and religious obediences can be reduced to one pattern in tune with the techniques displayed during the process. Nonetheless, the various applications, such as the spiritual praxis in conjunction with subsidiary rites and other activities, as well as the emphasis put upon certain meditational stages, and above all the goal to be attained, are important markers to determine the yogin's school.

The focus will be directed here upon a case and a specific historical and geographic context in which the ascetic, practising a particular technique of visualization, integrating the totality of the universe, surpasses the 'insuperable citadel' and, passing through a series of visual symbolic representations, attains the final spiritual goal.

1 The terms 'corporeity' and 'incorporeity' are introduced here for sake of convenience. However, as will be shown, the 'pseudo-individuality', or the person which is the agent of the process, is here designated on the basis of an indissociable combined 'corporeity' and 'incorporeity', or material and mental. See, pp. 194–6.

Introduction

India is famous for being the cradle of the oldest and still living tradition of yoga. It is indeed notorious that some particular practices or religious ideas that will eventually become landmarks of the classical Indian systems of thought, including Buddhism and Jainism, appear in the Upaniṣads.[2] While the dating of the Upaniṣads is still a debated question, scholars generally agree that the oldest among them pre-date Buddhism, though they were put down in writing much later. The Upaniṣads are a reservoir of amazing data on cosmological and religious representation of the spheres composing the entire world, of theories in which the physiology of breathing and vital energy (*prāṇa*) play a central role in the meditative process. On their part, eminent or superior practitioners (yogin), ascetic techniques and philosophical ideas are staged within the epics (*Mahābhārata* and *Rāmāyaṇa*) as protagonists of a mythological organization of the cosmos.

While this largely shared tradition of yoga may show striking textual parallels, particularly in matters of terminology or specific techniques,[3] it equally presents remarkable variation, revealing 'geographical' itineraries of transmission, with specific local and/or oral traditions possibly introduced by the masters themselves – all factors that may contribute to a better understanding of the underlying socio-historical changes. Apart from what we know from hagiography, however, very little may be said about the early Masters of Yoga – who instructed disciples in these techniques, each according to their respective personal 'composition'.[4] Moreover, textual tradition tells that, in particular circumstances and/or specific religious

2 Also called Vedānta, that is the 'conclusion of the Veda' or the 'definite ascertainment of the Veda'.

3 The terminology related to the techniques of corporeal-cum-mental training that we find in the early Buddhist treatises is abundant and partially shared with the early Indian tradition, as attested for instance in Patañjali's *Yogasūtra* (second to fourth century AD), possibly composed at the time of the exuberant flourishing of the Buddhist yoga treatises, in the first centuries AD. See Wujastyk 2018:38–42.

4 In Classical India, particularly from the fourth century AD on, the very rare chronicles, which refer to the lineage of Masters, as well as some of the extant Indian/ Indic manuscript's colophons, have preserved hagiographic-cum-historic data. A variety of Indian sources on Buddhist masters's vitæ have been included in the Tibetan historiographic tradition, dating from the twelfth to thirteenth century and later. The Chinese scholarly tradition on its part has preserved amazing data concerning the Indian, North Indian and Serindian Masters that were working in China as Teachers and translators of Indic texts, where the curricula of some 'Masters of dhyāna' are recorded. Incidentally, the images that the practitioner sees and experiences are precious indications for the Master of the type of teaching that he shall address to the disciple.

contexts, the treatises (*śāstra*) themselves were substituted for the Master (*śāstṛ*) in absentia. And writing, like painting, functioned as an 'ancillary' spiritual practice.

The importance of the early forms of 'body-mind' training (*yoga*), some still in vogue nowadays and 'adjusted' to modern societies, is evident in the flourishing of a series of treatises allegedly dated to the first centuries AD. These detailed techniques, together with the cultivation of moral principles (*śīla*) and insight (*prajñā*), constitute the path toward the final goal, a state or condition outside the ordinary and mundane world. These practices contemplate various stages in close connection with the levels, 'disks' or spheres through which the cosmos is structured, and which are spaced out along a central vertical axis. In his spiritual-cum-cosmic itinerary, the practitioner (*yogācāra*) visualizes (and in a sense 'visits') the transient and revolving world in which the various modes of existence (human, deity, animal etc.) are reborn and move in circle (i.e. the world of *saṃsāra*). The yogin progressively ascends to the summit, while travelling through the various cosmic spheres, each of them correlated to a meditative stage.

The process combines the activity of seeing or perceiving (*darśana*) and cognition (*jñāna*), in alternation, and culminates with the knowledge and vision (*jñānadarśana*) of things 'as they are' (*yathābhūta*), that is 'in their true nature'. If, as will be shown, some of the propaedeutic exercises of meditation may favour the attainment of singular perfection (*siddhi*) or 'magical' power (*ṛddhi*), the mastery of these 'arts' is considered inferior to the supreme goal that the yogin aims to attain, i.e. the apex of knowledge or omniscience (*sarvajñāna*).

Those techniques that were put down in writing at the beginning of the CE have been increasingly, and incessantly, discussed in the following centuries. The range of scholastic tenets professed by the Indian Buddhist schools at that time created one of the most important and extensive bodies of Buddhist literature, the treatises on the practice of yoga (*yogācāra*).[5]

Of particular interest to the present topic are those sections of the scholastic treatises dealing with specific practical exercises of visualization that focus upon the external representation of corporeal elements, and which

5 One of the oldest and most interesting treatises or *manuel de méditation*, the *Yogācārabhūmiśāstra* of Saṅgharakṣa, dates to the first, or to the beginning of the second, century AD, and very likely was composed in Kashmir. It was translated into Chinese, at first incompletely (second century AD), and then, a century later, completely. Saṅgharakṣa's treatise, together with the amazing corpus of Asaṅga's *Yogācārabhūmiśāstra*, and other texts, contributed to initiation of the most influential Indian tradition in China.

lead the practitioner to see and know, via the visualized image, the progressive detachment from and the successive fading (but not disappearing!) of 'corporeity', intended here as the 'material' component of the indissociable composite (of matter and mind) that constitutes the personal entity under which the 'self' (*ātman*) is wrongly subsumed.

Moving further, the practitioner (yogin) progresses toward other spheres of the world that are more and more subtle, or 'thinner', and in which, while 'corporeity' is fading away, 'incorporeity' or the 'mental' components of the 'pseudo-individuality' assume a preponderant role. This practice leads the yogin toward the highest condition and the highest cosmic sphere, where the practitioner is close to the 'city of *nirvāṇa*' a citadel that, for other practitioners, shall never be entered without it compromising the realization of the religious vow taken by the yogin to remain in the world in order to help the sentient beings, not yet liberated from the cycle of existence (*bhavacakra*) or *saṃsāra*.[6]

To further vivify the representation of the spiritual praxis, the careful reading of ancient sources tells us that subsidiary rites (invocation, eulogy etc.), ancillary activities (painting, writing etc.) or the emphasis placed upon a particular meditative stage, may each intervene in the process. Once again, the application of these rites and activities, and, above all, the intended purpose to be attained, are indicative of the specific religious commitment and beliefs of the practitioner.

Incidentally, and to return to the ideas conveyed by the treatises and manuals on yoga that we see flourishing in Classical India, one may observe that they present singular affinity with meditative practices and ideas (e.g. with regard to the process of an image's visualization, or the application of mindfulness) known through the works of coeval authors of Christian Antiquity,[7] while some of their translations in modern languages, at times, diverge considerably.

---

6 See, for example, Schlingloff 2006:161R6: *iha nagare yaḥ praviṣṭo na bhūyo nirgacchatīti* 'Wer hier in [diese] Stadt eingetreten ist, geht nich mehr heraus'. See also the section 'Didatics, allegory, the imaginary', below.

7 For instance, Johannes Cassianus (*c.*360–435), see the very inspiring book of Olivier Boulnois (2008:25–72).

> Dans la méditation selon Cassien, il s'agit de parvenir à la mémoire de Dieu. L'ascèse suit une progression méthodique, avec ses étapes, ses techniques, qui conduisent finalement à l'illumination. Or la mémoire se structure comme un bâtiment peuplé d'images, celles-ci sont repérées par leur place dans l'édifice, qu'on peut se représenter comme les cases d'un colombier (= Platon, *Théétète* 197d–198d). L'âme doit parvenir à l'édification', qui n'était pas à l'origine une

In the modern Western world, meditation in Buddhism is often associated with the teaching of Zen, Theravāda or Tibetan Masters, from whence originated those techniques that were introduced in the second part of the nineteenth century, first in Europe and Russia, and eventually in North America. As a consequence, the terminology related to these practices has been strongly influenced by the historical context of reception of these ideas, in an epoch when spiritual praxis of different kind and horizon were in vogue in the Western world.[8] In this respect, Alan Sponberg's words are still apt, particularly today, when terms such as yoga, mantra, or mandala are in common use and are frequently adopted in non-Indian or non-Buddhist contexts,

> As interpreter of an alien culture, we cannot be content simply to assign aspects of Buddhist experience to the best available category from our own culture. Rather we need to expand and elaborate our categories to better encompass what we find in the alien culture: in this case we must modify our understanding of meditation as a category of human religious experience in whatever ways are required to make sense of the Buddhist experience as it emerges from our study.
>
> (Sponberg 1986:20)

He invites us then to enquire about what Westerners,

> [A]re likely to include in the rubric 'meditation' or 'meditative practices', and perhaps of even more significance, on what we are likely not to include, consciously or otherwise.
>
> (ibid.:16)

> métaphore pieuse, mais la construction d'un espace intérieur aux places bien marquées et ornées d'images.
>
> (Boulnois 2008:70)

Incidentally 'la mémoire de Dieu' may here be paralleled with the remembrance of the Buddha (*buddhānusmṛti*) that together with the remembrance of his teaching (dharma), his community (*saṃgha*) and the remembrance of the deities (*devatā*), refers to a mental exercise conspicuously present among the fragmentary collection of manuscripts from Central Asia, including the Qïzïl manual (see section 'Didactics, allegory, the imaginary', below).

8 On this epoch and this context, see Brach in this volume.

We must admit, however, that the terminology related to the various stages of the process of meditation is difficult to translate, even for those having spent decades reading these ancient texts. The very sound principle that univocal terms of translation are hard to find is certainly applicable here. Not the least because, for reasons that far exceed the present scope, the terminology related to the singular stages of the meditative process changes according 'to time and space', as the ancient authors themselves already noticed; with the consequence that the list of categories related to meditation that the various schools and/or masters had established in a specific historical-cum-doctrinal context were eventually included into very large compendia composed by scholiasts. As a result, the terminology related to the various practices appears today noticeably blurred; and in their turn, the ancient authors, while trying to make sense of this gigantic construct, themselves created an inextinguishable stream of exegesis.[9]

The yoga practitioner and his practice

In the earliest Buddhist treatises the practitioner of yoga (a yogin), is often called *bhikṣuyogācāra* or 'monk and yogin': he visualizes, surveys and in some particular stages of the process even moves through the various cosmic spheres, and sees the place where the sentient beings are reborn. The exercise of the four successive stages of meditation (*dhyāna*)[10] generates in him a series of specific qualities, whose role is to function as counteracting agent of the main passions linking the monk-and-practitioner to the world of *saṃsāra*.

The process of meditation that is here very concisely summarized, and whose purpose is to liberate the monk-and-practitioner from the transient world by knowing and seeing the real nature of things, moves in alternation: the meditative process is by no means static (let alone ecstatic! – cf. Seyfort Ruegg 1967:165) and consists in a series of moments, in which a cognitive

9 For instance, there is the case of the term *samādhi*, which refers to the practice of intensive contemplation/concentration upon the object of meditation, and which, among others, designates the last stage of the four meditations (*dhyāna*). In the most common and general sequence constituting the path toward liberation, that consists of moral conduct (*śīla*), meditation (*samādhi*) and discriminative knowledge or insight (*prajñā*), *samādhi* is used as a generic term to designate the complex process of meditation.

10 The term *dhyāna* derives from the verb *dhyai-*, meaning 'to think intensively upon' a determined object. The stages of the *dhyāna*-practice consist of processes in which the mental activity (*citta*) is variously 'associated' with specific cognitive and mental activities (*caitta*) capable, among other things, of counteracting the noxious elements generated by the application of the passions (attraction, repulsion and stupefaction/dullness) to the meditated object.

'active' instant of intellection alternates with a cognitive 'inactive' instant of quiet or tranquillity of mind.

The *Yogācārabhūmi* of Saṅgharakṣa (*c.* first to second century AD),[11] one of the oldest Indian manuals addressed to the Buddhist practitioners of yoga presents a passage in which the author, among others, defines the meditative process and in particular the two cognitive moments just alluded to. 'Quiet' (*śamatha*), he says, is when the mind is correctly fixed (upon the meditated object) and is motionless, without distraction or negligence. While the moment of 'intellection' (*vipaśyanā*) takes place when the mind knows the teaching of the Buddha, knows how the world is produced, and knows the very nature of what is produced.

These alternating modes, as will be shown, are exercised when the yogin meditates upon the skeleton and the corpse in the process of decay. Following these and other preliminaries, the practitioner will progressively enter the four stages of meditation (*dhyāna*), at the end of which he will acquire special skills (*ṛddhi*), such as the capacity to move or travel (*gamana*) through the sky/air, or, as it is said by the fifth-century author Buddhaghosa, the power of 'elevating the body and moving like birds'; or the ability to move cross-legged through the space; also the power of having objects move, a feat which is abundantly recorded in narratives that tell how images of the Buddha travelled through the air, and for a long distance. The yogin will also gain the power of forming/creating metamorphoses (*nirmāṇa*), which allow them to transform into a tiger, or to create a tiger; and also, the ability to perform other amazing feats, such as shaking the earth, crossing walls, projecting masses of water. Moreover, the yogin may also obtain another category of 'abilities' giving superior knowledge (*abhijñā*), such as the thoughts of other beings, the remembrance of previous existences, or the faculty of seeing, with the divine eye (*divyacakṣu*), the sentient beings in the round of existence (*saṃsāra*).[12]

The process of moving or travelling (*gamana*) that occurs during a specific form of concentrated meditation (*samādhi*) is succinctly explained by Buddhasena, a renown Kashmirian master of meditation (*dhyāna*), active at the turn of the fifth century, and the author of one of the numerous yoga treatises, composed at this epoch. Buddhasena refers to the practitioner of yoga,

11 The text was first partially translated by the Parthian scholar An Shigao (148–170 AD), and then a complete version was translated by Dharmarakṣa (284 AD), a Buddhist religious Master born at the 'gate' of China. The passage alluded to here (T. 606, 211c17–213a21) was translated into French by Demiéville (1954:409).

12 This is explained in more detail below.

> who in the course of the four meditations (*dhyāna*) cultivates and produces the five superior knowledges. In the process of concentrated meditation with his mind fixed upon the meditated object he contemplates his own body. He conceives the notions of lightness and suppleness, gradually soars, immobile, with the object of meditation (his own body) present in front of him; he leaves the ground at a distance of a sesame seed, then of a barley seed, then gradually to a height of four fingers; while, step by step he moves from a seat to another and circulates at will. He flies and transforms himself freely, without obstacles. This is the sublime force of the superior knowledge of the *yogācāra*.
>
> (*Yogācārabhūmi* of Saṅgharakṣa T. 618, ii, 319a21–27; Demiéville 1954:411n.4).

How effectively these practices were done is hard to imagine, but they were at least inspiring to painters (Figure 8.1), and they were also matter of scorn from the Vinaya masters (see section, 'Preliminary practices to counteract the obstacles to meditation in socio-historical context'). Thaumaturgic skills and extraordinary yogic feats have indeed fired the imagination if not the imaginary of literary narrative in Classical India as well as in the Western world, obscuring for some the specific role that these practices were playing in the spiritual path. Indeed, unless the yogin had reached the highest stage/condition, where he perfectly masters the cognitive object without departing from his ethical commitment, the superior knowledge (*abhijñā*) and special skills (*ṛddhi*) were not recommended to the novice practitioners of either Buddhist or non-Buddhist Indian traditions of yoga,[13] as these practices, if not perfected, could well cause undesirable diversions from the final goal and could even preclude the access to it – a fact recalled in some hilarious narratives (for example, the passage translated by Schopen, below).

The body-mind composite entity or pseudo-individuality

The question may arise as to the 'agent' (*kartṛ*) of the cognitive and meditative process or to the status of the yogin. The majority of the Buddhist schools do not admit the real existence of a personal agent (*ātman*) and rather profess the idea that a personal individuality is but a name for a pseudo individuality subsumed under the complex of five interdependent components or aggregates: matter (*rūpa*), sensation/feeling (*vedanā*), notion (*saṃjñā*), mental constructions/actions (*saṃskāra*) and mental cognition (*vijñāna*). In short, these aggregates determine the mental-and-material (*citta-rūpa*) composite entity, responsible for accomplishing a deed (*karman*), and whose

13 See Patañjali's *Yogasūtra* III.16–50, listing the *siddhi*, and III.37 warning against.

Figure 8.1 *Qumtura, Ceiling painting with visualization of flying monks. Courtesy of Dieter Schlingloff, reproduced here after Schlingloff 2015:53, fig. 17 (Kapitel 4 'Der Zustand der Levitation').*

result directs the composite entity or pseudo individuality toward the various destinies (*gati*, lit. 'there where one goes') that incessantly move in the wheel of existence: infernal destiny (*nāraka*), errant spirits (*preta*), animals (*tiryañc*), gods (*deva*), semi-gods (*asura*) and humans (*manuṣya*).

The result or fruit (*vipākaphala*) of the deed (*karman*), accomplished by the composite entity or the pseudo-individuality, is projected by the karmic force into the entire world (*sarvaloka*), otherwise described as the world of sentient beings (*sattvaloka*) and its receptacle (*bhajanaloka*), the spatial environment where the sentient beings are moving and acting, with its natural and artificial landscape: mountains, lakes, trees, buildings etc. Going a step further, the deed (*karman*) performed by the pseudo-individuality projects its karmic force into a series of momentary instants (*kṣaṇa*) that constitute the present and future existence of the aggregate of mind and matter, that at the time of death assumes the form of an extremely subtle entity (*susukṣma*)[14] and after wandering in search of the proper 'support' will re-emerge in a new existence; while part of the karmic force is projected into the receptacle world (*bhajanaloka*) which is the fruit of the sum of the collective acts accomplished by all sentient beings.[15]

The socio-historical context of preliminary practices to counteract the obstacles to meditation

Allowed and prohibited monk's feats: the 'feminine' and the institutional call to order

The Buddhist early treatises on yoga are primarily addressed to a monk (*bhikṣu*), for whom the main 'daimon' that captivates the mind is the image of the 'feminine', in all its possible varieties. Rhetoric warning against the ugliness of a woman's body (for some authors the body *tout court*, thus also including the masculine one) invades the Buddhist literature. Narratives relating the temptations faced by meditating monks are depicted in the Vinayas,[16] and essentially directed at those meditating in secluded places. These passages are studded with hilarious scenes. Gregory Schopen, who dedicates his research to the gigantic collections of Vinaya, acutely observes that the monk's feats

14 This subtle entity, made of mind and very tiny matter is called *gandharva*, and for his subsistence consumes the subtlest element of matter, that is, wind. This echoes some ideas that circulated in Antiquity, see Peter Brown (2016:105), which reports a passage from a letter of Evodius to Augustine: 'Dans sa lettre à Augustin, Évodius montrait qu'il était lui-même favorable à une forme plus modérée de platonisme. Il suggérait que l'on devait penser que, même lorsqu'elle se trouvait hors du corps, l'âme était portée par une sorte de 'véhicule' matériel et avait conservé une sorte d'enveloppe extrêment fine.'

15 In short: *karman*, or the act accomplished by the pseudo-individuality, designated as 'person' (*pudgala*), 'self' (*ātman*) etc., is responsible vis-à-vis the entire world formed by the sentient beings (*sattavaloka*) and the receptacle (*bhajanaloka*); as the ancient texts say: the variety of the world is born from the *karman*. Ascetic practice envisions a perfect mastery of the mind, as the *karman* is effectively accomplished by it.

16 At least some of the Vinayas, or the corpora of the monastic rule of the various Indian schools (*nikāya*) of Buddhism, were translated and adopted, if not adapted, outside India in the course of their transmission and diffusion to the Asian world. The Vinayas appear as cumulative compendia of the rules of conduct for monks and nuns, allegedly all the way back to the historical Buddha, and successively augmented with new or newly formulated rules whose authority, if not authorship, is granted by the narrative, staged at the time of the historical Buddha, illustrating the case in point.

acquired in meditation and accomplished in solitary places could result in public disturbances, to the point that their institution, in some cases, felt obliged to intervene, calling the monk-practitioners to order. Schopen notes that when the *Mūlasarvāstivāda Vinaya* refers to ascetics or meditating monks,

> such monks almost always appear as the butt of jokes, objects of ridicule, and – not uncommonly – sexual deviants. They are represented as irresponsible and of the type that give the order a bad name. There are texts in our Code where, for example, ascetic, cemetery monks manage only to terrify children, where ascetic monks who wear robes made from cemetery cloth are not allowed into the monastery, let alone to sit on a mat that belong to the Community; tales whose only point seems to be to indicate that meditation makes you stupid; texts about monks who meditate in the forest and cannot control their male member and so end up smashing it between two rocks, whereupon the Buddha tells them, while they are howling in pain, that they, unfortunately have smashed the wrong thing – they should have smashed desire; and a tale about another monk who meditated in the forest, and to avoid being seduced by a goddess, had to tie his legs shut. The goddess being put off by that then flung him through the air, and he landed – legs still tied – on top of the king, who was sleeping on the roof of his palace. The king of course was not amused and made it known to the Buddha that it would not do to have his monks being flung around the countryside in the middle of the night. The Buddha then actually made a rule forbidding monks to meditate in the forest.
>
> (Schopen 2004:26)

The practice of meditation, and in particular the skills that the practitioner could gain from them, which appear to have been a subject of controversy, if not scorn, in the specific context of north-western Indian monasticism, seems to have been flourishing in different religious contexts, particularly in the fifth century, when we see the works of the Kashmiri masters paying much attention to the detailed description of levitation (ibid.:4). Some astonishing feats were transposed into the *didactic imaginaire*; as, for instance, may be observed in oases situated along the northern route of the Taklamakan desert (Xinjiang) where an impressive complex of caves (Figure 8.2) attest the presence of Buddhist communities and mural paintings reflecting, *inter alia,* a series of motifs related to meditation practice (Figure 8.3).

In these oases, considerable collections of manuscripts were found that have contributed to better define a chapter of the history of these communities. The texts reveal that poetry, drama and other liberal arts constitute elements

Figure 8.2 *Qyzyl caves, east side; photograph. From Grünwedel 1912:41, fig. 84a.*

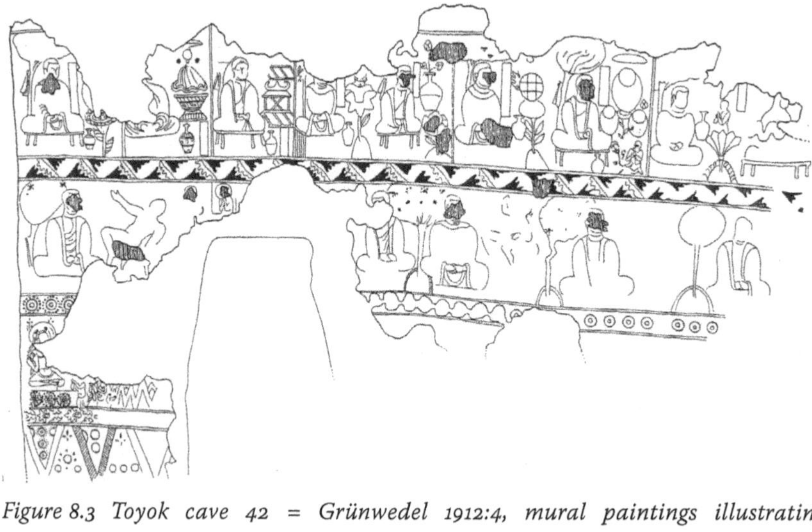

Figure 8.3 *Toyok cave 42 = Grünwedel 1912:4, mural paintings illustrating meditation/visualization's topics. Courtesy of Miyaji Akira (1995:29, fig. 13). See Yamabe 2004:402, n.10 and fig. 2 (right wall), pp. 403–4. Yamabe notes that the paintings evoke 'the context of visualization texts in general' and 'rather than that these paintings were based on any particular text, I think it is more likely that the texts and paintings individually preserve different aspects of the same large stream of oral tradition'.*

of the daily liturgy, such as the recitation of the name of the Buddhas, or of eulogies addressed to various entities, the recitation of protective formulas (*rakṣā*), and yoga practices. As said on another occasion (Scherrer-Schaub 2009:33–4), art and meditation, on their part, are phenomena of reciprocal attractions, as both practices have, to some extent, a common terminology, sharing photic and visual experiences and analogous practices. The painter indeed, like the practitioner of meditation, 'fabricates' or 'causes the existence' of the image. In the context of Buddhism in Early and Classical India, the practice of meditation, like that of painting, begins with gazing the object, and grasping its features, in due order, and as faithfully as possible, as the object must be seen 'as it is' (*yathābhūta*). The painter, on his part and in this particular context, reproduces the image with fidelity, in close resemblance to the external gazed-upon object. Possibly, the support chosen to fix one's gaze upon in the course of meditation, e.g. in the case of a particular exercise that aims at controlling the formation of the image and its features, may have collided with the other form of representation. This meditative practice can indeed also contemplate the fabrication of a disk of earth (*mattikamaṇḍala*), of dark colour that the practitioner places on a pedestal at the right distance in order to perfectly gaze it without being distracted by other colours that will be progressively controlled in the superior sphere of meditation.[17]

Preliminary practices counteracting obstacles to meditation: on the 'inordinate' desire

To return to the hilarious narratives of monks unable to master 'concupiscence' (*kāma*), we see the Buddha intervening in some of these scenes, comparing the objects of desire to a skeleton (*aṭṭikaṇkala*), a piece of rotted flesh (*maṃ sapesi*) and other unattractive objects. Gruesome scenes are frequent in monasticism and Buddhism is no exception. To counteract the excessive propensity to sensuous desire, the first recommended propaedeutic to meditation is the visualization of a corpse in a state of decomposition, an exercise known as the mental cultivation of the vision, or creation, of the horrible/unattractive (*aśubhabhāvanā*).

In an early epoch this practice, shared by ascetics in India and elsewhere, was most likely performed in burial places. With time, for various historical and socio-cultural reasons, paintings 'transposed' the real support of meditation into a virtual one, and depictions of this sort are not infrequent in Central

17 See Scherrer-Schaub 2009:5–6. In passing, it is worth mentioning the mural paintings of Qïzïl, where a painter is represented with a brush in his right hand and a pot in his left. In these regions some painters have also left their signature, if not their portrait.

Asia, particularly in the region where our micro-historical investigation is focused (see below).

Description of this practice are well known in scholastic treatises, and Asaṅga's *Yogācārabhūmiśāstra* gives the following instruction to the monk and practitioner of how to seize the image (*nimitta*):

> Go to a charnel/burial ground (*śmaśāna*) and grasp an image (*nimittam udgṛhāṇa*) from a blue [corpse] up to [the image] of bones and skeletons. If not, grasp an image from a charnel/burial ground in a painting or made of wood, stone or clay (*kāṣṭhaśmaśānakṛtād vā*). Having grasped [it] come back to the dwelling place (*śayanāsana*). Having come back, being in solitude, under a tree, or in an empty house, sit on a couch, a seat, or a cushion of grass. Having crossed the legs and having washed the feet, having put the body straight, making the mindfulness present in front, sitting, first tie the mindfulness/attention (*smṛti*) to the one-pointedness/concentration and the non-distraction of mind.
>
> (Yamabe 2009:53–4; translation slightly modified)

Incidentally, it may be noted that the detailed description of the process of the corpse's decay, that the ascetic could observe in particular places in which corpses were abandoned, besides hinting at the variety of mortuary rituals current in ancient India, equally points to expertise in physiology in the Indian tradition of medicine, and to the fact that yoga and medicine were closely related. The repulsive description of the corpse reflects a knowledge of the timing of the progressive stages of organic decomposition.

Moreover, and obsessed by casuistry as they were, the scholastic treatises assign to each variety of desire (*rāga*), manifested by this or that religious person, the corresponding counteracting agent. For instance, those who are attracted by colours, to them the Master will impose the mental cultivation of the corpse in decomposition and turning blue (*vinīlaka-vipūyaka*). To the religious person attracted by figures, the counteractive agent will be the image of the corpse devoured by animals (*vikhāditaka*, Figure 8.4), and so on. Finally, the skeleton is the ideal and generic counteractive agent for victims of all sort of passions (*sarvarāgin*). Furthermore, the cultivation of the repulsive (*aśubhabhāvanā*) must subsequently be enforced by doing refined practices, according to the preparation and rank of the ascetic (*yogācāra*). In this regard, the scholastic treatises take into account three kinds of ascetic contemplating the skeleton.

1. First, the *beginner* (*ādikarmika*). He shall expand the vision of the bones to the sea, and back again, reducing/compressing his vision. The text says,

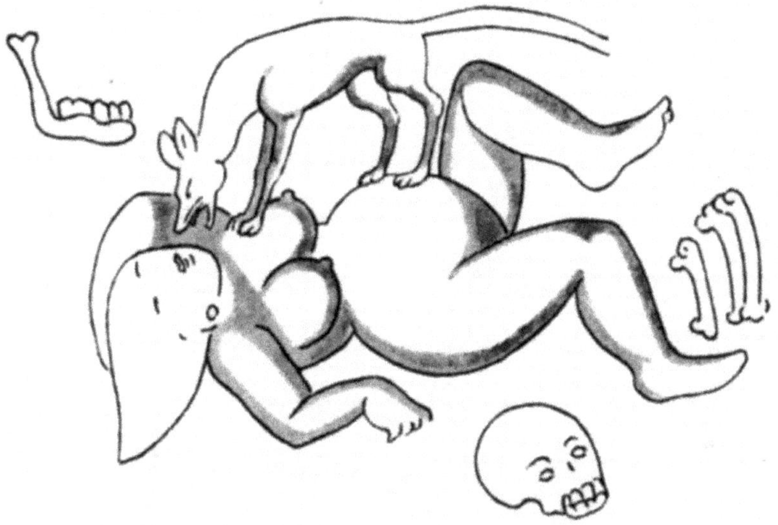

Figure 8.4 Qyzyl-Scakalhöhle n° 7. Image of a corpse devoured by animals. From Grünwedel 1912:181, Fig. 420.

> The yogin begins in fixing his mind upon a limb of his body, either the big toe, or the brow and so on; then he proceeds in purifying the bone, that is he moves apart the flesh, imagining that the flesh decomposes and falls down. He then progressively enlarges his vision and sees his entire body reduced to the skeleton. Then in order to improve the power of his vision the yogin repeats the visual experience with another person, with persons living in the monastery, the gardens, the village, the region, till when the universe surrounded by the ocean is conceived and seen filled with skeletons. At this point, he reduces his vision in order to fortify the power of vision, until when, again, he sees only his own body as a skeleton [Figure 8.5]. The mental cultivation of the repulsive (*aśubha*) is now ended, and the practitioner is called a beginner (*ādikārmika*) – according to the scholastic treatise Vasubandhu – Kośabhāṣya ad VI.9–11, 148–53.

2. The second practitioner, in reducing his vision, (starting with) the feet's bones up to half of the skull (*kapālārdham*), masters the practice.

> In order to fortify the power of a reduced vision and to make the mind even more concentrated, the practitioner disregards the feet's bones, and considers the other bones; in progressively reducing his vision, he disregards

Figure 8.5 *Qyzyl-Höhle der 'Seereise' n° 11. See Grünwedel 1912:147. A monk with, on his left, a skull, perhaps visualized by him. From Bussagli 1963 = Berlin MIK I B 8401.*

> the other bones until, in discarding from his vision half of the skull, he fixes his attention on the other half only. He is now a master (*kṛtaparijaya*); and he is in possession of the mastery of the act of attention.

3. The last practitioner is the one who, in keeping his mind fixed to the median point of the eyebrows, excels in the act of attention (*atikrāntamanaskāra*).

> While disregarding even the remaining vision of the half of the skull, he keeps his mind between the eyebrows. He is now the practitioner in whom the act of attention on the repulsive is completed.
>
> (*Kośabhāṣya* ad VI.9–11, 148–53)

In this process the yogin fixes his attention upon specific physiological points of his body, that were known to him from the ancient medical treatises.

The second propaedeutic exercise to meditation (dhyāna): the mindfulness or attention applied to respiration (ānāpānasmṛti)[18]

This practice, which is itself a cognitive act, is the counter-agent against the distraction caused by the activity of mind – reasoning, reflecting, thinking (*vitarka*) – and enforces concentration, thus granting a perfect knowledge of the meditated object.

> L'ascète, *après* s'être assuré d'une position physique parfaitement détendue, les yeux fermés, porte son regard intérieur vers la respiration. Il en observe le rythme naturel. Il observe le 'vent' expiré et le 'vent' inspiré. Il se concentre toujours davantage, en comptant les mouvements d'expiration et d'inspiration de un jusqu'à dix. Il répète ce cycle jusqu'au moment où il en possède la maîtrise parfaite. Le mémoire active (*smṛti*) veille à ce que ce compte soit régulier. Si l'ascète est distrait, intérieurement ou extérieurement, il doit reprendre le compte. La maîtrise consiste à savoir exactement ce que l'on fait sans laisser aucune place au trouble tant intérieur qu'extérieur. (...) Dans l'attention à la respiration, l'ascète doit 'suivre l'air qui

18 See *Kośabhāṣya* VI.12–13, VI.13a, 156–7: 'L'expiration-inspiration comme le corps' (*ānāpānau yataḥ kāyaḥ*)'. And, following the *Vibhāṣā*, Vasubandhu comments: 'lorsque le corps présente des vides (*śuṣirakāya*), lorsque la pensée appartient à une terre où il y a respiration (*āśvāsapraśvāsabhūmicitta*), alors il y a inspiration-expiration. Il y a inspiration à la naissance et au moment où l'on sort du quatrième *dhyāna*. Il y a expiration à la mort et au moment où l'on entre dans le quatrième *dhyāna*.'

> pénètre le corps jusqu'aux orteils et considérer les masses du corps comme des perles enfilées sur le courant d'air; suivre l'air expulsé à une distance d'une coudée, jusqu'aux vents supérieurs du cosmos.
>
> (Scherrer-Schaub 1988:138–9 and notes)

As will be shown, the perfect mastery of the circulation of the 'wind', the breath and vital force (*prāṇa*), delineates the imaginary itinerary visualized by the yogin in the Qïzïl manual that will be the focus of our inquiry in the following section. To better understand the process, it may be useful to refer to the pneumatic physiology attested in Indian ancient medical treatises. The essential role played by the 'internal wind' or the breath in the body and the correlative function of the 'external wind' that circulates in the cosmos are at the core of the pneumatic theory. As has been noticed, modern authors have largely neglected the Indian medical tradition, and consequently, some of their interpretations are biased.[19] What is of interest for us here, is the importance in the Qïzïl manual of the vital points from where the breath is exhaled, and circulates in various cosmic spheres and functions as the support of the object of cognition (*jñeya*) visualized by the yogin, before finally disappears again into the vital centre.

Didactics, allegory, the imaginary and ways of attaining the goal: the yoga treatise from Qïzïl

Albert von Le Coq, who directed the third German 'Turfan' expedition, in a letter addressed to the Berliner Museum für Völkerkunde dated 8 April 1906, relates the circumstances of the finding of the birch-bark manuscript (herewith MS)[20] that will be the focus here. Le Coq relates that Theodor Bartus, a member of the expedition, found what seemed to be a monastic library, at the Ming-öi of Qïzïl, near Kučā.[21] Fragments of the same text were eventually discovered in the surrounding oases of the Taklamakan desert, present day Xinjiang (China), namely in Šorčuq, and in Duldur-Aqur, a large monastery near Qumtura, by the French scholar Paul Pelliot. Despite the fact that the Qïzïl manuscript is fragmentary, the text, possibly originating from Kashmir (see Seyfort Ruegg 1967), contributed the confirmation of the existence of spiritual practices and meditational techniques that were imparted by masters to the monks and yoga practitioners, who, in consequence of their particular

19 See the still valuable work of Filliozat 1975 and Roșu 1978.

20 The text was published by Dieter Schlingloff (1964). For its history, see pp. 9–25; on the passage discussed here, pp. 9–10.

21 The location of the library is a debated question, see the illuminating article by Ching (2015).

mental dispositions and/or the cultural environment, were more receptive to yoga practice than to the argumentative method (*yukti*) applied to the exegesis and interpretation of the scripture (*āgama*).

After Dieter Schlingloff's ground-breaking work, the text has been referred to as the '*Yoga-Lehrbuch*' or 'manual on *yoga* practice', henceforth YL. The doctrines and techniques that appear in the text, and in particular the use of allegory, draw on a common Indian, if not Indic, background, whose historical complexity is worth exploring, though a full treatment far exceeds the present scope. Dieter Schlingloff and other scholars have noticed the unusual presence in the YL of metaphors and symbols, some of which were already known in early Buddhist texts, while others are echoed in Tantric literature. But there are also other aspects worthy of note.

Indeed, the text in its use of a 'normative imaginary' appears to be a kind of manual prescribing a form of substitution of evocative images that intervene to illustrate and punctuate, if not 'actualize', specific stages of meditative process and spiritual practice. The text, in this case, speaks of 'signs' (*nimitta*) that illustrate abstract or conceptual entities. For instance, the frequent and progressive staging of a woman in various roles is the 'sign' or 'image' of a series of feminine concepts central to the spiritual practice. It is equally the sublimation of the 'feminine' into its most concentrated form which the text calls a 'master-image' or 'embodiment' (*adhipatirūpa*). These images emblematically/symbolically represent particular constitutive qualities and lead the practitioner along a path towards the attainment of the intended final goal (and possibly even more, see below).

Metaphors, such as the images of a city, a sword and a bowl filled with oil, are known from early Indian Buddhist texts (*sūtra/sutta*), where they represent specific doctrinal data. Such metaphors function didactically in the construction of a structured memory. In the case of the YL, the use of metaphoric images, at once aesthetic, moral and conceptual, reveals a process structurally analogous to mnemonic techniques known elsewhere. The metaphors function as instruments to punctuate the meditative process, and the correlative displayed mental-and-visual experience. In the Qïzïl manual the meditative process concentrates upon a series of practices whose pattern is common to other yoga treatises, even if the categories appear in a different order. These practices whose role, as described, is to counteract specific obstacles to meditation and insight, and help with attainment of the final goal, are marked by the manifestation of particular signs (*nimitta*) connected with specific points of the practitioner's 'substrate' or corporeal body, to which the mental image is tied: for instance, the nostril (*nābhi*) or the median point between the eyebrows (*bhrūmadhya*). The 'signs' equally function as an opening to a series of 'visions' or perceptual experiences, in which the practitioner 'breaks' the frame sequence, and sees himself in the 'visualized'/'visited' scene, receiving a teaching from the Buddha, or being admonished or even implored by other actors that reside in the specific cosmic sphere he's 'visiting'.

Signs, metaphors, images: painting the cosmo-didactical path

Despite the fragmentary condition of the Qïzïl manual, it is nonetheless possible to follow some of the principles underlying the singular stages of the meditative process, such as the images connecting the inner to the outer world. For instance, and while explaining the cultivation of the attention focused upon the in-and-out-breathing (*ānāpānasmṛtibhāvanā*) of the present time, our text says (118R3) that when [the practitioner] breathes-in and breathes-out, at that moment, [he sees] a young child as the sign of the mental activity (*citta*). In [seizing the] in-breathing [he sees] the mental activity in the form of a young child sinking down in the internal sea, while in out-breathing [he sees] the little child withdrawing from the external sea (127R2). In scholastic treatises, the process of breathing and the movement of breath that connects the 'inside' of the practitioner to the 'external' world is accompanied by the image of a string of pearls (*muktāhāra*)[22] that leads the breath outside the body of the practitioner without, however, ever being disconnected or separated from his corporeal support.

Attempting to envision the entire fresco painted by the mind of the practitioner would lead us too far, so we focus here upon the images appearing in the Qïzïl manual that represent an alternative, if not opposed view, of the 'feminine' when contrasted with the 'feminine' that haunted the ascetics meditating in secluded places, who were desperately trying to get rid of desire (*kāma*). In the course of his meditative path, which is extremely complex, the yogin practises four 'mental cum moral qualities' that constitute his spiritual commitment towards the entire world, including the beings in distress moving in the ocean of *saṃsāra* (Figure 8.6), justly termed '*apramāṇa*' or 'immeasurable', as 'they apply to an immeasurable number of beings, and produce an immeasurable number of good *karmic* effects'. These 'qualities', the object of various stages of the meditative process, are benevolence (*maitrī*), joy (*muditā*), compassion (*karuṇā*) and equanimity (*upekṣā*), and are, from the grammatical point of view, feminine nouns. They are counteractive agents against all attitudes that cause harm to other beings (see Seyfort Ruegg 1967:157–8).

---

22 Puns and equivoques are frequent in Indian literature. Possibly here the term *muktāhāra* or 'string of pearls' could also be interpreted as *mukta-āhāra*, meaning that which is 'bringing near to liberation'.

Figure 8.6 Qyzyl, Cave of the Seafarers, wall painting, Berlin MIK III 8398. From Bussagli 1963. Beings in the sea of saṃsāra?

In meditating upon benevolence, the Qïzïl manual stresses the commitment taken by the yogin to alleviate the grief that afflicts all beings not yet liberated, and towards whom the yogin shall be 'like a mother' (*mātṛbhūta*). The text, while exhibiting a fantastic imaginary, says that, at this very moment, the heart's door (*hṛdayadvāra*, 143R6) of the yogin opens, and inside a sea of milk (*kṣırasamudra*) springs up. Then the yogin opens all the 'doors' of the body's channels, from which milk pours out, submerging the suffering beings.

The image of the mother appears in one of the oldest texts,[23] in which the Buddha praises the mental attitude of benevolence as being 'like a mother protecting her only son'. The emphasis put on the thought directed upon the aspiration (to realize) the Good of all sentient beings. (*sarvasatvāhitādhyāśayapravṛttaṃ cittam*, 145R2, 145V6)[24] definitively places the Qïzïl manual among those texts combining different practices that the scholastic classifications tend to attribute separately to the two main streams

23 The *Mettasutta* of the Sutta Nipāta.

24 Something that is close to ideas that are for instance present in *mahāyānasūtras*, such as *Kāśyapaparivarta* §§ 153–154, a passage which is kept in a fragmentary manuscript from Turfan published by Silk (2010: 900, 906–7).

of Indian Buddhism, or to specific schools, while the unavoidable changes introduced by the geographic and diachronic dimensions have smoothed away some of their divergent conceptions (see Schlingloff 2006:54–6; Seyfort Ruegg 1967:161–2). The Qïzïl manual, like several *mahāyānasūtra*s and some other texts, stages the Buddha, as a Master (*śāstṛ*), following the practitioner along his path and varying his teaching in accordance with the personal composition of the yogin. The Buddha appears in the visualized scenes, in which the practitioner sees himself and also various kinds of buildings laid out as a string of pearls; then Bhagavat ties a string of cloth to the yogin's head, confirming that they have correctly and successfully accomplished that specific practice (e.g., 128V3). It is as if, with this gesture, Bhagavat 'activates' the 'connection' between the sphere of the practitioner and the cosmic sphere 'visualized/visited' by the yogin, and connects the 'inner' to the 'outer' space, where the vital force and the wind circulate.[25]

Later on, the yogin visualizes the flow of milk coming out from the region situated deeply inside the median point between the eyebrows (*bhrūmadhyādhar nimnapradeśāt*), and this, after having split the disk (*maṇḍala*) of earth, appeases the griefs of all sentient beings that have fallen into bad destinies.[26] Splitting the disk of wind, the flowing milk returns, enters the nostril, and comes up again from the summit of the head to the Akaniṣṭha;[27] again, the milk's flow returns and disappears into the summit of his head. After other mirabilia, the yogin sees a pond of milk in his heart, where a sinking star (*nakṣatra,* 147V2)[28] is the master-image or the embodiment (*adhipatirūpa*) of the commitment taken by the yogin, to help the beings in distress. Then a rainbow-coloured woman appears and takes ambrosia from a pure bowl, and sprinkles it in the ten directions of the space, allying/uniting/embracing (*saṃyojayati*) the beings into the highest happiness.

The exuberance of the YL's imagery evokes the skills of Indian storytellers and moral fabulists. The finding, in various oases of the Taklamakan desert,

25 This seems to allude to ritual practice and, specifically, to the 'connection' between the body of the practitioner and the cosmic spheres, recalling analogous ideas appearing in the Upaniṣads, cf. Olivelle 1996:lii–lii, and Gonda 1965: 1–29; Smith 1989, cited therein.

26 The *apāyagati*, better known in scholastic treatises as *akuśalagati*, are inauspicious or evil destinies that preclude access to Buddhahood. The fact that our text clearly shows that the practitioner extends his commitment to help the suffering beings who have fallen into bad destinies is the mark of a pluralistic view.

27 The highest sphere of the 'material' world, residence of the homonymic class of deities.

28 Or a constellation that the practitioner situates on specific regions of the body, here his heart, seat of the mind.

of manuscripts of dramas, apologues, and other literary compositions, suggest that religious plays were part of the life of these communities, like music and dance, which are very well represented on mural paintings of the region. The practice of the yogins may well have influenced, if not inspired, some of the painting in the Qïzïl caves and in other oases. Their literary imagery most likely permeated the minds of the practitioners; conversely, the cosmopolitan milieu of these regions may also have contributed to the colour of some of the scenes staged in the text.

To return to the feminine qualities that the yogin exercises in his cosmo-didactic spiritual journey, it is worthwhile concluding with a scene staging the 'border line' separating the 'hearer' (*śrāvaka*s) who aspires to *nirvāṇa*,[29] from the bodhisattva who remains in the world to help the sentient beings and who has received the announcement made by the Buddha that in the future he will, in his turn, reach enlightenment (*bodhi*), and act as the steersman of the world (*jagatkarṇadhāra* YL 150R2), guiding the beings to cross the ocean of suffering.

The citadel of extinction (nirvāṇanagara) and the imperious commitment toward the sentient beings still moving around the wheel of existence

The process of meditating upon the 'immeasurable feminine qualities' culminates with 'equanimity', which, the Qïzïl manual notes, 'should have nothing whatsoever to do with heartless indifference' ('*maitrānusāreṇo upekṣā saṃtiṣṭhate, na nairghṛṇyadoṣāt*', 161V5). The cultivation of equanimity ends with a scene in which the practitioner visualizes the Buddha's complete extinction (*parinirvāṇa*) and at a certain moment – as in the preceding meditative visions – he sees himself into the scene. At first, while facing the scene, the yogin sees the 'city of extinction' (*nirvāṇapura*), where one of the numerous Bhagavats present sounds the gong to inform the disciples (*śrāvaka*) who are approaching that for them it is now time to enter the city, and this sound fills all the world's regions. Then, when the Bhagavat followers are about to enter the city of *nirvāṇa*, the doorkeeper announces 'he who enters the city, will never come out again!', as they will enter final extinction in the manner of a lamp being stopped by a multitude of clouds made of the subtle substance circulating in the space.

It is at this moment that the master signs of the eighteen qualities exclusively belonging to a Buddha appear in the body of the yogin, each group of them indicated by a specific sign (*nimitta*): the ten forces (*bala*)

29 That is the final extinction of the composite body-mind entity, the final goal of the Arhats having cut all links binding them to the world of *saṃsāra*.

are indicated by the ten images/statues (*pratimā*) of Buddhas riding on ten elephants; the four Buddha's confidences (*vaiśāradya*) indicated by the sign of four Buddha's statues, seated on the lion throne; the three mindfulness (*smṛti*) by three men holding bowls filled with oil; and finally, the sign of the great compassion (*mahākaruṇā*) appears in the heart of the yogin in the guise of a woman having the colour of space/white, shining like gold, and dressed in blue.

While other allegoric visions, which would have pleased the artists of the *Apocalypse* of Angers,[30] fill the scene, the yogin visualizes the Buddha's disciples (*śrāvakas*) entering complete extinction (*parinirvāṇa*); but at that moment the practitioner who was following them is stopped by the doorkeeper, who prevents him entering the city. Then, the practitioner visualizes the ocean of *saṃsāra* (Figure 8.6), where beings in distress implore him:

> Save us, you the Compassionate One! It is not proper for you to enter the city of complete extinction!

Then the woman who is the embodiment of Great Compassion appears in the heart of the yogin, and while holding the hands of the practitioner, says:

> Where would you go, abandoning the beings in distress?

At that moment equanimity withdraws and compassion descends into his heart, and the practitioner holds the entire ocean of the suffering beings in his arms. At the end of the process the yogin becomes 'radiant with the bodily marks of a Great Being' (*mahāpuruṣa).* This is what other texts found in the vicinity also teach, and this 'bodily cum spiritual transformations' was also taught in early Indian Buddhist treatises.

While the imaginary that the Qïzïl manual displays may lead the reader back to a series of canonical texts, there is no doubt that this astonishing text has been composed in a polymorphic narrative, literary and religious *milieu,* most likely, as noted, in Kashmir.

Moreover, the attributes and functions assumed by the woman that appears to the yogin in the meditative cum visionary process recall other

30 The tapestry illustrating St. John's Apocalypse was manufactured in 1373 and is now in the Château d'Angers. Despite the topic of the Apocalypse, its purpose and context are different, if not diametrically opposed to the YL's conspectus, though some of the scenes make use of structural items that evoke singular elements of the YL's imagery, as for instance in the scene of the falling down of the '*étoile nommée absinthe*'. See Delwasse n.d.:26.

themes that are present in polymorphic if not pluralistic treatises. And, as already mentioned: the woman of the Qïzïl manual, strangely, and above all intriguingly, recalls the figure of the Great Bodhisattva Avalokiteśvara in his feminine transmutation, but even more the figure of his *parèdre*, the goddess Tārā, the star, the saviour, the compassionate who, possibly, is painted on the ceiling of 'Höhle 3' at Murtuq.[31]

That, however, as the poet says, is another story.

References

Boulnois, O. 2008. *Au-delà de l'image: Une archéologie du visuel au Moyen Âge Ve-XVIe siècle.* Paris: Éditions du Seuil.

Brach, J.-P. 2022. 'In between body and soul: the 'Subtle body' as a spiritual technique in nineteenth century occultism'. In this volume.

Brown, P. 2016. *Le Prix du salut: Les Chrétiens, l'argent et l'au-delà en Occident (IIIe-VIIe siècle)*, trans. C.J. Goddard. Paris: Belin.

Bussagli, M. 1963. *La Peinture de l'Asie centrale de l'Afghanistan au Sinkiang.* Genève: Skira.

Ching, C.-J. 2015. 'Rethinking "MQR": on a location where texts were found in the Kizil Grottoes', *Journal of the International Association of Buddhist Studies* 38:271–93.

Delwasse, L. n.d. *La Tenture de l'Apocalypse d'Angers.* N.p.: Éditions du Patrimoine, Centre des monuments nationaux.

Demiéville, P. 1954. 'La Yogācārabhūmi de Saṅgharakṣa', *Bulletin de l'École Française d'Extrême-Orient* 44 (2):339–436.

Filliozat, J. 1975. *La Doctrine classique de la médecine indienne: Ses origines et ses parallèles.* Paris: EFEO.

Gonda, J. 1965. 'Bandhu in the Brāhmaṇas', *Adyar Library Bulletin* 29:1–29.

Grünwedel, A. 1912. *Altbuddhistische Kultstätten in Chinesisch-Turkistan.* Berlin: Druck und Verlag von Georg Reimer.

Kośabhāṣya – De la Vallée Poussin, L. 1971. *L'Abhidharmakośa de Vasubandhu.* Bruxelles: Institut belge des Hautes Études chinoises.

Miyaji A. 1995. 'Turufan, Toyoku sekkutsu no zenkankutsu hekiga ni tsuite: Jōdozu Jōdo kansōzu, fujō kansōzu. Part I', *Bukkyō geijutsu* 221:15–41.

Olivelle, P. 1996. *Upaniṣads.* Oxford: Oxford University Press.

Patañjali's *Yogasūtra* – Filliozat, P.-S. 2005. *Le Yogabhāṣya de Vyāsa sur le Yogasūtra de Patañjali.* Paris: Āgamāt.

Roşu, A. 1978. *Les Conceptions psychologiques dans les textes médicaux indiens.* Paris: Collège de France.

31 See Grünwedel 1912:306, commenting on the image reproduced here.

Scherrer-Schaub, C. 1988. 'La Mémoire dans le bouddhisme indien'. In P. Borgeaud (ed.), *La Mémoire des religions*, pp. 135–44. Geneva: Labor & Fides.

— — — 2009. 'Scribes and painters on the road: inquiry into image and text in Indian Buddhism and its transmission to Central Asia and Tibet.' In A. Pande (ed.), *The Art of Central Asia and the Indian Subcontinent in Cross-cultural Perspective*, pp. 29–40. New Delhi: National Museum Institute.

Schlingloff, D. 1964. *Ein Buddhistisches Yogalehrbuch*. Berlin: Akademie Verlag.

— — — 2006. *Ein Buddhistisches Yogalehrbuch: Unveränderten Nachdruck der Ausgabe von 1964 unter Beigabe aller seither bekannt geworden Fragmente* (eds J.-U. Hartmann und H.-J. Röllicke). Düsseldorf: EKŌ-Hauses der Japanischen Kultur.

— — — 2015. *Die Übermenschlichen Phänomene: Visuelle Meditation und Wundererscheinungen in buddhistischer Literatur und Kunst. Ein religionsgeschichtlicher Versuch*. Düsseldorf: EKŌ-Hauses der Japanischen Kultur.

Schopen, G. 2004 [2000]. 'Art, beauty, and the business of running a Buddhist monastery in early Northwest India.' In his *Buddhist Monks and Business Matters. Still More Papers on Monastic Buddhism in India*, pp. 19–44. Honolulu: University of Hawai'i Press.

Seyfort Ruegg, D. 1967. 'On a yoga treatise in Sanskrit from Qïzïl,' *Journal of the American Oriental Society* 87(2):157–65.

Silk, J. 2010. 'Test sailing the ship of the teachings: hesitant notes on *Kāśyapaparivarta* §§ 153–154.' In E. Franco and M. Zin (eds), *From Turfan to Ajanta: Festschrift für Dieter Schlingloff on the Occasion of his Eightieth Birthday*, vol II, pp. 897–924. Bhairahawa: Lumbini International Research Institute.

Smith, B.K. 1989. *Reflections on Resemblance, Ritual, and Religion*. New York: Oxford University Press.

Sponberg, A. 1986. 'Meditation in Fa-hsien Buddhism.' In P.N. Gregory (ed.), *Traditions of Meditation in Chinese Buddhism*, pp. 15–43. Honolulu: University of Hawaï Press.

Wujastyk, D. 2018. 'Some problematic yoga sūtras and their Buddhist background.' In K. Baier, P. Maas and K. Preisendanz (eds), *Yoga in Transformation: Historical and Contemporary Perspectives on a Global Phenomenon*, pp. 23–47. Göttingen: V&R unipress.

Yamabe, N. 2004. 'An examination of the mural paintings of Visualizing Monks in Toyok Cave 42: in conjunction with the origin of some Chinese texts on meditation.' In D.Durkin-Meisterernst, S.-C. Raschmann and J. Wilkins (eds), *Turfan Revisited: The First century of Research into the Arts and Cultures of the Silk Road*, pp. 401–7. Berlin: Reimer.

— — — 2009. 'The paths of Śrāvakas and Bodhisattvas in meditatives practices,' *Acta Asiatica: Bulletin of the Institute of Eastern Culture* 96:47–75.
YL. See Schlingloff 1964.

9

In between body and soul

The 'subtle body' as a spiritual technique in nineteenth-century occultism

Jean-Pierre Brach

The present chapter is concerned with the renewal, so to speak, of a very specific theme in Western occult spirituality during the second half of the nineteenth century. This particular theme – the astral body and its projection – is situated at the crossroads of animal magnetism, sexual and ritual magic and crystal-gazing, at a crucial moment of their historical evolution, when they are confronted with the spread of Spiritualism, in its strict understanding as 'table-turning' and as 'communication with the spirits of the departed' (Cuchet 2012; Oppenheim 1985).

The 'new' practice of mediumship, and its implications for individual as well as for collective religiosity, is largely responsible for some of the transformations undergone by some fringe aspects of (mostly) non-denominational Western spirituality, equally concerned with contacting spirits and obtaining messages from the celestial hierarchies. In certain circles, this pursuit took a distinct turn towards magic and occultism – particularly from the 1860's onward – as both of these were perceived as a more 'active' and responsible attitude to the process of self-realization than a merely 'passive' mediumship. To the already existing vocabulary of magnetism, 'fluid(s)', electricity, vital force, cosmic fire etc., is added a 'new' syncretic understanding of the nature of the cosmos, on the one hand, and of the inner self on the other hand, as participating in one and the same substance, perceived in terms of 'energies', 'vibrations' and immaterial – 'subtle' – occult forces (Bramble 2013, 2015). This tendency is rapidly reinforced by the accretion of vulgarized 'Egyptian' (*Kha*) and Hindu/Buddhistic terms and notions (such as *prana*, *tattvas* etc.) widespread in the occult/spiritualistic literature of the period (Butler 2011:86–98; Djurdjevic 2014:1–33).

For instance, H.S. Olcott (1832–1907), one of the founders of the Theosophical Society, wrote that 'magnetism is the key to Indian philosophy' (Bramble 2013:200) and equates *prana* with 'ether' or with the so-called 'astral light', a term borrowed from Eliphas Lévi (1810–75).

In the writings of P.B. Randolph (1825–75) and others, a growing importance is also given to the intermingling of psychic and bodily fluids, mainly the sexual ones, in the production of dissociated states of consciousness and occult phenomena, also as supports of magical action and communication with spirits (Deveney 1997a:295–308). In other words, and certainly in reaction to the mostly bookish approach favored by many armchair spiritualists of the high Victorian era, Western occultism of the second half of the nineteenth century abetted mostly practical goals, and insisted on the acquisition of experiential, inner knowledge of the spiritual nature of man: one of the first public statements (1876) from the founders of the new Theosophical Society actually said: 'we seek to obtain the knowledge of the nature and of the attributes of the supreme power and of the most elevated spirits by means of physical procedures'; and 'White magic is Theosophy – a science founded upon a practical and experimental knowledge of pure spiritual beings and of the powers of one's own immortal soul' (Deveney 1997b:60).

An ancient tradition

Whether we speak of the 'astral body', 'subtle body' or 'double' etc., none of these designations seem satisfactory, at least from an academic perspective (Cox 2022; Samuel and Johnston 2013:1–9). All we know, and this is vague enough, is that, using this terminology, we are supposedly dealing with the imprecise and easily deluding category of 'spirits', 'vapours' or 'fumes', in other words with the *corpora subtilia* which supposedly border on the material, visible and tangible, as well as on the volatile, ethereal, immaterial aspects of reality (Göttler and Neuber 2007:i–xxvii). The idea of a 'subtle' order of reality (i.e. less 'gross' than the material or physical level), appears to have come, at least in part, from the original necessity of translating some Hindu notions into Western categories. Yet the traditional Western vocabulary – inherited from classical Antiquity and, naturally, consisting in designations of the emic kind – of the *corpora subtilia* or of the *vehiculum aethereum* is convenient as an Early Modern Western characterization of the 'subtle body'. As pointed out long ago by D.P. Walker (1958:121), such notions actually conflate data and doctrines pertaining to theology, natural philosophy and medicine, which all acknowledge 'corporeal spirits' (such as those at work in perceptions) supposedly akin to the substance of the soul, yet assigned to certain bodily functions – it being understood that the more immaterial or incorporeal something appears, the more 'spiritual' in nature it is usually made out to be (Plato *Phaedrus* 247b; *Timaios* 41e).

According to these ancient sources, the idea we are mainly concerned with is that of a fundamental ontological mediation between body and soul. There are basically four main aspects to this mediation: an anthropological one – stressing the necessity of a hierarchical link between the parts and functions of the soul that appear linked to the body, and those which seem independent from it; an eschatological one – after the disappearance of the terrestrial body, there may be an immaterial, yet corporeal, soul capable of surviving death; a psychological and cognitive one – a 'vehicle' of the soul, responsible for the imaginative function (which acts as intermediary between reason and the senses, as the summit of the irrational part of the soul, though eventually submitted to reason as such) but which needs gradual purification so as to enable man to receive divine visions; a demonological one – in which a pneumatic or aereal wrapping serves as body to the demons.

To these four aspects, Aristotle adds the notion of a body which is essentially superior to the corporeal elements, inasmuch as it is made of a substance assimilated to the celestial *pneuma*, which serves in turn as the *substratum* for the activities of the human soul (Aristotle De gen. an. 736b, 37–8).

In Plato's *Timaios* (31c), the vehicle is of an astral nature and linked to the soul before it actually descends into a body. In direct connection with this, for our purpose, we must actually take into account a fifth, later and central, aspect of it: the theurgic one, given the fact that the rites of theurgy supposedly anticipate in this life the *post mortem* ascension of the soul and of its vehicle to their celestial origin, by purifying them, and also construe the vehicle itself as an important instrument of spiritual achievement (Shaw 1995:70–80).

Finally, Proclus asserts the existence of different vehicles for the rational and the irrational parts of the soul, the first one immortal (and an instrument for the apprehension of divine realities), the second and pneumatic one, mortal (Proclus *Elements of Theology*; Siorvanes 1996:131–2).

The main theme resulting from these considerations is thus the necessity to mediate between the physical and intelligible levels of reality, on both the ontological and the cognitive levels.

Besides these glimpses and very general tenets borrowed from the Greek authors, modern occultists also gather information about the 'astral body' from such Renaissance thinkers as Marsilio Ficino (1433–99) and H.-C. Agrippa (1485–1535). According to Ficino, the intermediary *spiritus* either clings to the higher, intellective part of the soul (*mens*) or to the lower, inferior part of it. If separated from the physical body, the intellectual soul is rendered more powerful and is therefore able to wander freely about the world and to govern other bodies than its own (Ficino 2001–6:XIII, 4).

According to Agrippa, a close follower of Ficino in many respects, it is by the agency of the 'ethereal body' – which is made of the same astral substance as the heavens (the *corpusculum ethereum,* according to Ficino (ibid.:XVIII, 4) – that the immortal soul is enclosed in the material body (Agrippa 1992:36–7). After the occurrence of physical death, individual affects and desires persist in the soul (ibid.:41); also, the possibility exists for the soul to influence other people's thoughts and desires (ibid.:43). As explicitly recognized by several occultists, mostly from their reading of Agrippa, the power of the mind is reputed to be everything in ritual magic: ritual gestures, words, symbols and paraphernalia are only accessories, inasmuch as they simply help the mind to concentrate on its intended goal and strengthen the will of the operator.

Immaterial bodies

Although it has enjoyed an enduring favour in the cultural history of the West, the general theme of the 'subtle body' is not – as believed by some – a permeating and widespread feature of nineteenth-century occultism in general. It is in fact picked up anew by precisely those writers that mainstream Spiritualists, from 1860 onward, criticized for attempting to derail Spiritualism towards magic and occult practices, and, in so doing, relinquishing, in their view, the pursuit of a common good for selfish goals and illusory self-accomplishment. As a matter of fact, one of these writers, E. Hardinge Britten (1823–99), went as far as characterizing (*c.*1875) the 'liberation of the double' as the supreme achievement of magic, presented as the 'new spiritualism' (Deveney 1997b:5–17). She was also one of the first (with H.S. Olcott) to publicly interpret the phenomena of the seance room not as the exclusive result of disembodied spirit agency, but as caused by living human beings acting by and through their astral bodies.[1] This gave rise, a little while later, to the more ambitious theory of the 'hidden hand', which attributed even the birth of the spiritualist movement and its rise to the immaterial action of 'higher adepts', who seldom ever manifested themselves in the flesh (Chanel, Deveney and Godwin 2000:63–8).

Moreover, from this same perspective, the 'double' of a living person may be dominated and controlled by another entity, whether a living man or woman or a disembodied spirit of an order either superior or inferior to that of mankind (we shall come back to this point). Accordingly, astral projection may be described according to a fourfold division (Deveney 1997b:2).:

1 For a further discussion of these points and others, see Deveney 1997a:3–4; Thompson 2019.

- as happening involuntarily and in a haphazard way (as in sleep, stress, trauma or dream);
- as caused by the action of another, exterior, person;
- as the result of a deliberate and conscious process (as a consequence of which it may even become visible);
- as the inhabitation of the 'double' in another person's body.

Now, an important factor to be reckoned with is that there exists a fundamental link between the occult constitution of man and the practice of astral projection (Blavatsky 1888–9:217–26).

Such a link is nowhere more obvious than in the early teachings of the Theosophical Society (*c.*1875–82), where liberation of the double is presented as a basic component of the quest for individual immortality (supposedly 'a judaeo-egyptian kabbalistic doctrine' – Chajes 2016:33–43; Deveney 1997b:45, 2016:97–8), in other words to 'become a god', a spiritual achievement that is, in principle, open to all, yet which must be conquered and cannot in any way be taken for granted.

According to H.P. Blavatsky (as early as 1877) the universal and supreme law of harmony prescribes that in this earthly life (and exclusively during this life) the human soul – conjoined, therefore, to its body – must be (re)united with its ultimate origin, the divine sun or spirit, in order to develop a 'body of light' (or individualized monad) capable of surviving death and of retaining its individual consciousness (Blavatsky 1877: I, 315–18; Deveney 2016:98).

In and of themselves, both the human body and soul are perceived as mortal, and condemned to dissolution when physical death occurs. Fortunately enough, there exists in man, overhanging this dual element, a ray of the universal and eternal spirit, and man must therefore become a threefold entity, in which the soul, considered as the 'vital astral body', if conjoined to and illuminated by the divine spirit, may become an immortal entity, a 'god'. After physical death, this god-like entity – still retaining consciousness of its individuality – may freely progress through the hierarchy of spiritual spheres until it reaches nirvana and unites with the universal sun or divine spirit (Deveney 2016:102; Irwin 2017:167–83).

In line with such views, astral projection becomes an essential operation, as it is construed as an indication of the fact that the fusion of the individual monad with the divine spirit has in fact started, and that conscious control over the process in question is currently being obtained.

The goal of practical occultism is, thus, to enable one to enter nirvana (which is not at all understood as implying annihilation in this context) consciously, that is as an individual monad conscious of itself, and not solely as the spiritual but impersonal higher part (spirit) of man.

Following these indications, to be 'reborn' is actually to be able to live in one's astral body or 'body of light', that is to be able to travel the ethereal worlds, free of the material body, while retaining a clear consciousness of one's own individuality, as well as the memory of what has been perceived or learned during those trips.

Spiritual identity

However, in the early 1880s Blavatsky started to depict individual consciousness as the false personality in man, logically destined to disintegration and oblivion after death. A while later in her *Secret Doctrine* (1888: I, 334), thanks to a significant swerve in her numerical theories about man's inner constitution (Fitger 2019), we learn that among the constituent parts of man only *atma*, *buddhi* and the upper portion of *manas* (which are not individualized, anyway, and consequently have no bearing whatsoever on individual consciousness) actually survive death, while the lower *manas* (and the four remaining inferior parts) goes to the *devachan*, where, in an unconscious state, it supposedly awaits its next reincarnation on earth. In such a context, two different ways are being pointed to in order to achieve this 'personal' kind of immortality: either to achieve the process while, hopefully, benefiting from a long earthly existence in one's own physical body; or to be able to transfer one's individuality – whilst actually preserving it – into another person's body (Crow 2012; Deveney 2016:103, 106).

Getting practical

Unfortunately, there are no detailed or organized descriptions in the relevant literature of the techniques involved, apart from some rather vague indications about the necessity of periods of fasting, of sexual continence or abstinence, of a vegetarian diet and of refraining from tobacco and alcohol, as well as of exercising control over material thoughts and desires – general rules which were strongly recommended to all active members during the first years of existence of the Theosophical Society, but which after 1885 stopped being implemented relatively rapidly, or fell into disuse (Deveney 2016:103–4).

To these recommendations one may add, in a restricted number of cases, the use of drugs (hashish, opium, cannabis and others) in order to bring about altered states of consciousness. As with the practitioners of animal magnetism[2]

2 A classic, yet particularly strong emphasis on the importance of will-power in the practice of animal magnetism is found in Baron Jules-Denis Dupotet's (1796–1881) treatise *La Magie dévoilée* (1852, privately printed in Paris), a very influential text well-known to P.B. Randolph, Eliphas Lévi and H.P. Blavatsky, among others (and

and of magic,[3] the insistence is very much on developing (and making use of) will-power, and there are hints at ways of concentrating the will successively on different *chakras*, possibly combined with the presence of magnetic sleep and breathing exercises (Deveney 1997b:51; Leland 2016:93–140).

Among members of a contemporary and rival occult order (the 'Hermetic Brotherhood of Luxor'), the practice of sexual magic (essentially inherited from Randolph's teachings) was seen as a privileged instrument for communication with the celestial hierarchies, as well as with the order's secret chiefs or 'Instructors'. Developing 'clairvoyance' and the higher type of spiritual intuition, mainly through the practice of contacting higher entities via the magic mirror, was considered a preliminary achievement to astral projection, and to the pursuit of a consciously awake trance state, allowing the seer not just contemplation of, but complete assimilation to (and even identification with) the celestial entities supposedly perceived in the crystal (Chanel, Deveney and Godwin 2000:74–82; Deveney 1997b:9, 54–5).

'Je' est un autre

A quite peculiar aspect of 'astral projection' (which we have already mentioned in passing) is what Randolph and E. Hardinge Britten, among others, called the practice of 'blending': 'the taking over of a living subject's body and mind (or of a recent corpse) by a living adept, or by some – disembodied or never embodied – entity from the celestial hierarchies' (Deveney 1997a:103–19, also 1997b:10, 16–7).

This means that a recognized potentiality of astral travel can be to temporarily occupy the vacant body of someone else – that is, after its soul has been momentarily pushed aside or substituted by that of the adept – with a spirit, which may either be that of the adept himself or of someone else, but in the latter case one attracted and dominated by the magician's magnetic power. Such practices, also known as 'life transfer', have to do, on the one hand, with the second way – alluded to above – of acquiring immortality

later translated into English). On a particular blend of animal magnetism, mirror magic and drug use, see Hanegraaff 2017.

3 A similar insistence on will-power is found in the 'introduction' to E. Lévi's famous magical work *Dogme et rituel de la haute magie* (1854–6); English translation by Arthur E. Waite (1857–1942) as *Transcendental Magic, its Doctrine and Ritual* (1896) – see Brach 2021. Such a theme, also present for instance in E. Hardinge Britten's productions, became a byword of contemporary, and later magical, occultism, up to and even beyond Aleister Crowley himself (1875–1947). The main *topos* behind this continued emphasis was, originally, to extoll the magician (supposedly active, powerful and knowledgeable) at the expense of the spiritualist medium (belittled for being passive and ignorant).

and, on the other hand, with the manner in which the masters or instructors may impart knowledge and teach the less ordinary disciples (as in the cases of both Blavatsky and Randolph). The 'life transfer' process is considered, by Blavatsky and the Theosophists, as the highest accomplishment of theurgy, and was actually called the 'awful seventh rite, known solely to the "Grand Hierophant" who alone knows how to transfer his own vital energy and astral soul into the adept he has chosen for his successor (*tulku*)' (Blavatsky 1877:II, 564–5, *tulku* pointing of course rather plainly to Tibetan religious culture; see also Deveney 1997b:10, 2016:103). We may note immediately that, as uncanny as it may seem, such a 'science of entering another body' (along with its varied purposes) nevertheless has historically documented yogic and Tibetan counterparts (for Asian sources on these practices, see Lopez 2003:125–6; White 2009:122–66).

A fact not to be overlooked, is that there is explicit insistence on the Theosophists' part on the fact that 'mediumship' of any sort has absolutely no place in these considerations. In a more specific – but not necessarily more humble – twist of this theory, found in the teachings of Randolph (and of the Hermetic Brotherhood of Luxor), it is said that 'blending' can also be supported by sex magic in order to be able to infuse certain knowledge and powers in the future fetus at the instant of climax. It almost goes without saying that the possibility of sexual relationships with celestial entities is also being considered – although in a rather vague manner! (Deveney 1997a:303–7).

Conclusion

It looks like the time has come, not precisely to draw conclusions, but to reflect back on some of the material we have examined.

Concerning the success of the theme of the 'subtle body', mostly in the last quarter of the nineteenth century, the decisive influences are those of Spiritualism in general, of the Theosophical Society and of earlier occult literature, of 'orientalism' and of popularized scientific discourses about the nature of physical reality, as opposed to finer, immaterial forces (Asprem 2014:209–27; Howe 2015:171–93).

As supposedly made of a subtler, more refined type of matter than the material body, the 'double' is perceived as pertaining to a higher energy level and, by the same token, as corresponding to another and superior plane of existence, therefore as having to do with the very substance of consciousness, at least in some of its altered, higher states. The roots of such a notion of an intermediary ontological level are found in previous (Western as well as Eastern) cultural world-views, which include the existence and conceptual relevance of the 'Great Chain of Being'[4] as an accurate description of the actual structure and relations of the macro- and microcosmos. In between spirit and matter, body and mind, a common 'middle' term or substance warrants unity and continuity between ontological levels, which are otherwise differentiated. This 'subtle matter' also serves as an explanation for the operations of magic, being at the same time – like the 'fluid' of old – presented as both an agent and a propagation milieu for such an agent, equally at work in man and in nature; but it also linked to individual subjectivity and to self-realization, insofar as these are experimented in some sort of a middle zone between consciousness and the body proper, both understood as closely knitted together and as sheaths for one another. Yet, as magic would have it, the 'double' and its projection are not just meant to describe and explain, or to act solely as a theoretical model: they are also construed, and perhaps above all, as an instrument of knowledge and of power, that is of control over the unseen aspects of our minds, of our bodies and of the world(s), with goals that boast of 'knowledge of the mysteries of nature' as much as of spiritual enhancement, inner transformation and – no less – ultimate deification.

Accordingly, along the quite specific lines we have been following, Spiritualism is not simply understood as a powerful instrument for the reform of Christianity but, coupled with occultism, as the practical contents of a new religion per se, intended to supersede Christianity, and as the rightful heir to ancient magic and witchcraft.

Magic is thus considered as deriving from the existence of natural powers in man, and as totally independent in its efficacy from ethical preoccupations, faith or denominational affiliations and creeds. It is also perceived, in this context, as fundamentally different from mediumship, insofar as one of its main purposes is to transform passive mediumship into active occultism, directed by conscious will and open to empirical and controlled spiritual (as well as scientific) experimentation.[5] Moreover, magical powers are conceived of as accessible to all, present in all, and developable by all – so that in no way can their possession be the exclusive privilege of a priesthood or, more generally, of the masculine sex, nor can they be appropriated by any historical religion or reduced to theoretical pursuits; so that, as finally put by E. Hardinge Britten (or by the elusive 'Chevalier Louis de B.') in *Art Magic* (1876): 'The source of all spiritual powers and functions resides [...] in the astral spirit or spiritual body of man' (Mathiesen 2001:43).

4 Lovejoy 1936 remains, of course, a classic on this theme.

5 This anticipates in some measure what A. Crowley later (1909) termed 'scientific illuminism,' which figures as the subtitle of Crowley's journal *The Equinox* (published 1909–13).

References

Agrippa, H.C. 1992. *De Occulta Philosophia* (ed. V.P. Compagni). Leiden: Brill.

Asprem, E. 2014. *The Problem of Disenchantment: Scientific Naturalism and Esoteric Discourse, 1900–1939*. Albany, NY: SUNY Press.

Blavatsky, H.P. 1877. *Isis Unveiled*: blavatskyarchives.com/theosophypdfs/blavatsky_isis_unveiled.pdf (accessed 23 January 2016.

——— 1888. *The Secret Doctrine*: www.sacred-texts.com/the/sd/index.htm.

——— 1888–9. *Collected Writings* (ed. B. de Zirkoff, 15 vols ,1933–1991). Wheaton, ILL: The Quest.

Brach J.-P. 2021. 'Psychic disciplines: the magnetizer as magician in the writings of Jules Dupotet de Sennevoy (1796–881)'. In G.D. Hedesan and T. Rudbog (eds), *Innovation in Esotericism from the Renaissance to the Present*, pp. 185–200. Basingstoke: Palgrave Macmillan.

Bramble, J. 2013. 'Sinister modernists: subtle energies and yogic-tantric echoes in early modernist culture and art'. In G. Samuel and J. Johnston (ed.), *Religion and the Subtle Body in Asia and the West. Between Mind and Body*, pp. 192–210. Abingdon: Routledge.

——— 2015. *Modernism and the Occult*. Basingstoke: Palgrave Macmillan.

Butler, A. 2011. *Victorian Occultism and the Making of Modern Magic: Invoking Tradition*. Basingstoke: Palgrave Macmillan.

Chajes J. 2016. 'Construction through appropriation: Kabbalah in Blavatsky's early works'. In J. Chajes and B. Huss (eds), *Theosophical Appropriations: Esotericism, Kabbalah and the Transformation of Traditions*, 33–72. Beer Sheva: Ben-Gurion University of the Negev Press.

Chanel C., Deveney, J.P. and Godwin, J. 2000. *La Fraternité Hermétique de Louxor (H. B. of L.): Rituels et instructions d'occultisme pratique* (trans. C. Chanel). Paris: Dervy.

Cox, S. 2022. *The Subtle Body. A Genealogy*. Oxford: Oxford University Press.

Crow, J. L. 2012. 'Taming the astral body: The Theosophical Society's ongoing problem of emotion and control', *Journal of the American Academy of Religion* 80 (3): 691–717.

Cuchet, G. 2012. *Les Voix d'outre-tombe: Tables tournantes, spiritisme et société au XIXème siècle*. Paris: Seuil.

Demarest, M. 2011. *The Emma Hardinge Britten Archive*: www.ehbritten.org (accessed 10 February 2016.

Deveney, J.P. 1997a. *Paschal Beverly Randolph: A Nineteenth-Century Black American Spiritualist, Rosicrucian, and Sex Magician*. Albany: SUNY Press.

——— 1997b. *Astral Projection or Liberation of the Double and the Work of the Early Theosophical Society*. Fullerton, CA: Theosophical History (Occasional Papers VI).

——— 2016. 'The two theosophical societies: prolonged life, conditional immortality, and the individualized immortal monad'. In J. Chajes and B. Huss (eds), *Theosophical Appropriations: Esotericism, Kabbalah and the Transformation of Traditions*, pp. 93–114. Beer Sheva: Ben-Gurion University of the Negev Press.

Djurdjevic, G. 2014. *India and the Occult: The Influence of South Asian Spirituality on Modern Western Occultism*. Basingstoke: Palgrave Macmillan.

Ficino, M. 2001–6. *Theologia platonica* (ed. J. Hankins, trans. M.J.B. Allen, 6 vols). Cambridge, MA: Harvard University Press.

Fitger, M. 2019. 'The *tetractys* and the *hebdomad*: Blavatsky's sacred geometry unveiled': independent.academia.edu/MFitger (accessed 9 October 2023).

Göttler, C. and Neuber, W. (ed.) 2007. *Spirits Unseen: The Representation of Subtle Bodies in Early Modern European Culture*. Leiden: Brill.

Hanegraaff, W.J. 2017. 'The first psychonaut? Louis-Alphonse Cahagnet's experiments with narcotics', *International Journal for the Study of New Religions* 7(2):105–23.

Hardinge Britten, E. 1876. *Art Magic: Or Mundane, Sub-Mundane and Super-Mundane Spiritism*. Boston: William Britten.

Howe, L.A. 2015. Spirited Pioneer: The Life of Emma Hardinge Britten. PhD thesis, Florida International University (digitalcommons.fiu.edu/etd/2292).

Irwin, L. 2017. *Reincarnation in America: An Esoteric History*. Lanham, MD: Lexington Books.

Leland, K. 2016. *Rainbow Body: A History of the Western Chakra System from Blavatsky to Brennan*. Lake Worth, FL: Ibis Press.

Lopez, Donald S. 2003. *Fascination tibétaine: du bouddhisme, de l'Occident et de quelques mythes* (trans. N. Münter-Guiu, K. Buffetrille and G. Stein). Paris: Autrement.

Lovejoy, A.O. 1936. *The Great Chain of Being: A Study of the History of an Idea*. Cambridge, MA: Harvard University Press.

Mathiesen, R. 2001. *The Unseen Worlds of Emma Hardinge Britten: Some Chapters in the History of Western Occultism*. Fullerton, CA: Theosophical History (Occasional Papers IX).

Oppenheim, J. 1985. *The Other World. Spiritualism and Psychical Research in England, 1850–1914*. Cambridge: Cambridge University Press.

Samuel, G. and Johnston, J. (ed.) 2013. *Religion and the Subtle Body in Asia and the West. Between Mind and Body*, Abingdon: Routledge.

Shaw, G. 1995. *Theurgy and the Soul: The Neoplatonism of Iamblichus*. University Park: Penn State University Press.

Siorvanes, L. 1996. *Proclus: Neo-platonic Philosophy and Science*. New Haven: Yale University Press.

Thompson, R.C. 2019. 'The chevalier's secret: Emma Hardinge Britten and the dawn of American occultism', *Literature and Theology* 33(4): 451–75.

Walker, D.P. 1958. 'The astral body in Renaissance medicine', *Journal of the Warburg and Courtauld Institutes* 21:119–33.

White, D.G. 2009. *Sinister Yogis*. Chicago: Chicago University Press.

10

The lotus mandala and Prince Sutasoma in Bali

A poet-priest's techniques and experiences of the sacred

ANGELA HOBART

Everything visualized should be made of transparent light –
just like a rainbow (or shadow) is transparent light – vivid yet
non-solid – and should be experienced as pure, perfect and vast.
(*sadhana* of Chenrezig or Avalokiteshvara, see Holmes 2009)

In Bali and Java, Indonesia, a *dalang* (in the local language, as he will be called throughout the chapter – essentially a poet-priest) is the central force of the revered shadow theatre. Like bards elsewhere in the world, a *dalang* performs in small isolated villages and towns, telling stories from the mythological past. He projects shadows onto a screen for the benefit of his audience. While most stories are loosely derived from the classical Hindu epics, the *Mahabharata* and *Ramayana*, others like the Sutasoma story can be traced to the Pali *jatakas*, texts compiled in the fifth century AD in Sri Lanka, that recount Buddha's previous rebirths as a *bodhisattwa*[1] before becoming the enlightened one.

1 The spelling of Balinese follows the official Indonesian system introduced in 1972. Diacriticals are generally not used in Balinese, particularly in shadow theatre. It is a poetic language which incorporates numerous languages – Sanskrit, Old Javanese, Indonesian, English and others – depending largely on the *dalang*'s knowledge and the context of the performance. There is variation in how indigenous terms are spelt. I have tended to use the prevalent Indonesian usage or adopted the common spelling used by learned Balinese.

A *dalang* is a ritual priest, who seeks wisdom and ultimate enlightenment or liberation, referred to in Bali as *moksa*. At the same time, he is a visionary artist and skilful technician who follows definite procedures and practices when performing shadow theatre at night. In this role he acts as healer, as well as moral and spiritual guide, who both entertains and contributes a redirection of the consciousness of the spectators, remaking their realities. By his practices and narration, he can be described as shamanic Buddhist, being concerned with both his own attainment of enlightenment, as well as with the welfare of the villagers (cf. Samuel 1993:9).[2]

Most spectators during a performance watch the shadows of flat leather puppets projected on the screen. The shadows – sharp and steady or diffuse and quivering – evoke myths of gods, nobles, servants, sages, ogres and wild creatures. Shadows more generally hint at magical realms that extend in our technological era to the vibrant unknown. As T.S. Eliot writes in *The Hollow Men*:

> Between the idea and the reality,
> Between the motion and the acts falls the Shadow.
> Between the conception and the creation,
> Between the emotion and the response falls the Shadow.

The shadow theatre exists, or has existed, from China to Turkey, Morocco and Western Europe. It is well known in South-east Asia, especially in Cambodia, Thailand, Malaysia, Java and Bali.

In this chapter, however, I will be focusing initially on East Javanese poetry, which I argue has subtly left its imprint on Balinese shadow theatre, with special reference to the Buddhist poem *Sutasoma* written during the period of East Javanese classical literature that flourished between the eleventh and fifteenth centuries, approximately. Scholarly *dalang*s, particularly, are drawn to the poem of Prince Sutasoma because of its didactic and philosophical content, which is inspirational for them because of its luminescent quality. It has also the capacity to guide spectators, both young and old alike, in everyday

---

2 The history and nature of Buddhism in 'premodern' Tibetan societies is complicated. Samuel (1993) distinguishes between shamanic and clerical Buddhism. Both have enlightenment as their prime goal. Clerical Buddhism has similarities with monastic and scholarly Buddhism; shamanic Buddhism is directed towards the welfare of the lay community, mainly through (Tantric) rituals. These took on a great variety of forms as they entered South-east Asia. Both orientations are found in Java and Bali, though clerical Buddhism primarily developed in Java. Shamanic Buddhism prevails still in Bali.

Figure 10.1 Painting by I Mandera. Sutasoma teaching the wild creatures. Photographed by A. Hobart.

village customs and regulations, and to enchant them with the magical charm and beauty of the stories narrated.

Intriguingly, the genre left an imprint on a recent drama in London. In 2015/16 *The Firework-Maker's Daughter* (by Pullmont 1995) was shown in The Royal Opera House. It incorporated effects from the shadow theatre and gamelan music. In the story, Lila, the daughter of a firework-maker, goes off on a perilous journey during which she meets a white elephant, his caretaker Chulak, and a tiger. The journey is essentially an initiation rite, through which Lila gains wisdom and realizes the ongoing mutual dependency and interaction between everything, and hence the importance of flexibility and friendship or cooperation with even the seemingly most unsuitable Other. These themes also resonate in the Buddhist Sutasoma story on which this chapter focuses (Figure 10.1).

Introduction to Indonesia

The Republic of Indonesia comprises about 1,000 inhabited islands, and is known for its biodiversity. With a population of about 240,000 million people, it is the also the most populous Islamic, or nominally Islamic, country in the world. At crossroads for sea routes and international maritime trade along the Silk Road between East and South Asia, it has interwoven multiple cultures for thousands of years. The country has hundreds of distinct ethnic and linguistic groups and elements of the great religions – Hinduism, Buddhism, Tantrism, Islam and Christianity – have long blended with indigenous traditions of ancestor worship, sorcery and animism.

The archipelago shares a history of Dutch colonialism, rebellion against it, and the horrors of genocide. At the same time, like the rest of the world, it is undergoing globalization and rapid technological development. This multifaceted historical background is reflected in the national motto '*Bhineka Tunggal Ika*': 'Unity and Diversity'. The phrase can also mean 'in pieces, though one' – obliquely alluding to the genocide from 1965–6, when thousands of communists, or alleged communists (members of the PKI – *Partai Kommunis Indonesia*), were massacred in the country. While ensuing tensions and unrest have to some degree been smoothed out, wounds and scars from that period still remain (Hobart 2014).

Java

East Javanese classical poetry and the Sutasoma story

Buddhism and Hinduism entered South-east Asia around the first century. The earliest zenith of Buddhism was in south Sumatra, in a region designated as Srivijaya, and ruled by the Sailendras. There are essentially no remains of this dynasty, but Chinese pilgrims in the eight century (Fontein 1990:29), probably on their way to or from the Nalanda, the great learning centre in India for Buddhism, documented meticulously the existence of monasteries and a large college in Srivijaya, where the *Dharmapada* and Sanskrit were taught.

Buddhism spread throughout South-east Asia and elsewhere, and took on many forms, amalgamating with local belief systems. From the eleventh century to modern times visionary techniques intrinsic to Tantrism, referred to in Tibet as Vajrayana Buddhism, left their mark in the Himalayan region and South-east Asia (see Samuel's chapter in this book). This is evident in what is one of the most majestic monuments ever built, Borobudur in Central Java, dating to the ninth century, and to which I want to make fleeting reference before turning to classical literature of Java. It is sufficient to point out here that Borobudur has been referred as a Tantric Buddhist mandala (meaning 'circle' or diagram, *yantra*, Miksic 1990:50–3).[3] Samuel (1993:236) describes a mandala as a form of 'pure vision' opposed to the impure vision of ordinary

3 Mandalas can be either two dimensional or three dimensional, like Borobudur, with Buddha statues intrinsic to its architectural structure. A mandala is comparable to a diagram called a yantra. A great variety of mandalas existed around the time of Borobudur, which is the most complex Buddhist monument in the world. It is

life. The mandala vision is truer and more correct than the practitioner's normal perception of reality. Hence, a pilgrim who is sincerely motivated to attain wisdom and compassion, ultimately enlightenment, experiences his visit to the three-tiered Borobudur as a practice or 'technique' of meditation. As a mandala it is graphically comparable to a pure flowering lotus that unfolds the divine, through its architectural structure and exquisite narrative of reliefs the on the balustrades and walls.[4] These predominantly recount tales from the Buddhist scriptures which, among others, refer to Prince Sutasoma's pacification of both a cruel human-headed monster and a tigress who wishes to devour her cubs (Kempers 1976:113, 116). The mandala configuration that underlies this magnificent monument resonates within the classical poetry to which I now turn.

There are different versions of classical literary poems (*kakawin*) in Java that the scholar Zoetmulder (1974:173) calls '*religio poetae*'. Many poems come from the well-known Hindu epics, the *Ramayana* and the *Mahabharata*. With the *Mahabharata* I am referring to the condensed versions of eight *parwa*, or subdivisions. These epics originally derived from India. In the context of this chapter, however, I want to draw attention to the two major poems, *Arjuna Wiwaha* (Arjuna's Wedding) and *Sutasoma*, that are ascribed to the court-poet, sage (*wiku*) and scribe. Both are written in an Old Javanese (*kawi*) that contains some Pali and Sanskrit terms, on palm-leaf manuscripts or paper, at a time when poetry flourished at the royal courts of East Java (from about the mid-eleventh to fifteenth centuries – Holt 1967:66). Whilst the armatures of the East Javanese poems derive from India, these are elaborated upon in Java, and a number of them are unique in their erudite, eloquent and philosophical content. This applies in particular to the two poems. The first, *Arjuna Wiwaha*, was composed by the court-poet and sage (*wiku*) Mpu Kanwa in the mid-eleventh century in honour of King Erlangga (for a summary, see Zoetmulder 1974:234–37). Mpu Tantular was the author of *Prince Sutasoma* in the fifteenth century (for summery, see ibid.:329 –41). Both poems are renowned in Java and Bali, and stories from them are narrated, still nowadays, in shadow plays in Bali.

---

not only a mandala, but has also been considered a sacred mountain (symbolic of Mount Meru) and a stupa (Miksic 1990).

4 Samuel (in this book) writes that visualization in 'deity yoga' in Tibet focuses on imaginatively bringing Tantric deities into presence. While this applies to a Balinese poet-priest's practice during a performance, he seems not to observe internal yogic practice or 'subtle body' practice' (generically Known in Tibet as *risa rlung* or 'channels and prana' practice).

Their erudition comes to the fore in *Arjuna Wiwaha*, one passage of which describes Prince Arjuna's encounter with the god Indra, who was disguised as an elderly Brahmin. Zoetmulder (ibid.:209–10), via direct analogy to the shadow play, narrates how this god expounds on the true values of power and pleasure. The phenomenal world and all appearances in it merely attract and ensnare the senses (of the spectators watching). The characters projected on the screen are leather figures, puppets, and the events that befall them are merely illusions, *maya*, 'a display of sorcery without reality'. Implicitly, a performance is merely 'a play, and a delusive play at that, which would be incapable of deceiving a true sage' (ibid.:210).[5]

In Bali the poem of *Prince Sutasoma* still enjoys considerable popularity with scholarly clerics, or *dalangs* as they are called there (and henceforth in this chapter), scholars and spectators. Though these days it seems to be rarely enacted in Java. Although the roots of the *Sutasoma* poem go back to an early Pali *jataka* (pre-Buddhist) story, it was considerably transformed by Mpu Tantular, who was a Buddhist himself and a cleric-poet at the court of King Rajasanaraa or Hayum Wuruk at the height of the of Majapahit kingdom in the fifteenth century (see Hobart 1990 for the historical background and transformations of the poem), Whilst the poem is Mahayana Buddhist in orientation, it is a distinctive product of the late East Javanese period, marked by the growing syncretism of Buddhist and Saiva cults, and tinged with Tantric concepts of deliverance by magical means (Holt 1967:68). The poem is both didactic and metaphysical, and this makes it particularly poignant. This comes to the fore in the following episode of the poem, which I also witnessed performed as one of the spectators of a Balinese shadow play.

Prince Sutasoma is called by many names in the Javanese poem: as a Bodhisattva, Buddha, Gautama, Sakayamuni, Bajrajana or Wairocana (Absolute Buddha) who exemplifies the 'Centre' or the undifferentiated, perfect Void, *sunyata*. Essentially, it emerges that Prince Sutasoma is Lord Buddha himself. In the poem the prince, like the historical Buddha, leaves his palace to practice an ascetic way of life (*tapa*) and meditate (*semadhi*) at the cemetery of Mount Meru. On his path to the cremation grounds he meets a Sivaite and Buddhist priest, who accompany him. Having reached Mount Meru he encounters the Durga (the goddess of death), in her terrifying form, who praises him for his Buddha nature – as one who has subdued his passions and whose heart is filled with unceasing compassion (cf. Zoetmulder 1974:331).

5 Mpu Kanwa dedicated the poem *Arjuna Wiwaha* to King Erlannga whom he deems as enlightened as Prince Arjuna in *the parwas*. Erlangga, too, in the poet's perception, is not deceived by the world of forms and shadows, but strives to bring welfare to the people (Zoetmulder 1974: 435).

The goddess gives Prince Sutasoma a protective mantra that enables him to destroy all hostile and evil powers. On leaving Mount Meru the prince enters a dense wood where he meets three wild creatures, a cruel elephant-headed giant, a venomous serpent and a tigress in the process of devouring her cubs. Sutasoma tries to dissuade the latter from her evil intention and action, but the tigress pounces on him. Sutasoma willingly sacrifices himself to bring back dharma (the doctrine and ultimate reality) to mankind. Yet the god Indra brings him back to life, saying he is needed as humans have lost their equilibrium, and malevolence and suffering are rampant in the mundane world. The three creatures heed Indra's instructions and become the prince's faithful pupils and follow the practice of Tantric yoga of non-duality (*adwayayayoga*), the explicit aim being to reach the state of absolute purity (*pikayun nirmala*) and inconceivable emptiness (*acinttyasunyaga*) that ultimately leads to enlightenment. Mpu Tantular concludes his poem by writing that Buddha and Siwa in their (deepest) reality are identical (ibid.:248), although more credence is given to the former's path of liberation. This is in tune with the late East Javanese period of the fifteenth century, and contemporary Bali, where there are both Buddhist and Siwaite priests, though their distinction is nominal.

In order to gain the insights of the court poetry in East Java it is crucial to add a few words about the introductory stanza of the poems that Zoetmulder (1974:173–85) refers to as *manggala*. A *manggala* is basically a literary form of Tantric yoga unknown in Sanskrit, though elaborately discussed in many Indian texts and difficult to understand. Essentially, a major poem is conceived of as an aesthetic form of meditation, that is, a complex Tantric yoga practice that involves the inner descent of a poet's 'self', referred to (in Buddhist Tantric terms) as *istadewata* (ibid.:177), or the 'god of Beauty' to Sublime Consciousness. This mystic space in the microcosm is symbolized by the heart lotus, a four- or eight-petalled lotus (*padma*) surrounding the corolla, or the *nawa-sangaa*, in Bali (Figures 10.2a and 2b). The monument Borobudur, as mentioned, is also envisioned as a mandala comparable to a beautiful lotus. From this perspective, it is noteworthy that a court-poet in East Java compares his poem to a receptacle or 'temple', *candi* (ibid.:176), that ideally illuminates and beautifies both himself and his devotees or audience, who, even if only for a brief moment, experience 'ecstatic rapture' (ibid.:173) in surrendering themselves to the overwhelming power of the aesthetic experience. Essentially, a scholarly poet's path is one in which his 'ego' (in psychological terms) transcends duality. Once the sense of 'ego' vanishes 'the veil of *maya*, illusion, is rent and destroyed' (Tucci 1961:29). The poet's 'self" then merges with the Sublime Consciousness (also 'Elevated Consciousness' or 'Field of Light') that is 'the innermost core of the essence (*sari*) of beauty ... penetrating all things in every direction' (Zoetmulder 1974:181).

Figure 10.2a The nawa-sanga.

In tune with the aesthetic and spiritual experience that East Javanese classical literature seeks to evoke, court poetry abounds in similes, metaphors and other figurative forms of speech (ibid.:211–21; see also Brandon 1970:2–3). They emphasize the importance of cosmic unity in poetic Javanese thought, while at the same time stressing that beauty is inherent in all phenomena. Analogies throughout are made, for instance, to dance performances, epic recitations and *mawayang*[6] that may be the shadow play, (see the above passage of *Arjuna Wiwaha*). *Widu*, by analogy with the skilful *kuwang* bird, singer of songs, may refer to the poet or *dalang* who performs the shadow play (Zoetmulder 1974:211). The booming of frogs in the river sounds like xylophones (*sarong*) or the wind blowing over empty bamboo cylinders, like flutes played in a performance (Brandon 1970:3).

6 The term *wayang* (or *ringgit*) in Java or Bali also implies puppet. In Bali *wayang* is associated with *bayang*, which means shadow.

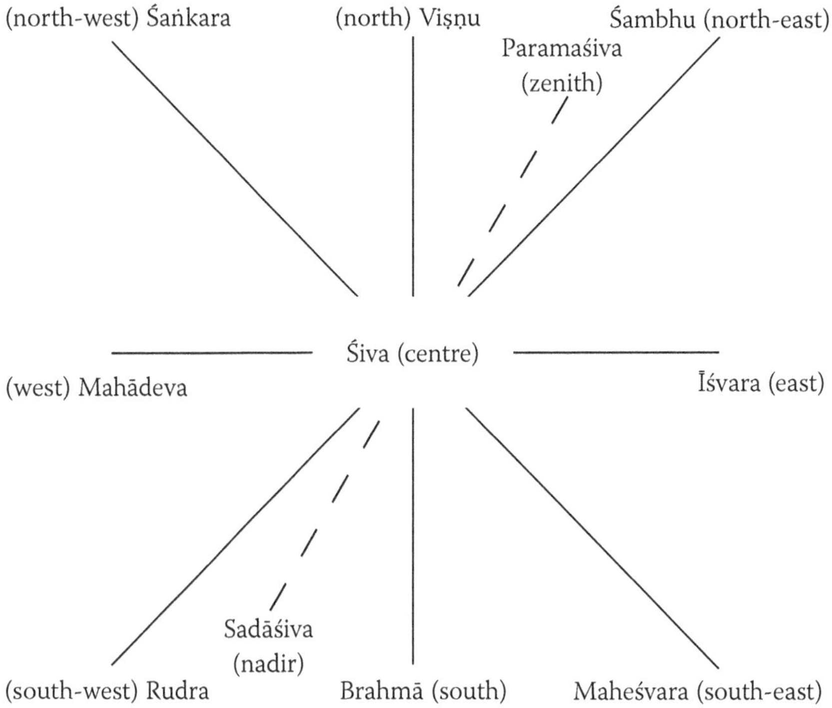

Figure 10.2b Nawa-sanga system of Java and Bali. After Pott 1966:135.

It is evident that classical East Javanese poetry and theatre, especially the shadow theatre, already existed in the twelfth century, perhaps even earlier. The poems composed in the early Javanese period had undoubtedly an important spiritual and aesthetic role in court life in that period. The unique heritage of the East Javanese literary past is subtly echoed by contemporary Balinese scholarly poet-priests or *dalang*s in their rituals, or when they perform the shadow play, as will emerge as my account turns to Bali.

Bali

From Java to Bali

Bali's population of over two million is concentrated in the fertile south-central part of the island, considered the heartland of culture, having been exposed to early Indo-Javanese influences from the eleventh century onwards. Sufism and Islam hardly penetrated the island, although there are Islamic communities, especially in north Bali. In Bali, Hinduism and Tantric Buddhism blended with ancient beliefs that left their imprint on the religious life of the people.

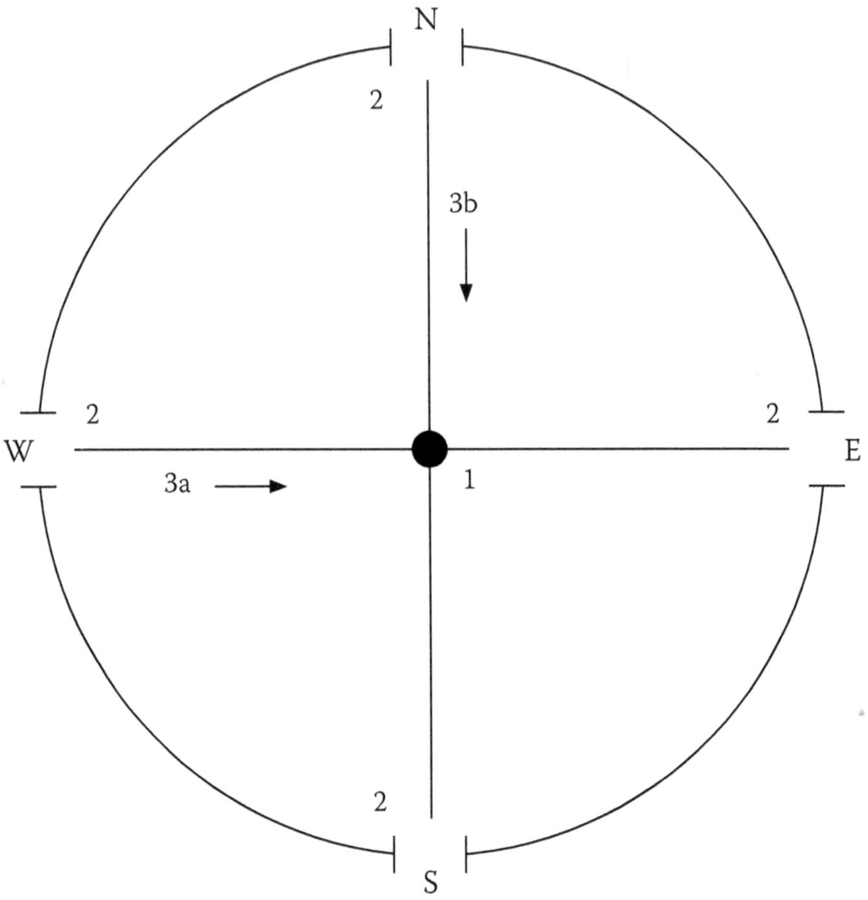

Figure 10.2c Diagram of the lotus mandala.

1. *The sacred centre – represented by Siwa, a luminous point of consciousness. Siwa's vehicle is the lotus.*
2. *Entrance gates – the four cardinal directions whose associated colours from east to west are: white, red, yellow and black or blue. Siwa at the centre is multicoloured. The directions are represented bu the sevant-clowns: Tualen, Delem, Sangut and Wisnu.*
3. *Two intersecting pairs of opposites:*

   a. creative versus destructive or goodness versus obscuration, the ruwa-bineda (the cosmic opposites). In the play of Sutasoma the prince and his associates who follow the path of dharma oppose the wild creatures of the wood.

   b. The axis mundi – represented by the Kakayonan. It signifies the Cosmic Mountain or Tree of Life that ascends from the underword to earth or heaven.

The social structure is based loosely on the Indian caste system. Generally, Balinese say that the high castes (*triwangsa*) – *brahmana*, *satriya* and *wesia* – are descendants of aristocrats who came over to Bali after the great dynasty of Majapahit disintegrated in the fifteenth century under the onslaught of the Islamized sultanates. The commoners, the *sudras* (literally *jaba*, outsiders to the palaces) comprise over ninety per cent of the population. The ancestors are intrinsic to the kinship structure, with descent being conceived of as a spiritual relation of identity, and ascribed patrilineally. Each household has a temple containing shrines dedicated to the family's lineage ancestors, to whom homage is given with rituals throughout the year to ensure that they guide and protect the descendants.

Irrespective of the bombings of 2001 and 2003, Bali has remained a major tourist resort, though the clientele has changed. Over a million foreign tourists are estimated to have visited the island in recent years – mainly from Australia, China, Japan and South-east Asia. Tourism has little affected the techniques and principles underlying the major art forms in Bali, such as shadow theatre, traditional architecture and gamelan music, although new dance and drama forms have been developed in response to popular trends that have infiltrated societies worldwide.

The shadow play has remained essentially a rural, down-to-earth drama genre in Bali, in contrast to its counterpart in Java, where it evolved into a sophisticated drama form at the Islamic courts of the Sultans of Surkakarta and Jogykarta. Poems such *Sutasoma* would have reached Bali only after the Majapahit expedition in 1342, when the island became a dependency of the great empire. With the triumph of Islam in Java in the fifteenth century and the decline of the Majapahit era, Hindu-Javanese influence waned in importance. Yet it continued to be preserved at Balinese courts, especially in the south-central part of the island, where old Javanese texts were studied, translated and narrated. The shadow theatre is still the main vehicle through which these texts are disseminated to village communities.

The Balinese shadow theatre

The main occasion for a shadow-theatre performance at night is in connection with the anniversary of a temple, once every 210 days. They may sometimes also be given in association with rites of passage in wealthier households. Spectators do not pay for attending a performance. The shadow play (Figure 10.3) is often chosen and paid for by the village community or family, as it is held in high esteem for the spiritual and moral contents of the stories narrated (one of the core values being sacrifice, as will emerge in the subsequent section of this chapter). During the show the *dalang* sits in a small, elevated, temporary booth with four metallophones (*gender*) accompanying the narration, while the

Figure 10.3 A shadow-theatre stage in Bali. Photograoh courtesy P. Horner.

puppets are projected onto the screen. Most of the spectators are youngsters and elderly men (Figure 10.4), huddled together on the ground in front of the booth while watching the dancing shadows on the screen, some drinking hot lime juice or coffee while smoking clove cigarettes. Performances continue for about three to four hours. The atmosphere is relaxed and informal. The main characters of the story are immediately recognizable by their forms, which are standardized, and the skeleton of the stories are usually already known by the public.

The servant-clowns of the nobility are characters with special appeal, as their antics are lively and their speeches often replete with jokes, humour, anecdotes and imagery. These servants are crucial, as they improvise extensively on passages taken from the classical literature and translate the archaic Javanese (*kawi*) dialogues spoken by the deities, the nobility and ogres (which is inaccessible to most villagers) into local Balinese. *Dalang*s themselves may be rusty in speaking *kawi*, which thus is often garbled. Yet it is important that the epic characters speak the veiled language, for this contributes to the sacred nature of a magical shadow-theatre performance.

The dalang, poet-priest and his training

There are varied ritual specialists on the island – Brahman priests (*pedanda*), village priests (*pemangku*), various healing specialists (*balian*) and so forth.

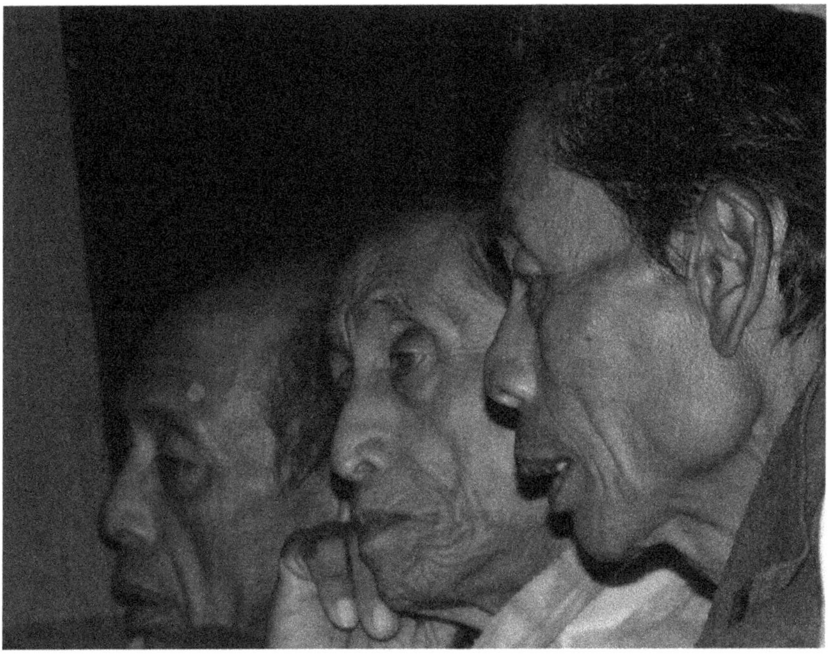

Figure 10.4 Male audience at shadow theatre. Photographed by A. Hobart.

They all have to be initiated before being allowed to practice. In the case of a *dalang* he has to be initiated with his puppet case by a Brahman priest. The puppet chest is usually a family heirloom that is kept in the household temple when not in use.

In his role, a *dalang* has special affinity with mediums or shamans on the archipelago. They all have the potential to create a magical, illusionary world for the benefit of the spectators. Yet a *dalang* is also a storyteller, musician, manipulator of the puppets (*wayang*) and a spiritual and moral guide who seeks to propel the spectators into a magical temporary reality that arguably refers to a mandala (a cosmic diagram and technique for meditation). This image becomes progressively more vivid when exploring the practices and intentions of a *dalang*.

*Dalang*s vary considerably in their skill and 'purity' (*pikayun nirmala*). In the local idiom, '*dalang*' is derived from '*galang*' (clear), implying someone who illuminates the deeper meaning in the stories. *Dalang*s are usually male and low caste. The art of performing shadow plays is commonly transferred down the patriline. The main teachers of an aspiring poet-priest are his older relatives, though he also learns by watching performances of other *dalang*s of repute. These may be very mobile, travelling great distances if they are widely renowned.

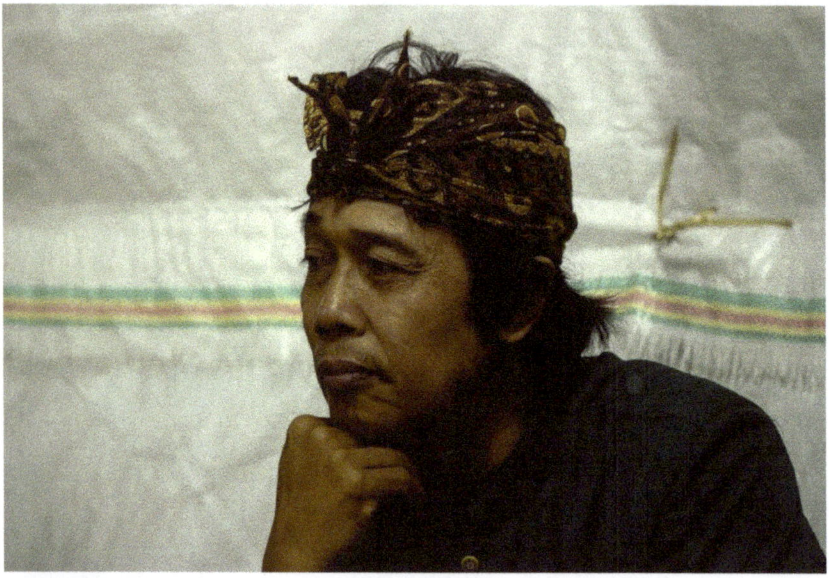

Figure 10.5 Portrait of poet-priest I Wija by Angela Hobart.

There are about one hundred *dalang*s on the island these days, and they basically fall into two types. There are those who excel in performing. Their shows are dramatic and may be replete with bawdy jokes. While scholarly *dalang*s, the second type, are also skilled performers, they are well versed in, and have profound understanding of, the philosophy embedded in the classical literature. The scholarly I Wayan Wija (Figure 10.5) is one of these. He has travelled and performed widely – in Japan, India, the U.S. and various European countries. Some such *dalang*s give special performances, *wayang sudamala*, which are exorcist in intent, to reconstitute the realities of ill or suffering humans. *Mala* means impure, unclean (Hooykaas 1973:6) and is used to denote bodily deformities and blemishes; it also refers to a child born in the week of Tumpek Wayang, who is prone to illness or accidents inflicted by the demon-king Kala. A *dalang* during the ritual prepares special purifying water (*toya penglukatan*) to restore health and well-being.

It is pertinent to ask at this point whether the shadow play falls into the category of theatre or ritual (Turner 1982). It is essentially both. It is theatre, in the sense that there is clear-cut distinction between the audience and the actors (that is the *dalang* and the puppets or shadows projected on the screen). However, the ritual component is pronounced in this genre that emphasizes the liminal, 'the between' which Stoller (2009:6) refers to as the space of imagination, or a space that is indeterminate and ambiguous, and which the Balinese refer to as the 'unseen', *niskala*. Stories narrated by a *dalang* project the spectators into a mythical drama in sacred space and time. The

Figure 10.6 The poet-priest, dalang I Wija paying homage to the gods while facing his household.

ritual aspect of the story is further characterized by repetitions, ambiguities and aesthetic detailing that allow for transformations of experience.

As a recognized ritual practitioner, it is important that a *dalang* meditates regularly in or facing his household temple (*sanggah*) (Figure 10.6), and conducts rites to the gods and demons to appease them. This is sometimes referred to as yoga, though they are more commonly called *nunas ica ring ida batara* (giving homage to the gods) or *muspa* (worship). He maintains a disciplined and mindful lifestyle. In his meditative practices and way of life he strives to reduce the six passions (lust, anger, arrogance, greed, jealousy and envy) and avoid intoxication through passion or drink. Pursuing such a path leads both to liberation (in the Buddhist conception), as well as to an attitude of altruism, whereby the *dalang* is of service to the people by contributing to their happiness and veneration of life in all its variety and beauty, as well as to their general well-being.

Given that a *dalang* is a ritual practitioner, as well as an entertainer, healer and teacher of his audience, it is important that performances of mythopoetic power, or of agency in the environment and social context, are given. Here Kapferer's words come to mind:

> Symbolic forms (e,g., shadow theatre performances) are active in the creation of their realities and have effect or bring about changes in the

> circumstances of existence through the aesthetic dynamics of their composition.
>
> (Kapferer and Hobart 2005:9)

Specific practices and techniques have to be adhered to by an aspiring *dalang* so as to become adept enough in his art that he can move and enthral spectators, as well as become inspired himself. With the term 'techniques' we are not only referring to artefacts or 'tools' that have use-value, but with 'technical strategies that enchant' (Gell 1988:7), i.e. they serve symbolic or magical and spiritual ends which effect both himself and the spectators. They are also intrinsic to his training. The main formal techniques and practices required are as follows:

Knowledge of the mystic treatise

The *Dharma Pawayangan* ('Laws of Puppet Performance', see Hooykaas 1973) contains the philosophical and spiritual background to the shadow play, and mantras for puppets and performances. The manuscript also alludes to the mandala configuration that, as will emerge, underlies shadow-theatre performances in Bali, as well as probably in Java. The stage, together with the equipment and music – the microcosm (*buwana alit*) – replicates the universe (*buwana agung*). The lamp above the *dalang*'s head is the sun. The screen is the sky or face of the world. The puppets symbolize all that is in it. The banana stem into which they are placed is the earth. The *dalang* is the 'Creator God', referred to in a performance as Siwa, the central god of the cosmos, i.e. the fundamental classificatory systems in the Bali (the fivefold, *panca dewa*, and ninefold, *nawa sanga*, division of the cosmos – Figures 10.2a and 2b). In this sublime mystic manifestation, the *dalang* (i.e. Siwa) is invisible to the spectators watching the shadows dance on the screen in front of them.

*Dalang*s, however, stress that spiritual knowledge does not just come from studying the mystic treatise, but from practising the rituals and their lifestyle. This gives them capacity to evoke the invisible, veiled realm, *niskala* the deities, spirits of the environment, ancestors and demonic beings; in contrast to the visible realm, *sekala* forms and phenomena of the mundane world:

Knowledge of the myths

The myths mainly originate in the classical literature, particularly the *Mahabharata*, and form the skeleton for most plays.[7] As already mentioned,

---

7 Most stories in shadow theatre are loosely based on the *Mahabharata*, the narrative of the tragic conflict between first cousins – the five Pandawa brothers, descended from gods, and the Korawas, ogres incarnate – over who should rule

the story of *Sutasoma* stems from the east Javanese poem *Sutasoma*. All *dalangs* improvises imaginatively on the basic plot, some of course more wittingly and with more insight and understanding of the classical literature than others.

Understanding of the disposition and motivation of the puppets, the actors

A standard collection comprises about one hundred puppets. New puppets are made by copying old ones. They have a curious lingering affinity with characters on reliefs in east Javanese temples (*candi*) that gives them an aura of sanctity.[8] They can be divided into two groups that oppose each other on the stage: the relatively virtuous dharma group and their ignoble adversaries (see *ruwa-bineda*),[9] although this dichotomy in a narrative is not strict, for there are various shades between characters. Puppets can be classified into distinct categories:

1. The celestial beings, the deities and celestial nymphs.
2. The high castes, the *satriya*, to whom Prince Sutasoma belongs (Figure 10.7). They are the largest group. The towering headdresses of characters such as Sutasoma or Kresna indicates their high status.
3. The *sudra*, the low-caste servant-clowns, *parekan*, the mediators between the spheres, heaven, earth and the underworld. (Figure 10.8). In contrast to most other characters, they do not appear in the classical literature but derive from the folk tradition. They serve the main characters in plays, and are pot-bellied, eccentric and uncouth looking. There are four main servants, *parekan*, Tualen, Delem, Merdah and Sangut, who in the mystic treatise the *Dharma Pawayangan* are associated with the gods of the four cardinal directions and their associated colours: east, white; north, black or blue; west, yellow; and south, red (Hooykaas 1973:130–2). Of these, Tualen (equivalent to Semar in Java) is the most important *parekan*, clown and

---

the kingdom of Hastina. Numerous heroes from both camps are killed during the Bharatayuda War. The goodness of the Pandawa emerges in opposition to the Korawas in performances.

8 Javanese puppets, unlike their Balinese counterparts, are highly stylized in order to remove any human semblance because of the Islamic proscription of image making (Holt 1967:135).

9 The opposition of the Pandawas and Korawas is associated with the dualities often mentioned in Tibetan texts that arise from the individualizing force Illusion force of illusion, maya. E.g. in the Mahamudra prayer is written: 'May the pure motivation and action of myself and all beings, infinite in number, be free from any kind of dualistic notion.' Dualisms are often mentioned in a *dalang*'s narration, and referred to as *ruwa-bineda*.

Figure 10.7 Silhouette of Sutasoma. Photographed by A. Hobart.

Figure 10.8 Silhouette of The servant-clown Tualen. Photographed by A. Hobart.

mediator (identified by *dalangs* with Siwa) at the centre of the cosmos (Figures 10.2a – 2c).[10]

4. The demons (*buta*) and ogres (*raksasa*).
5. Animals, plants, chariots, others.

Skill in dancing the puppets

The dance should accord with the pitch and vocal qualities associated with the characters in the story. The rhythmic dancing (*sesolahan*) imparts the illusion of a conquest of gravity, that is, 'freedom' (Langer 1976:194). Like the shadows, the voices are disembodied. Both the dance and the voices accentuate the mythopoetic power of the performance and narration.

Representation of the Kakayonan

Kakayonan, the tree-of life or mountain or cosmic mountain (Figure 10.9), has great significance in any performance. A show always begins and ends with the appearance of this intricate and beautiful leaf-shaped figure. It also marks the beginning and end of scenes. The figure is visualized as the *axis mundi* that stands at the primordial centre of the universe and intersects the three realms of existence: the underworld, the human and the celestial realm (Eliade 1954:18). As such, it is reminiscent of the ancient pyramid-ziggurat and the Buddhist stupa. The Kakayonan or tree of life, like the imagination, is a source of endless regeneration.

Play the musical instruments

The music in the shadow theatre is a subject in its own right. The ethnomusicologist McPhee (1970:146) described it as 'the most sensitive form of musical expression in Bali.' Compositions that sparkle with intricate configurations are played by an ensemble of four metallophones, called *gender* (Figure 10.10). Technical skill and rhythmic coordination is required between the *dalang* and musicians to produce the shifting melodic modes and dynamic

10 Colours (of puppets) are said to be the purest 'essence' (*sari*) of the gods; unlike India, where statues of main gods are located in prominent temple shrines. Hence, for example, colours of banners hung from important shrines in temple complexes during festivals symbolize the five- or ninefold gods of the division of the cosmos (Figures 10.2a – 2c). I am not discussing in this short chapter the body colours of puppets in association to their character and disposition, apart from drawing attention to Tualen's body colour. He is the only puppet whose body colour is a mixture of all the colours, to identify him with Siwa, who is multicoloured at the centre of the cosmos, or *nawa-sanga*. It is unsurprising in this spiritual context that only the *dalang* sees Tualen and his specific body colour. The spectators in front of the screen see only the silhouettes of the puppets (the actors).

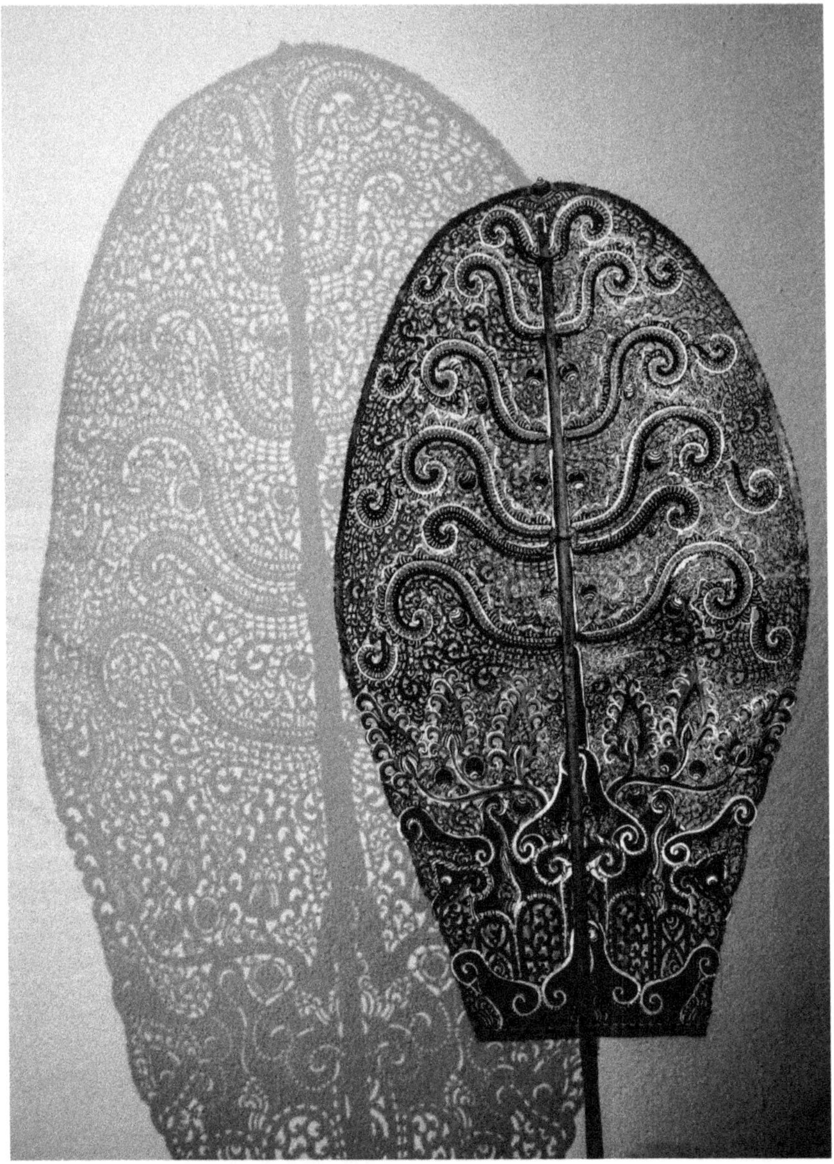

Figure 10.9 The Kakayonan (or Tree of Life) as a silhouette and puppet visible to the dalang. Photgraphed by M. Hobart.

accents that draw the spectators into the sacred time-space created by the drama. The music gives organic unity and sonorous beauty to the narration.

This genre of theatre is given, essentially altruistically, to an audience to entertain, enchant and instruct them in the moral values of the community, a

Figure 10.10 The metallophones, gender. Photographed by A. Hobart.

core one of these being the importance of sacrifice,[11] which crops up in most of the narrated stories. The performance and narration of the story subtly and imperceptibly contribute to the spectators' well-being and guides them to follow the path of dharma. However, for a scholarly *dalang* a performance is more than this. For him it is a ritual, a form of Tantric meditation with profound spiritual meaning, as will emerge when we look at an actual performance.

Unfolding the lotus mandala in Bali: preparations of a dalang before a performance

Before a show a *dalang* pays homage to the gods at his household shrine (*taksu*, 'inspiration') in the household temple, focusing his thoughts (*masikiyang pikayunan*) on the god Siwa. The significance of this orientation towards the god at the centre of the cosmos emerges in the manuscript *Dharma Pawanganan*, in which is written:

> The enlightened *dalang* incorporates the earth, the ogres and the gods.
> His other name is 'leader', for he is Siwa, Sada-Siwa, Parama-Siwa (different aspects of the Siwa; Pott 1966:135–6) and the Unfathomable God.

11 Sacrifice is a complex subject that has been discussed by many scholars. Kapferer (1997:185–220), for example, argues that the regeneration of the human is at the heart of sacrifice. Through his death the victim essentially has the capacity to re-imagine and redirect human consciousness and to remake relations in the world.

For 'Tintya'[12] is the 'supreme god of unity'.
All worlds are united in him.
Empowered he chooses his position.
This is the origin of him who is called *dalang*.
Empowered he commands speech.

(Hooykaas 1973:16)

Siwa (or Absolute Buddha) is the supreme god of the fivefold division of the cosmos, *panca-dewa*, mentioned earlier, as well as its expanded version, the well-known *nawa-sanga* (Figure 10.2a – 2c) which includes the intermediate directions. These schemes represent in their entirety a lotus – four or eight petals placed symmetrically around the corolla.

Martin Brauen (1998:28) emphasized the mandala character of Borobudur (see above), which propels pilgrims to progress from the gross to the subtle, mysterious realm, eventually to experience the perfect void (*sunyata*). A unique mandala configuration can also be made out in examining the structure underlying the shadow theatre, the most revered genre of theatre in Bali. This is illustrated in diagram: the mandala comprises a central point, a circle and two intersecting pairs of opposites (Figures 10.2a – 2c).

The lotus, an image of luminosity (Figure 10.11), is also the centre point of both the *nawa-sanga* and the mandala configuration underlying shadow theatre. The lotus (or liver as some locals refer to the centre) is not only Siwa's vehicle, Buddha's seat is often an open beautiful lotus. The blossom grows in mud in shallow water, and rises out of suffering and impurity. The designation 'lotus mandala' is an apt for the mandala that underlies and structures a *dalang*'s performance and narration. The story of Sutasoma recounts how the prince attains enlightenment after he has overcome all the obstacles on his path by purifying and taming the wild creatures encountered.

Dalang I Wayan Wija's performance in Switzerland

Before turning to the magical shadow play given by I Wayan Wija in the Theatre Dimitri in the small village of Versacia in south Switzerland in 2016,[13] I want to say a few words about this scholarly *dalang*. I Wija is known for his sweet (*manis*), lyrical singing and the gracefulness and beauty with which he dances the silhouettes. He is considered the most erudite, scholarly and

12 Tintya is also called Tunggal, the supreme god of unity, known to most modern Balinese as Sang Hyang Widi Wasa.

13 Theatre Dimitri was founded by Jacob Dimitri (1935–2016) and his wife. It became one of the four theatre schools in Switzerland for graduate students in performing arts, and an inspiring meeting ground for actors and others to share experiences.

Figure 10.11 The Lotus. Photographed by A. Hobart.

spiritually elevated *dalang* presently in Bali. On occasion, locals say he is divinely inspired (*metaksu*), as he has the capacity to inspire and 'enchant' (*ngelangunin*, which has affinity with the *kawi* term *lango*) the audience with the eloquence and beauty of his performance.

I Wija was born in 1959 in Sukawati, in south Bali, a location known as the village of *dalang*s. When only six years old he became interested in shadow theatre, making puppets out of jackfruit leaves. As a youngster, he had a keen interest in dance and music and studied with the well-known musician, I Made Rajin, among others. I Wija learned the art of shadow theatre from his father, grandfather and uncle down the patriline, all accomplished *dalang*s, as well as by assisting the renowned scholarly *dalang* I Nyoman Granyam in his performances. I Wija is both innovative and flexible. He created new puppets representing large dinosaurs or dragons, sometimes out of mirrors, to be used in animal fables and Tantric tales. Whilst acclaimed in his region and abroad, I Wija's popularity has waned somewhat in Bali over recent years, due to modernization and secularization. Aspiring young *dalang*s are less metaphysical and more journalistic in their approach.

In 2016 Wayang Wija was invited by the Centro Incontri Umani (Centre for Humanitarian Studies) to give a shadow-play performance in Ticino, south Switzerland. The venue selected was Theatre Dimitri, established in 1971 by Jacob Dimitri, a clown of repute in Switzerland and a versatile musician who had studied with Marcel Marceau. The theatre is particularly suitable for Balinese theatre because of the sacred place of the servant-clowns in a performance. Frolicking clowns are depicted on many of the walls.

Prelude to the performance in Theatre Dimitri

A *dalang* is a world-maker during a performance. All the techniques concerning the aesthetic or symbolic forms brought up earlier – the dance, the plastic arts, narration and music, with special reference to gender – contribute to the dynamic field of forces and affect between those involved: including the *dalang*, musicians and assistants, and the audience.

As this is a genre of theatre as well as ritual, a scholarly *dalang*, like I Wija, both entertains and instructs the spectators on the moral values and precepts inherent to the society. He also subtly guides them to pursue a path of dharma (the Buddhist doctrine), which ultimately leads to liberation.

However, for a scholarly *dalang*, a performance has deeper meaning. Essentially the performance is a Tantric yogic practice or 'instrument' and 'tool' in Zuetmulder's words (1974:181; he repeatedly stresses this point throughout his work on East Javanese poetry). Thereby, an accomplished *dalang* seeks to merge with the supreme god in the centre of the lotus mandala. This process has, it can be suggested, affinity with the dynamic process of composing a court poem at the height of the era when East Javanese poems flourished. This is illustrated by I Wija's performance of the Sutasoma story in south Switzerland in 2016. The process is inherent to all shadow-theatre performances throughout Bali.

The story of Prince Sutasoma projects both the spectators and the *dalang* into a mythical epoch in sacred space and time. The ritual performance is characterized by repetitions, ambiguities and aesthetic detailing that allow for the transformation of experience. In the Sutasoma story the enlightened prince confronts ogres and wild creatures with his humility and beauty of body and spirit. Tualen and Merdah are the servants of Sutasoma, while the brothers Delem and Sangut serve as the wild creatures. An essential episode in the story is Sutasoma's sacrifice, and his being brought back to life by the god Indra. Short extracts of dialogues from the Sutasoma story are reproduced below. All have moral import. The servant-clowns translate and expand on what the epic characters have said, as is usual. As the audience consisted mainly of Swiss, there was more clowning than is common in I Wija's own habitat, and the performance was shorter than usual, lasting about two hours.

Figure 10.11 I Wija recites a mantra before beginning the narration. Photographed by M. Hobart.

Unfolding the lotus mandala in the Sutasoma performance in Theatre Dimitri

The manner in which a *dalang* enters the stage highlights his spiritual orientation. I Wija initially purified the place of the performance by asking permission from Mother Earth, Ibu Pretiw, to perform, He sweeps and purifies the surface of the floor with the tip of his gown. The musicians sat behind him and one assistant handed him the puppets. Offerings were given to the gods and the delicate scent of incense enveloped the stage (Figure 10.12). He always begins the performance by waving the elusive figure, the Kakayonan or *axis mundi*, in front of the screen. This preliminary dance signifies the five great elements, the *panca-maha-buta* – air, wind, fire, water and earth – that are responsible for creation and form the essence of both the microcosm and macrocosm.

The mantras he chants at this stage, before narrating the story, are crucial. Two are summarized. The first reiterates the importance of the Kakayonan, or *axis mundi*, in the shadow play.

> On dancing the Kakayonan the *dalang* believes that the gods of the cardinal points alternate:
> Sambu takes the place of Wisnu, Wisnu that of Sankara,

> Sangkara takes the place of Mahadewa, Mahadewa that of Rudra,
> Rudra takes the place of Brahma, Brahma that of Mahesvara,
> Mahaesvara takes the place of Iswara,
> Iswara that of the Kayon (or Kakakyonan)
> The Kakayonan takes the place of the Pure All-Powerful Mind,
> The Pure Mind takes the place of the God Poet (i.e. Siwa at the Centre).
>
> (Hooykaas 1973:33)

This radiant lotus mantra is a powerful tool of meditation at the beginning of any performance. The gods of the *nawa-sanga* are rotated clockwise until they all merge with Siwa at the centre of the lotus (which in the microcosm is designated as the 'heart-lotus', that is, the seat of a scholarly *dalang*). This process has, I suggest, proximity to that of an East Javanese court-poet, Tantular, in composing the *manggala* of a poem, when he experiences momentarily 'aesthetic rapture' or absorption through oneness with the 'god of beauty' (Zoetmulder 1974:185). In effect, during the play when his consciousness is illuminated, I Wija becomes the central god of the cosmos, Siwa. This dynamic empowers the poet-priest to generate a 'pure vision' of the universe or a map of the world – in effect a mandala.

The Kakayonan is the cosmic axis for the magical play, given for the benefit of a *dalang*'s 'self' or 'soul' (Pott 1966:15) in his path to enlightenment, but also to inspire the spectators to follow an enlightened path. Numerous other mantras are chanted at the beginning of the show to protect the *dalang* from destructive forces and sorcery, as well as to entertain and enchant the spectators, as evidenced by the mantra 'Pangeger':

> May the goddess of love, Ratih, be in my voice so that it is as sweet as a flute, an orchestra, or a song. May the god of love, Kama Jaya, be in my dance, May the spectators become aware of their love and forget their suffering.
>
> (cf. Hooykass 1973:43)

A final mantra before beginning the narration is dedicated to the creator god Brahma, to request him to descend 'to give the puppets life' (*panurip wayang*), so that they glow.

Guiseppe Tucci (1961:25) says that a mandala is not only a cosmogram but also a 'psychocosmogram', implying:

> the scheme of disintegration from the One to the many and of reintegration from many to the One, to that Absolute Consciousness, entire and luminous.

This dynamic loosely underlies the succession of stages and shifts of any shadow-theatre performance and the story narrated therein. For example, in the play given at the Theatre Dimitri in south Switzerland, based on the journey of Sutasoma through the woods, two principal phases can be distinguished. During the first phase of 'disintegration' the spectators are presented with the obstacles encountered by Sutasoma, which obscure his path to liberation. In the second phase of 'reintegration', the spectators observe how the prince attains supreme illumination from which all beings can benefit. I Wija's narration of the story highlights this transformational dynamic. Examples of dialogues are included to give an inkling of the compelling quality of the performance. They are idiomatic and repetitive, and hence here paraphrased throughout. As the performance was given in Switzerland, the dialogues contain more English words than usual.

Phase I: the drama of disintegration

The poet-priest I Wija introduces the play by explaining that ogres are threatening to destroy the world. Thus, Prince Sutasoma, called Batara Buda, Lord Buddha, is born. Sutasoma, like Buddha, quietly leaves his palace with his servants one night in search of enlightenment. His journey leads him to the death temple (*pura dalem*) on Mount Meru. While meditating, the terrifying apparition of the goddess Bagawati (goddess of power, Batari Sakti, that is, Durga, the goddess of death) appears (Figure 10.13). Sutasoma humbly pays homage to her. She is moved by the beauty of his speech and grace of movement, and gives him a mantra that purifies him. It also gives power (*sakti*), but to be used only for good, dharma.

Sutasoma and his companions then continue on their way deeper into the woods. They reach an open space, where heads, bones and hair are strewn around. The elephant-headed ogre, Gaja Waktu, has caused this havoc. Prince Sutasoma admonishes the ogre. Tualen, his servant, translates and improvizes on the prince's words in local Balinese.

Gaja Waktu [in *kawi*] Who are you [to Sutasoma]? Authority and radiance emanate from you.

Delem Who are you? No one ventures here. Are you a sage, a celestial musician or a god?

Sutasoma [in *kawi*] I am a human. My name is Sang Sutasoma and I wish to prevent you from causing more devastation.

Tualen He is Sang Sutasoma, the son of King Ketu of Nastina, who follows the path of dharma. You are consumed by greed (*kemomoan*) and indulge in lustful desires. Sutasoma feels compassion (*kepiolasan*) and pity (*kangen*) for all beings. If you continue your evil ways you will suffer (*samsara*) in the hereafter and not attain liberation.

Figure 10.13 Silhouette of Sutasoma encountering Goddess Bagawati (Durga) on Mount Meru. Tualen's head is shown. He is accompanying his master, Sutasoma. Photographed by M. Hobart.

Sutasoma, through the power of his thought, subdues the ogre, who humbly requests to become his pupil. A similar encounter is narrated between Sutasoma and a cruel serpent, who is also pacified.

The prince, accompanied by the elephant-headed ogre and serpent, goes deeper into the woods. On their way they meet numerous creatures – elephants, monkeys, kangaroos, frogs, fish and ogres – with whom they may converse, sing, dance, frolic or admonish or simply bypass, as with a charging elephant and dancing demons (Figures 10.14 and 15). In these scenes the *dalang* articulates a 'pure vision' of an animated mode of living, in which all beings experience heightened sensibility and responsiveness to one another. This fosters a realization that all beings are entwined in a world of constant

Figure 10.14 Silhouette of charging elephant in Sutasoma story. Photographed by M. Hobart.

Figure 10.15 Silhouette of two demons dancing. Photographed by M. Hobart.

flux. In such a world, the prince's compassion and sense of beauty and equality to all are poignantly evidenced for the spectators.

Further into the forest, Sutasoma and his companions meet a wild tigress who is about to devour her cubs. The following dialogue ensures.

> Sutasoma [in *kawi*] Mother tigress, desist from this wicked act.
>
> Merdah Mother tigress, do not devour your cub. You are setting them a poor example. Later they too will become bad parents, cruel and greedy. They will also not treat you well when elderly.
>
> Tigress [in *kawi*] I'm hungry and am hence devouring my children. All animals have fled and there is nothing to eat.
>
> Tualen In her hunger, mother tigress is no longer aware of her limitations (*batas*).

This leads to the second phase of the story, in which Sutasoma seeks to appease the tigress.

Phase II: the drama of integration

In compassion, Sutasoma willingly sacrifices himself to the tigress, offering her his body. He dies as she claws his chest and imbibes his blood. But it acts like *amerta*, the elixir of immortality, and she becomes aware of her ignorance. In misery, she tries to kill herself. The goddess of death, Durga, descends (Figure 10.16) and prevents this, and brings Sutsoma back to life as he is needed to bring 'light to the darkness' in the world (*galang petent*), which is experiencing Kali *juga*, the cycle of destruction. Sutasoma, through the violence of his death and the purity of his compassionate nature, is transfigured and transported to a more exalted spirit realm. Sutasoma's spirit, having been purified, returns to *sekala* (the mundane world). The poet-priest is motivated in the drama to identify with Sutasoma (Lord Buddha or Siwa). Thereby, he experiences the reintegration of the many to the one, that is, the luminous consciousness at the centre of the lotus mandala. Through this cosmic process the centre of both the microcosm and macrocosm momentarily merge, as epitomized by the elusive shadow of the Kakayonan, the *axis mundi*, which appears after the sacrificial act. It can be suggested that Prince Sutasoma becomes aware that 'his Buddha-nature is ultimately not separate from the compassionate and wisdom potential intrinsic within the universe' (Samuel 2015:495).

In the performance the pupils, including now the tigress, request the prince teaches them:

Figure 10.16 Silhouette of god Indra bringing Sutasoma back to life. His spirit re-enters his body. Photographed by M. Hobart.

Merdah [translating and improvizing on Sutasoma's Old Javanese] Children, the dancing shadows illustrate the illusionary nature of the world (*dunia maya*). Nonetheless, it is important to heed the principal of complementary opposites intrinsic to the mundane world of humans, *ruwa-bineda*: right/left, benign/destructive, male/female, sun/moon, day/night, and so forth. Ultimately, a seeker must transcend the dualities and become aware that they are transitional and conditional.

[In the story the opposites are between Sutasoma and the wild creatures.]

You cannot have one without the other. Equanimity and compassionate balance should ideally be sought between them. Yet balance is not constant. It has to be continually reasserted in tune with an ever-changing world (*sami metamahan*).

It is important for a person to realize that the principle of *ruwa- bineda* is linked to the forces manifest in all creatures: thought (*idep*), voice (*sabda*) and energy/action (*bayu*). How these three elements interconnect in a person is variable. It is, however, important that they harmonize with one another (*mangda pada pada*). Prince Sutasoma's appearance, intentions, speech and actions are beautiful and respectful to all.

Tualen [expanding of Merdah words] Yet religious dogma should not 'control' [in English] a human. He/she would then become narrow-minded and 'stupid' [English] (*buduh*). Such an attitude leads to conflict and 'fanaticism' [*fanatisme* in Indonesian].[14]

Diversity is enriching and harmonizes with a key principal of the Indonesian state, '*bhineka tungal ika*' (unity in diversity). Respect, amity and compassion should be shown to all.

Sutasoma [in *kawi*] In order to follow the path of dharma you should concentrate and be balanced.

Tualen My children, Gaja Waktra, serpent and mother tigress, once you 'concentrate' (*nyikyang pikayun*) and are not 'impure' (*leteh*) nothing can disturb you. This is the 'path of Buddhahood' (*ngemargiyang kebudan*).

The performances came to an end when the poet-priest places the Kakayonan, the *axis mundi*, now still, in the middle of the screen, that is, at the centre of the lotus mandala. The scholarly *dalang*, I Wija, recited a few mantras in concluding the performance and the audience left the arena.

Discussion after the performance: the role of the servant-clowns, parekan

The four main servants, Tualen, Merdah, Delem and Sangut, deserve special attention, Representing the gods of the four cardinal points, they are the protective 'gateways' to the mandala. In Borobudur the demon on top of the four gateways to the monument is called Kala ('time'), who in his gaping mouth devours all obstacles to liberation (Miksic 1990:51), implicitly implying that a pilgrim to the monument is entering a sphere of sacred time (*niskala*) in contrast to mundane time (*sekala*).

---

14 In passing, I Wija brought up as an example the Wahhabi movement, a militant form of Islam in Indonesia linked to extremism and even terrorism.

The servant-clowns, *parekan*, have a crucial role in the dynamics underlying a show that evokes a pure vision of the universe, a mandala, as created by the scholarly *dalang*. The senior servant Tualen (Figure 10.8) stands out as he also symbolizes (to the *dalang*) the central, sublime god (Siwa or Absolute Buddha).

The servant-clowns' unique status in the shadow theatre is poetically summed up in Shulman's words regarding the Indian clown:

> The clown ... argues for the reality of the inner worlds of vision, intuitive perception... He exemplifies the world status as *maya* – at once tangible and real, and immaterial; entirely permeable by the imagination; always baffling, enticing, enslaving.
>
> (O'Flaherty 1984:120)

The servants are the mediators who interlink the cosmic spheres with the characters in the story and the audience, most of whom sit in front of the screen watching the dancing shadows. The servants translate and elaborate on what the epic characters say in often obscure, enigmatic Old Javanese (*kawi*). They are also the clowns, jokers, buffoons and jesters who entertain old and young alike with their bawdy jokes and comic antics. In their multiple roles, the servants create space to muse and reflect on the nuanced notions and emotions embedded in the dialogues that may be veiled, ambiguous or indeterminate. In this way they potentially alleviate suffering and restore community equilibrium, empowering beholders to revitalize their realities.[15] A performance essentially fails if the *dalang* is not skilled in animating the servant-clowns, who are the main figures propelling the audience into the visionary universe of the shadow play. The spectators might simply walk off. The servant-clowns are deeply human – in part by being low caste, like most of the audience. In Berger's (2013:98) expressive words, just by performing at street level they persuade everyone in the audience,

> between guffaws of laughter, that they could love one another, and with their skills and bare hands they momentarily release a kind of grace...

In a performance the servant-clowns, the *parekean*, highlight a *dalang*'s concern to contribute to the welfare of the villagers, and ultimately to direct

15 Babcock (1984:124) argued that ritual play and clowning, worldwide, encourage a state of mind that seeks out contradiction for its nourishment. 'The saints do not laugh nor do they make us laugh but the truly wise` men ... make us laugh with their thoughts and make us think with their buffoonery.'

their consciousness to enlightened compassion. In behaviour and speech, they characterize key qualities of Prince Sutasoma: his humanity, compassionate wisdom, openness to new perspectives and freedoms, and acceptance of contradictions. These qualities are becoming rarer in everyday life. Yet they remain as proof of peoples' desire for cooperation, as still prevails in markets, old universities or rituals and temple celebrations (cf. Kapuscinski 2008:81). In Bali, my main research area, the willingness to cooperate, referred to as *gotong-royong*, is epitomized in the traditional irrigation system. All aspects of rice cultivation require selflessness and commitment to working together (Lansing 2006). In our contemporary era there is a reduction in human relationships. Civilians may be threatened by senior government officials or scholars, who are often self-interested, and seek to isolate or separate themselves from the other, or the 'outsider'. Although technological developments and globalization have benefited some, especially in the medical domain, their negative impact on society is indisputable. Technology seems to be replacing face-to-face relations and the capacity to show kindness to the other, intensifying loneliness for many, especially in urban environments.

However, images like the circle, the mandala or tree-of-life have retained their significance throughout the ages and allude to flexibility, as well as stability and equilibrium inherent in relationships. Tucci (1961:37) wrote that 'such visions and flashing apparitions occur through some mysterious intrinsic necessity of the human spirit'. Tucci also noted that Carl Gustav Jung was the first scholar to become aware of this.

Let me draw brief attention to the tall pine trees in the Ticino in south Switzerland (Figure 10.17), where *dalang* Wija performed the Sutasoma story. In fierce storms trees, like humans in the grip of strong emotions, are vulnerable to the whirling winds that blow the branches to and fro. Yet, as epitomized by the pine tree, the trunk is still, solid and deeply rooted in the ground. Trees or mandalas, with particular reference here to the lotus mandala that underlies the drama of the Sutasoma story, hint at the luminous and compassionate potential inherent to the human being and the universe, the micro- and macrocosm, when the many have been integrated into the one, the centre, or 'Primordial Unity' (ibid.:1969:53). Such translucent images are sources of regeneration and renewal. Their vitality through the ages and in the present helps subvert the contemporary discourses of materialism, corruption, fascism and individualism intrinsic to many societies and at the core of Western problematics (Kapferer 2014). In the case of the shadow play, its agency is intensified as it is intentionally performed to enchant and redirect human consciousness to the aesthetic and spiritual dimensions of existence.

Figure 10.17 Old pine tree in south Switzerland. Photographed by A. Hobart.

Conclusion

This chapter focused on the ancient and present-day mandala designs that underlie ancient Javanese monuments and the magical shadow theatre. Mandalas, Tantric cosmograms, originated in India and later spread to Tibet and South-east Asia. They are intrinsic to both Buddhism and Hinduism. Yet mandala configurations are found worldwide and in varied forms. For instance, the intricate and well-researched diagrams intrinsic to Navaho sand paintings used to guide patients along the path of renewal (Sandner 1981:157–60) come to mind.

As we have seen, the majestic Buddhist monument of the ninth century, Borobudur, is based on the mandala design. Prince Sutasoma is shown on one of the many reliefs on the monument. The use of the mandala configuration in the revered shadow theatre in Bali and Java is unique to this part of the world. As Zoetmulder (1974) argued, ancient Javanese poems are a form of 'Tantric yoga' and this practice may well be echoed nowadays by the 'instruments' and 'tools' used by a *dalang* in a performance. In this role a scholarly *dalang*, or poet-priest, can be loosely described as shamanic Buddhist. Giving a performance is, for him, essentially a meditative exercise that empowers him to unite temporarily with quiet (emptiness) or the supreme god Siwa (or Absolute Buddha), when his 'inner being is as a pearl of unblemished purity' (Zoetmulder 1974:176). Intrinsic, however, to his pursuit for liberation is his concern for the well-being of the village community – a concern to enchant and guide the spectators imperceptibly to enhanced modes of consciousness.

A shadow play in which a *dalang* narrates the story of Sutasoma, Lord Buddha, is unusual. Sutasoma stands out from all other mythic figures, by his gentleness, beauty, wisdom and compassion. It is worth asking at this point what is implied by the term compassion in this chapter. A quote by Albert Einstein (1950) is apt in this context:

> The human being (experiences him or herself) as part of the universe – a part limited in time and space. Our task must be to free ourselves from this prison by widening our circle of compassion to embrace all living creatures and the whole of nature in its beauty.

Another quality alluded to in the drama – one vital for attaining enlightenment, as well as for well-being, cooperation and amity – is humility. Sutasoma's act of sacrifice to appease the hungry mother tigress epitomizes his humility in engaging with the other, not giving in to anger, pride or fear. This concurs with the approach of Emmanuel Levinas, who witnessed the horrors of Auschwitz, which was to encourage acceptance and converse with the other, even to take responsibility for the other, who is closer to the transcendental, 'the absolute alterity', than the I who is talking (Hand 1989:7). Intriguingly, this attitude is also echoed in the traditional Swiss-German greeting when meeting someone: *Guess Sie Gott* (I greet God in you). Thus, in giving a performance of Prince Sutasoma in Switzerland, I Wija was in tune with a strand inherent in Swiss culture. In Bali the following proverb (given to me by I Ketut Suta Temeja) points to the importance of humility:

> *Sekadi beras sane misi, yening jegjeg niki pujung, jening munduk niki medaging.*
>
> Like a rice plant that has many husks, if it stands upright these are empty of grain. If bowed they contain grain (ready to be harvested). This is analogous to a human, who can be either arrogant and proud (with his nose in the air) or humble.

In other words, a person who has enlightened compassion for others also has humility. In the story of Prince Sutasoma this attitude leads to awareness that humans are intertwined with one another, the environment and the cosmos, that there is an intuitive sense of beauty inherent in all phenomena and that there is deep fellowship with all creation.

References

Berger, J. 2013. 'The burden in visions of art'. In *Visions of Paris: Daumier*. London: Royal Academy of Arts.

Brandon, J. 1970. *On Thrones of Gold: Three Javanese Shadow Plays*. Cambridge: Harvard University Press.

Brauen, M. 1998. *The Mandala: Sacred Circle in Tibetan Buddhism*. Boston: Shambhala.

Eliade, M. 1954. *The Myth of the Eternal Return*. Princeton: Bollingen Series XLVI.

Einstein, A. 1955, https/www.brainpickings.org/2016/11/28/einstein-circle-of-compassion

Fontein, J. 1990. *The Sculpture of Indonesia*. Washington: National Gallery of Art.

Gell, A. 1998. *Art and Agency: An Anthropological Theory*. Oxford: Oxford University Press.

Hand, S. (ed.) 1989. *The Levinas Reader: Emmanuel Levinas*. Oxford: Basil Blackwell.

Hobart, A. 1980. 'The enlightened Prince Sutasoma: transformation of a Buddhist story', *Indonesia* 49(April):75–102.

——— 2014. 'Retrieving the tragic dead in Bali: regenerating rituals after the 1965–6 massacre', *Indonesia and the Malay World* 42(124):307–36.

Holmes, K. 2009. *How to Practise the Sadhana of Four-Armed Chenrezig*. Langholm: Kagyu Samye Ling Monastery.

Holt, C. 1967. *Art in Indonesia: Continuities and Change*. Ithaca: Cornell University Press.

Hooykaas, C. 1973. *Kama and Kala: Material for the Study of the Shadow Theatre in Bali*. Amsterdam: Verhandelingen der Koninklijke Nederlandse Akademie van Wetenshappen.

Kapferer, B., 1997, *The Feast of the Sorcerer: Practices of Consciousness and Power*, Chicago: The University of Chicago Press.

——— 2014. *2001 and Counting: Kubrick, Nietzsche and Anthropology*. Chicago: Prickly Paradigm Press.

Kapferer, B. and Hobart, A. 2005. *Aesthetics in Performance: Formations of Symbolic Construction and Experience*. New York: Berghahn Books.

Kempers, B.T. 1976. *Ageless Borobudur*. Wassenaar: Servire.

Kapuscinski, R. 2008. *The Other*. London: Verso.

Langer, S. 1976 [1953]. *Feeling and Form*. London: Routledge and Kegan Paul Ltd.

Lansing, J.S. 2006, *Perfect Order: Recognising Complexity in Bali.* Princeton, Princeton University Press.

McPhee, C. 1970. 'The Balinese Wayang Kulit and Its Music'. In J. Belo (ed.), *Traditional Balinese Culture*, pp. 146–97. New York: Columbia University Press.

Miksic, J. 1990. *Borobudur: Golden Tales of the Buddhas.* Berkeley: Periplus Editions.

O'Flaherty, W.D. 1984. *Dreams, Illusions and other Realities.* Chicago: University of Chicago Press.

Pott, P.H. 1966. *Yoga and Yantra.* The Hague: Martinus Nijhoff.

Samuel, G. 1993. *Civilized Shamans: Buddhism in Tibetan Societies.* Washington: Smithsonian Institute.

——— 2015. 'The contemporary mindfulness movement and the question of non-self', *Transcultural Psychiatry* 52(4):485–500.

Sandner, D. 1981. *Navaho Symbols of Healing: A Jungian Exploration of Ritual, Image and Medicine.* Rochester: Healing Arts Press.

Stoller, P. 2009. *The Power of the Between.* Chicago: The University of Chicago.

Tucci, G. 1961. *The Theory and Practice of the Mandala* London: Rider and Company.

Turner, V. 1982. *From Ritual to Theatre.* New York City: Performing Arts Journal Publications.

Zoetmulder, P.J. 1974. *Kalangwan: A Survey of Old Javanese Literature.* The Hague, Martinus Nijhoff.

CONTRIBUTORS

Jean-Pierre Brach, Directeur d'études/Research Professor, EPHE Paris.

Marie-Hélène Congourdeau, Chargée de recherches honoraire, CNRS, UMR 8167 Orient Méditerranée.

Rachida Chih, Senior Research Fellow, Center for Turkish, Ottoman, Balkan, and Central Asian Studies (CETOBAC) – School for Advanced Studies in the Social Sciences (EHESS).

Patrick Garrone, Independent Researcher.

Vincent Goossaert, Directeur d'études/Research Professor, EPHE, PSL.

Angela Hobart, Founder and Director of the Fondazione Centro Incontri Umani Ascona, Honorary Reader at Goldsmiths College and Honorary Professor of Medical Anthropology at University College London.

Moshe Idel, Professor Emeritus at the Department of Jewish Thought, Hebrew University, Jerusalem.

Geoffrey Samuel, Emeritus Professor at Cardiff University, UK; Honorary Associate, University of Sydney, Australia.

Cristina Scherrer-Schaub, Honorary Professor, University of Lausanne; Former Directeur d'Études/Research Professor, EPHE Paris.

Thierry Zarcone, Directeur de recherches/Research Professor, CNRS.

INDEX

alchemy *see* inner alchemy
Agrippa, H.C. 7, 219–20
air 63, 65, 68, 77, 120, 126, 135, 195, 199, 253, 264
Aristotle, neo-Aristotelianism 65, 83, 86, 219
ascetics, asceticism 1–3, 5–6, 11–18, 20, 22, 32, 35, 39, 45, 49–50, 57, 85, 118, 127, 134, 183, 189–90, 198–9, 201–2, 208, 234
astral body, forces 4–5, 7, 85, 217–24, 226
axis mundi 238, 247, 253, 258, 260

Bali 5, 229–65 *passim*
Barlaam of Calabria 63, 70, 72, 75–7
bhikṣu, bhikṣūṇī 12, 16, 20, 194, 198; *see also* monks
Blavatsky, H.P. 221–24
bodhi *see* enlightenment
bodhicitta 26–7, 30–2
breathing 1, 3–4, 6–7, 14, 32, 60, 63–70, 72, 75–7,100, 117–18, 122, 124, 126–7, 129–31, 138, 140–1, 173, 175, 180, 190, 206, 208, 223
Buber, M. 88, 90, 100, 106
Buddhaghos.a 14, 195
Buddhism 1–7, 11–18, 20, 22, 24, 27–35, 69, 77, 166–7, 173–5, 177, 179–81, 183, 189–91, 193–6, 198–9, 201, 207–12, 217, 229–37, 243, 247, 250, 252, 255, 258, 260–1, 263–4

Cairo *see* Egypt
cakra, chakra 6, 22, 25–7, 33, 120–1, 134–5, 138, 223
caste 239, 241, 245, 261
China, Chinese 4, 6–7, 14, 16, 22, 31, 117, 131, 138–41, 163–83 *passim*, 190–1, 195, 206, 230, 232, 239
Christianity, Christians 2–3, 6, 57–77 *passim*, 81, 83–8, 90–1, 93, 95; *see also* Jesus Christ
colours 100–3, 121, 134–5, 201–2, 210–12, 238, 245, 247
Confucianism 163, 173, 177, 180–1, 183
consciousness 1–2, 4, 6, 14, 27, 31–3, 48–9, 107, 119, 125–6, 129–30, 139, 151–3, 160, 218, 221–5, 230, 235, 238, 249, 254, 258, 262, 264
Cordovero, M. 81, 103–5, 107
corpses 5, 45, 179, 195, 201–3, 223

Dabeizhou 166, 168, 173–4, 180
dalangs 229–30, 234–56 *passim*, 260–2, 264
dance 1, 87, 211, 236, 239, 244, 247, 250–4, 256
Dārā Shikūh 125–31
dark 39, 47, 49, 63, 130, 258
David ben Yehudah he-Hasid 80, 100–3
death 4, 11, 13, 24, 32, 44, 48, 51, 53, 60, 69, 118, 129, 132, 156–8, 164, 171, 174, 198, 219–2, 234, 249, 255, 258
al-Demirdāsh, Demirdāshiyya 42–4, 50–2
demons 4–5, 57–8, 60, 64, 70, 75, 85, 219, 242–4, 256–7, 260
desires 18, 27, 45, 48, 64–6, 68, 104–5, 172, 179, 199, 201–2, 208, 220, 222, 255, 262
dharma 13, 24, 28, 193, 235, 238, 245, 249, 252, 255, 260
dhikr 1, 3–4, 46–9, 51, 53–4, 69–70, 95, 117–27, 129–41, 152
disciples 39–40, 42, 44–50, 52, 54, 66, 69, 75, 89, 105, 120, 124, 129, 131, 133–4, 166, 169, 171–3, 190, 211–12, 224
disorder 5, 149, 155–8, 161, 179
drugs 5, 158, 169, 222–3

ecstasy 85, 93, 96, 102, 150, 194, 235
Egypt, Egyptian 42–53, 57–8, 81, 217, 221
Eliade, M. 90–2, 150, 158
enlightenment 14, 29, 31, 33–4, 166, 211, 229–60, 233–5, 249–50, 252, 254–5, 262, 264–5
Eranos 1, 176

faith 48, 50, 69, 89, 122, 141, 225, 235
fasting 3, 5, 39, 47, 51, 53, 118, 222
Ficino, M. 7, 219–20
fire 64, 74–5, 120, 135, 217, 253
Frazer, J. 90–1

Gangūhī, A. 125–6, 130
gestures 1, 6, 117, 127, 129–30, 210, 220
Gnosticism 6, 81, 140
God, gods, goddesses 1, 3–4, 28–9, 39, 42, 44–8, 52–4, 57–8, 60, 64–70, 72–7, 85, 87–9, 97–9, 103–4, 118, 120, 122, 126, 132, 138, 152, 166, 169, 171–3, 180, 182–3, 197, 199, 213, 220–1, 223, 230, 234–5, 243–5, 247, 249, 250, 252–6, 258–60, 264; *see also* names of individual gods
gospels 3, 57, 60
grace 65, 74–5, 86, 104, 106, 126, 261
Greece, Greek 7, 60, 74–5, 81, 83, 88, 90, 93, 219
Gregory of Sinai 63, 66–9, 77
Gregory Palamas 63, 69–77
gurus 18, 26, 29; *see also* lamas

Hamayon, R. 150–2, 154, 157
Hardinge Britten, E. 220, 223, 226
heart 3, 46, 48–9, 58, 60, 63–70, 73–7, 118–21, 124, 129, 131, 209–11, 234–5, 249, 254
heaven 47, 60, 63–5, 68, 118, 168, 220, 238, 245
Hegel, Hegelianism 87–8, 91–2
Hermeticism 85, 93, 103–4, 223–4
Hesychasm 1, 3, 57–8, 60, 63–5, 69–73, 75–7, 85, 93, 98
Hindu, Hinduism 6–7, 13, 22, 31, 81, 85, 90–1, 93, 100–3, 126–7, 217–18, 229, 232–3, 237, 239, 263

illness *see* sickness
illumination 5, 39, 46, 93, 132, 221, 235, 241, 254, 255
Imdād Allāh, H. 125, 129–31
India, Indian 5–6, 11–17, 21, 23–4, 27–31, 34, 91, 102, 119–22, 125–7, 130–2, 134, 138, 141, 189–213 *passim*, 218, 232–3, 235, 239, 242, 247, 261, 263
initiates, initiations 5, 29–30, 42, 44–6, 48–50, 70, 124, 130, 137–8, 155–6, 166, 168–9, 171, 231, 241
inner alchemy 4, 173, 175–7, 180–1
Iran *see* Persia
Isaac of Nineveh 60, 64
Islam, Islamized 2–3, 5, 13, 39, 42, 51–4, 69–70, 81, 83, 85, 95, 103, 119, 122, 132, 141, 149–58, 161, 231–2, 237, 239, 245, 260; *see also* Sufism

Jains, Jainism 11–13, 29, 190
Jesus Christ 3, 57, 60, 64, 66–8, 73, 75; *see also* Christianity
Jews, Judaism 4, 81–108 *passim*, 221
Jin'gaishan 166–7, 169–72, 175–6, 178–9
Junayd, A. 117–18, 120, 122, 131
Jung, C. 176, 262

Kabbalah, Kabbalism 1, 4, 6, 34, 81–5, 88–90, 93–108, 221
Khālid, M. 50, 118, 124–5, 132–4
khalwa 2–3, 39–42, 44, 46–52; *see also* seclusion
Khalwatī, U., Khalwatiyya 40–2, 44–5, 49–52
al-Khānī, Q 45–6
Kizil *see* Qizil
Konya 69–70, 76
Kubra, N. 69, 117–18, 127

Laihe, C. 166–7, 169, 171, 182
lamas 18, 20–2, 26–7, 29; *see also* gurus
laṭā'if 117, 119, 133–5, 137–8
Levi, E. 218, 223
light 27, 47–8, 50, 60, 64, 68, 73–5, 96, 119, 121, 129, 164, 168, 218, 221–3, 229, 235, 258
love 44–5, 66, 68, 74, 105, 254, 261
Lovejoy, A.O. 86, 225
Lü, Patriarch 165–6, 169–80, 182

magic 2, 4–5, 7, 16, 28, 34, 83, 85, 101, 104–5, 177, 191, 217–18, 220, 223–6, 230–1, 234, 240–1, 244, 250, 254, 263; *see also* theurgy
Mahabharata 190, 229, 233, 244
Mahāyāna 14–15, 24, 27–8, 30, 32, 209–10, 234
mandalas 4–5, 7, 28–31, 34, 100–2, 193, 232–3, 235, 238, 241, 244, 249–50, 252–4, 258, 260–3
mantras 26–7, 31, 60, 193, 235, 244, 253–5, 260; *see also* recitation, repetition
manuals 2, 14, 120, 122, 129, 131, 133, 138, 168, 172–4, 176–7, 181–2, 192–3, 195, 206–13
masters, mastery 2–3, 5, 20, 39–40, 42, 44–51, 53–4, 66, 69, 105, 119, 124, 127, 131–2, 138, 151, 164–72, 175–7, 180–2, 190–1, 193–6, 198–9, 201–3, 205–7, 210–11, 224, 256

meditation 1, 4–7, 12, 14–15, 19, 23, 32–3, 48, 51, 60, 66, 117, 129, 134, 138, 164, 166, 168, 173, 175, 180–3, 189–96, 198–201, 205–9, 211–12, 233–5, 241, 243, 249, 254, 255, 264
mediums 4, 169–70, 173, 217, 223–5, 241
Meir ibn Gabbai 97–8
Meister Eckhart 88, 90
mindfulness 4, 15, 77, 118, 192, 202, 205, 212, 243
milk 53, 209–10
monasteries, monasticism, monastics 13, 15–18, 20, 22, 28–30, 34, 57–61, 63, 66, 70–1, 77, 86, 169, 173, 179–80, 182, 198–9, 201, 203, 206, 230, 232
monks 2–5, 7, 16, 18, 20, 29–30, 34, 58–62, 64, 66, 70, 72–3, 75–7, 167, 194, 197–9, 201–2, 204, 206; *see also* *bhikṣu*, monasteries
morality 13, 164, 173, 178–80, 183, 191, 194, 207–8, 210, 230, 239, 241, 248, 252
Moses 3, 47
mothers 166, 179, 209, 253, 258, 260, 264
Mount Athos 64, 66, 70, 71
Mount Sinai see Sinai
Muslim see Islam
mystics, mysticism 1, 4–6, 42, 46, 53, 57, 63, 66, 81–2, 84–90, 92–6, 101–3, 105–8, 117–18, 120, 124, 134, 139, 158, 161, 235, 244–5

names 3–4, 6, 40, 43, 46, 53, 57, 60, 66–70, 85, 94, 96, 98, 101–3, 121, 129, 134, 138, 153, 166, 174, 180, 199, 201, 234, 249
Naqshbandī order 39, 49–51, 53–4, 117–25, 130–6, 138–9, 141
navel 63–4, 66, 69–70, 72, 76–7, 124, 135, 137–9
neoplatonism *see* Plato
Nicephorus the Hesychast 64–5, 68–70, 76
nirvana 192, 211, 221
numinous, the 5, 87, 106, 149, 156–8, 161

occult, occultism 5, 7, 48, 104, 217–26 *passim*
Olcott, H.S. 218, 220
Otto, R. 87–8, 90, 99
Ottomans 42–3, 45, 49, 118–20, 125, 132–3, 138; *see also* Turkey

painting, paintings 23–4, 73–4, 164, 191–2, 196–7, 199–202, 208–9, 211, 213, 231, 263
Pāla, Pali 14–17, 229, 233–4
Persia, Persian 39–42, 49–50, 69, 81, 102, 121, 124, 126, 135, 158
Plato, platonism 57, 65, 70, 76, 83, 87, 93, 97–8, 105, 119, 192, 198, 219
Plotinus 57, 60
poems, poets 83, 169–70, 199, 229–45 passim, 252, 254–5, 258–64 *passim*
posture 1, 3, 6–7, 47, 64, 66, 68–9, 72–3, 76–7, 126, 130, 132, 152–3, 180
praṇa 3, 22, 32, 190, 206
prayer 1, 3, 39, 42, 47, 51–4, 58, 60, 63–4, 66–77, 83, 89, 94–6, 100–2, 104–5, 107, 126–7, 129, 164, 245
prophecy, prophets, The Prophet 44, 48, 53–4, 93, 95–6, 103, 119, 121, 126–7, 134
puppets, puppeteers 5, 230, 234, 236, 240–8 *passim*, 251, 253–4
Pure Land 4, 14, 174, 181
purification 14, 26, 46, 49, 72, 76, 103, 205, 219, 242, 250, 253, 255, 258

qi 4, 31, 164, 173, 177, 181
Qizil caves, manual 193, 200–1, 203–4, 206–13
Quran 46–7, 53–4, 118–19
al-Qushayrī, A. 40, 48
al-Qushshāshī, A. 46–8
Qyzyl see Qizil caves

rabbinism 4, 81–4, 88, 94, 96, 99, 106–7
Ramayana 190, 229, 233
Randolph, P.B. 218, 223–4
recitation 3–4, 24, 26–7, 46, 54, 104, 124, 126, 128, 130, 168, 170, 173–4, 179–80, 201, 236, 260; *see also* mantras, repetition
repetition 1, 3, 6, 24, 26, 31, 69, 118, 122, 124, 174, 205, 243, 252, 255; *see also* mantras, recitation
retreat 2–3, 17, 22–3, 30, 39–54, 159, 180; *see also* seclusion, solitude

Ṣāḥibzāda (K.F. Aḥmad) 136–8
śamatha 15, 195
saṃsāra 191–2, 194–5, 208–9, 211–12, 255
Schleiermacher, F. 87, 90, 99
Scholem, G.D. 88–90, 92, 96–7, 107
Schopen, G. 198–9

seclusion 1–2, 39–40, 44, 50–1, 53–4, 126, 198, 208; *see also khalwa,* solitude
secrets 46, 48, 73, 88, 90, 97–8, 106, 119–21, 124, 132, 167, 176, 223
sex 5, 20, 32, 179, 199, 217–18, 222–4
shadow theatre 5, 229–44 *passim*, 247, 250–3, 255, 259, 261–4
shamans, shamanism 1, 4–5, 69, 149–58, 160–1, 230, 241, 264
Shirokogoroff, S.M. 150, 155
sickness 5, 134 155–8, 177, 242
silence 3–4, 39, 48–9, 52, 66, 118, 122, 180
Sirhindī, A. 120, 131–2, 137
sleep 4, 46–7, 50, 118, 155–8, 160, 173, 199, 221, 223
solitude 2–3, 39–40, 44, 51, 58, 118–19, 202; *see also* seclusion
souls 2, 5, 39, 45–7, 49, 57, 60, 63–5, 67–8, 70, 72, 74, 76–7, 89, 98, 100, 105, 120, 132, 135, 156–8, 167–8, 177, 218–21, 223–4, 254
Siberia 149–61 *passim*
Sinai 3, 47, 60, 63, 66–8
skulls 120, 134, 138, 203–5
spiritualism 5, 217–18, 220, 223–5
spirit-writing 4, 170–1, 174, 176–7, 180–1
Sri Lanka 13, 15, 229
subtle body 4–7, 22–3, 27, 31–4, 117, 119, 121–2, 125, 131, 133–4, 139–41, 218, 220, 224, 233
suffering 24, 27, 30, 64, 67–8, 158, 167, 177, 209–12, 235, 242, 250, 254–5, 261
Sufism 1–4, 6, 22, 39–40, 42–51, 54, 69–70, 76, 93, 100, 102–3, 117–22, 124–7, 129–32, 134, 136–41, 152, 237
Sutasoma, Prince (and his story) 5, 229–35, 238–9, 245–6, 250–65 *passim*
sūtras 11, 14–15, 28–9, 100, 190, 207, 209–10
Symeon the New Theologian 63–4

Talmud 82–3
Tantrism 1, 3, 7, 14, 16–18, 20, 22–4, 26–34, 120, 134, 141, 174, 207, 230, 232–5, 237, 249, 251–2, 263
Taoists, Taoism 4, 7, 69, 117, 135, 138–9, 141
Tashkent 118, 124, 133–4, 159; *see also* Uzbekistan
Theosophical Society 7, 218, 221–2, 224; *see also* theosophy
theosophy 82–4, 96–8, 100–1, 105–6, 218; *see also* Theosophical Society
Theravāda 14–15, 193
theurgy 7, 34, 82, 84, 93, 96, 98–101, 104–6, 219, 224; *see also* magic
Tibet, Tibetan 2–3, 11–35 *passim*, 100, 190, 193, 224, 230, 232–3, 245, 263
Tishby, I. 89
Torah, the 4, 83, 94, 96–8
training 2–3, 13–14, 16–18, 20, 22–3, 27, 33–4, 53, 124, 170, 173, 180–3, 190–1, 240, 244
Turkey, Turks, Turkish 42–2, 50–1, 53, 66, 69, 120–2, 131, 134, 230; *see also* Ottomans

Upanis.ads 12, 190, 210
Uzbekistan, Uzbeks 124, 134, 155–6, 160; *see also* Tashkent

Vajrayāna *see* Tantrism
Vajrasattva 26–7
Vinaya 11–12, 30, 196, 198–9
vipaśyanā 15, 195
visualization 1–6, 14–15, 22, 26–8, 30–1, 100–3, 117, 129, 140, 166–7, 173–5, 179–81, 189, 191–2, 194, 197, 200–1, 204, 206, 208, 210–12, 229, 233, 247
void 39, 48, 234, 250

Wenchang 165, 169–70, 172–5, 177–9
Wija, I W. 242–3, 250–5, 260, 262, 264
writing 191–3; *see also* spirit-writing

Xinjiang 121, 124, 134–5, 152, 199, 206

Yide, M. 165–6, 171–2, 175
yoga, yogin 2–3, 5–7, 14, 18, 20–2, 26–34, 69, 91, 100, 117, 119–20, 126–32, 134–6, 138, 141, 189–96, 198, 201–3, 205–12, 224, 233, 235, 243, 252, 263

Zhilin, S. 165, 168–9, 171–5, 177–9, 181–3
Zoetmulder, P.J. 233–5, 263
Zohar, Zoharic 103, 107

www.ingramcontent.com/pod-product-compliance
Lightning Source LLC
Chambersburg PA
CBHW051435270326
41935CB00019B/1828
* 9 7 8 1 9 1 2 3 8 5 5 6 0 *